THE LIBRARY
ST. MARY'S COLLEGE OF MARY
ST. MARY'S CITY, MARYLAND

SO-BNA-963

THE
PUERTO RICAN
EXPERIENCE

This is a volume in the
ARNO PRESS collection

THE
PUERTO RICAN
EXPERIENCE

Advisory Editor

Francesco Cordasco

Editorial Board

Eugene Bucchioni
Maximiliano Soriano
Diego Castellanos

See last pages of this volume
for a complete list of titles

80 PUERTO RICAN FAMILIES IN NEW YORK CITY

HEALTH AND DISEASE STUDIED IN CONTEXT

BEATRICE BISHOP BERLE

With a New Foreword

ARNO PRESS

A New York Times Company

New York — 1975

Reprint Edition 1975 by Arno Press Inc.

New Foreword by Beatrice Bishop Berle
Copyright © 1975, by Beatrice Bishop Berle

Copyright © 1958 by Columbia University Press

Reprinted by permission of Beatrice Bishop Berle

The Puerto Rican Experience
ISBN for complete set: 0-405-06210-9
See last pages of this volume for titles.

Manufactured in the United States of America

Library of Congress Cataloging in Publication Data

Berle, Beatrice Bishop, 1902-
   80 Puerto Rican families in New York City.

   (The Puerto Rican experience)
   Reprint of the 1958 ed. published by Columbia
University Press, New York.
   Bibliography: p.
   1. Puerto Ricans in New York (City) 2. Hygiene,
Public--New York (City) 3. New York (City)--Social
conditions. I. Title. II. Series.
[F128.9.P85B47 1975]   362.8'4   74-14221
ISBN 0-405-06211-7

FOREWORD

The request for permission to reprint this little book came as a pleasant surprise. Four years ago a medical anthropologist reported that the Mount Sinai Hospital library copy of "80 Puerto Rican Families" was in shreds and that neither she nor the library could afford to pay $32—the price of a worn copy in a second-hand bookstore. This testimony notwithstanding, three publishers whom I approached with an outline to bring the book up-to-date turned it down. "This is neither medicine nor sociology." "Correct," I replied. "It is an interdisciplinary study intended to focus the attention of physicians, nurses, social workers and para-medical personnel on *people*—the sick and the well, living in a given environment. It is a study in human ecology."

A reprint is not a revision so that it is not possible either to rewrite the text or to bring all the statistical material up to date. A brief account of the activities of the family neighborhood clinic which continued after the publication of this book and a few remarks on the current situation of Puerto Ricans in East Harlem is all that can be attempted in a brief foreword.

The methods used in this study were quite unconventional. While some data were collected through the usual sources—census reports, hospital records, newspaper articles, scientific journals, etc., data from residents were obtained in the course of a medical social service operation. The assistance offered and promised gave us an insight into the problems of individuals and families which would not be revealed through a structured questionnaire.

By the time the book went to press, the service operation was taking over our little office at 311 East 100th Street so I decided to accept this challenge and to organize a family neighborhood practice as a continuing venture in human ecology. Two contiguous apartments were rented which raised the monthly rent of $11 for three rooms to $60 for eight rooms. The Fund for Human Ecology under the leadership of Harold G. Wolff, Professor of Medicine (Neurology) at Cornell University Medical College, gave us a yearly grant of $30,000 for five years. The anthropologists and other participants in the original study went on to other projects. I was fortunate in persuading Margaret Grossi, a young pediatrician then, today Associate Clinical Professor of Pediatrics at Cornell University Medical College and Director of Child Health Services in the Department of Health in New York City, and Elsie Jackson de Rubio, a public health nurse, today Director of Community Affairs and Clinical Professor of Community Medicine at New York Medical College, to join me.

The three of us took what in older times would have been called a vow to work together as a group for five years in this neighborhood. We employed other physicians and other nurses on a part-time basis over the five year period. The East Harlem Protestant Parish contributed the salary of another splendid public health nurse and their clergy, notably the Reverend Norman Eddy, and lay groups were generous in providing social and spiritual services.

This meant that over the five year period we rendered medical, health and social services to some 200 families and 300-400 separate individuals not identified as family members—a total of approximately 2,000 people, Puerto Ricans, blacks, whites and others living within a five block radius of 100th Street between 1st and 2nd Avenues. We discouraged relatives and friends from distant parts and referred them to other facilities.

Restricting patients to the neighborhood made it possible for each family and patient to be known personally both in the office and on the street to at least one of the permanent staff members. Each new staff member was presented with the family record folder and received a personal introduction to his patient.

Routine urinalyses and hemoglobin determinations were carried out in the clinic. Other essential laboratory tests were obtained through a commercial laboratory and through the Health Department.

Referrals to specialty clinics at Mount Sinai and other hospitals were made when necessary. A report from the hospital or a reading of the hospital record with the permission of the patient and the gracious cooperation of the record room librarian made it possible to interpret the hospital findings to the patient and to follow him in our family clinic after consultation or discharge. Patients requiring in-patient treatment were admitted to Metropolitan Hospital where our interest in individual patients was usually not appreciated. At Mount Sinai and Bellevue Hospitals, our physicians had staff appointments so that a patient needing hospitalization could be admitted even over the objections of the house staff who assured us that a child with pneumonia, living in an apartment heated with a smoking kerosene stove, and sharing a bed with a sibling, was not an "interesting case" and could return to the O.P.D. for daily penicillin injections, trudging through five blocks of snow and slush. Although Dr. Grossi and I were both on the staff of New York Hospital, rarely did we obtain a bed for one of our patients. They were not teaching material—just sick people.

Both the late Dr. Wolff and the late Dr. Allan Guttmacher supported our point of view—the latter sent us a few residents who gained experience treating women for venereal disease, unwanted pregnancies and menstrual problems in their home environment. A few fourth year students were assigned to us by Cornell University Medical College. One of these who had read all the medical literature on acute leukemia stared in wonder at the throat of a child with follicular tonsilitis —he had never seen one before.

Imbued as we were with the concept of the interaction between health and the total environment, we would have liked to substantiate and quantify the impression that increased medical utilization occurred in all members of a family during periods of stress, such as the father losing his job, but our small budget did not permit us to do this.

We realized also that 100th Street was not the frontier and that a family neighborhood clinic had no business to exist in New York City if it were not integrated with a comprehensive medical care program through affiliation with a teaching hospital. When Dr. Wolff died in 1961 and the grant from the Human Ecology Fund came to an end in 1962, we tried unsuccessfully to persuade New York University, Mount Sinai Hospital and Cornell University Medical College to take us on as a satellite clinic, or to give us the opportunity to set up a similar facility in close proximity to New York Hospital or to Bellevue Hospital. No one was prepared to take us on.

Since then billions of dollars have been spent and are being appropriated by government, trade unions and industry to finance medical care and health insurance plans, but the association between illness and life situations frequently remains unperceived nor has effective primary medical care been achieved yet. A survey of the Puerto Rican scene and of the East Harlem Health District in 1974 suggests that though the health indices of this area are following the upward trend noted for the rest of New York City, much remains to be done. But the East Harlem Puerto Rican scene must be considered in the context of the Puerto Rican population of New York City as a whole. According to the 1970 census report, one in 10 individuals living in the 8,000,000 New York City complex is Puerto Rican. Almost one in 4 (23%) is described as non-white, the remaining two thirds being classified as white. In our neighborhood in 1950, 34% were said to be Puerto Ricans; 41.5% American Negroes, and the remainder divided between native and foreign non-whites. The 1970 census estimates that 37% of the population of East Harlem are Puerto Ricans. We are not able to assess the significance, if any, of this slight increase. Comparing years of schooling in this group with the 1950 figures when a college graduate was a rare bird, almost half in the 17-44 age group claim from 4 years of high school to 3 years of college and 6% are college graduates or better. It is still a young population with a smaller percentage over the age of 65 than is found in other areas. While three out of four Latins (term includes natives of other Caribbean islands as well as Puerto Ricans) came to East Harlem more than ten years ago with the largest net migration between 1950-1960, 63% of those in the 17-44 age group have lived at their current address no more than five years.* We do not know whether these changes of address are changes of address within East Harlem nor can we fit this group into the continually changing inflow-outflow migration pattern from Puerto Rico to the continent and from the continent to Puerto Rico which showed a greater number of Puerto Ricans returning to the island than coming to the continent in 1963 and 1964. Are the newcomers who arrive in East Harlem and those who leave going up or down the social escalator? From personal experience, we know that among our former patients, many older people still living in the neighborhood are surrounded by their children and grandchildren residing in the new housing projects nearby, while the descendants of others have moved out to Long Island, following the pattern of upward mobility characteristic of earlier European migrants and marrying into non-Puerto Rican families. A few of these have joined the growing professional class of Puerto Ricans who are filtering across the United States while affirming their identity with Puerto Rican culture. Others return to Puerto Rico because they "didn't make it" or because they did make it and wish to live a less agitated life on the island. Still others strive to make their mark in politics. Altogether, New York is more like San Juan than it was 25 years ago—witness the hybrid "Spanglish" language heard on all sides, and San Juan is more like New York with all the problems of metropolitan life including drugs.

Today, drugs are perceived by a majority of the resi-

---

*(East Harlem Community Health Study (E.H.C.H.S.) prepared by Louise Johnson, Ph.D of the Department of Community Medicine of the Mount Sinai School of Medicine.)

dents of East Harlem as the most serious problem to which doctors should devote their attention (E.H.C. H.S.). Twenty years ago, doctors, including myself, swept the heroin problem under the rug. Then, sending addicted relatives to Puerto Rico where there was said to be no heroin was a happy solution; alas, no longer available. In fact, some of us who became so-called "experts" on the addiction problem have been called to Puerto Rico to assist with their drug problem. Although Norman Eddy and other members of the East Harlem Protestant Parish were struggling valiantly to succor incarcerated addicts, the drug problem was not faced by our clinic until 1960 when Dr. Marie Nyswander who had treated heroin addicts in her private practice secured a grant from the Health Research Council of New York City and together we tried to detoxify and to treat heroin addicts whose families were our patients. A year later, Dr. Nyswander joined the staff of Rockefeller University where she and Dr. Dole discovered that methadone was an effective agent in the treatment of heroin addiction. In 1973, the New York City Narcotics Registry reported that of 29,000 addicts registered with them for the first time, 14% are classified as Puerto Rican (residence not analysed), 28% as non-white, 30% as white and the rest as other or unknown ethnic origin. Of the 11,000 heroin addicts on the several methadone maintenance programs in New York City in 1974, 23% are Puerto Ricans, 46% non-white and 25% white. Lincoln Community Mental Health Center Methadone Maintenance Treatment Program in the South Bronx reports that of 231 patients admitted between March and November, 1971, 70% were Puerto Rican, 75% of these were receiving Welfare on admission to the program; 66% of these were still on Welfare two years later as compared to 39% Welfare recipients in the total catchment area.* Apparently the Puerto Rican group is taking advantage of one of the available treatment facilities. The overall figures only confirm what everyone knows: poverty and drug addiction move along parallel lines.

In East Harlem there are four methadone maintenance clinics located in the northern end of the district and four half-way houses based on drug free programs. Although several studies indicate that the crime rate has diminished as the number of patients on methadone treatment has increased, a majority of East Harlem residents continue to view drug addiction as the major problem to which physicians should address themselves, and crime in the streets as a valid reason for not going out at night. A fundamental solution to either drugs or crime is not in sight.

Health has always been and still is a major pre-occupation for the East Harlem population and a greater proportion of Latins compared to other groups are concerned with this problem (E.H.C.H.S.). The New York City Health Department reports that the epidemic of venereal disease in New York City is most widespread in the ghetto areas, the East Harlem rate being half that of Central Harlem. East Harlem now ranks 11th from the top of those districts with the highest infant mortality. Formerly it was 7th from the top. The infant mortality rate in this district is lowest among Puerto Ricans compared to white and non-whites; 44% of those born

*Langrod, John, et al, Community Based Treatment of the Hispanic Addict, Albert Einstein College of Medicine, Bronx State Hospital, Drug Abuse Service. Presented at the International Conference on Alcoholism and Drug Abuse, 1973.

in this district are children of Puerto Rican mothers. It is too early to assess the full impact of the liberalized abortion law on the reproductive pattern of Puerto Ricans. But these figures do not give a true picture of the morbidity and disability rate in this community.

Our experience with Puerto Rican patients suggested that health was equated with employability and that sickness constituted the only socially acceptable excuse for not working. We have no reason to consider that this reasoning has changed although the structure of the E.H.C.H.S. questionnaire did not bring out this point unless one were to interpret the greater utilization of medical facilities by people in households who had no income from work as a combined desire to seek relief from illness while receiving confirmation that one is really sick because one sought medical attention. At any rate, the overall hospitalization rate in this district is higher than for the rest of the nation.

There are now a greater number of providers of medical care in East Harlem than formerly. In addition to the established hospitals—Mount Sinai, Flower Fifth Avenue, Metropolitan, Joint Diseases, there are three regular Child Health Clinics; one pediatric treatment clinic which operates on a full-time basis and renders acute walk-in pediatric services as well as the traditional preventive health care services. An additional pediatric treatment clinic is operated by Mount Sinai.

Of the 350 free-standing Medicaid clinics in New York City at present, ten are estimated to be located in East Harlem and are presumed to care for most Medicaid clients as only a small proportion of private physicians wish to bother with the red tape involved in the care of Medicaid patients.

The quality of medicine practiced by Medicaid clinics

leaves much to be desired. According to Dr. Lowell E. Bellin, New York City Health Commissioner, abuses, duplication and discontinuity of health care are frequent. But most physicians operating Medicaid clinics in East Harlem speak Spanish and in spite of their deficiencies and quasi-malpractice they sometimes take a more personal interest in their patients than do hospital personnel. The conditions which led us to write this book in 1958 have not changed materially. "Medical personnel dealing with the people shouldn't be so indifferent. They should treat people with kindness. There should be more Spanish-speaking doctors and nurses. They should pay more attention to people in the neighborhood." (E.H.C. H.S.) It is the same old refrain and leaves the loose ends to be picked up by the *botanicas* and spiritualists who continue to flourish. Spanish Harlem could hardly qualify as a health resort.

In closing, let us walk down 100th Street once more. The Puerto Rican resident on this block is still a poor man by American standards although the mean number of years of schooling for this group has risen from 7.2 years in 1950 to 9.73 years in 1970—he still does not have many marketable skills.

In East Harlem as a whole, two out of five of the households reported no income from employment the week preceding interview, and in those where someone was employed, the majority had no more than $100 a week take-home pay for the household. Income from Welfare and Social Security provided maintenance for nearly all who had no employment income and supplemented the income of some who were employed (E.H.C. H.S.).

As I was looking at the pile of rubble which once housed our clinic, a young man hailed me across the street. "Don't you remember me—you took care of me when I had the measles. I live at 312, Apt. E, with Mother. There she is sitting on the stoop. Now I know everybody on the block. Soon it won't be that way no more." He was referring to the new high rise building which was going to replace the old tenement site where I was standing. But perhaps he is wrong—neighborhoods will not be destroyed but strengthened. The City Planning Commission has announced the inauguration of a series of miniplans tailored to the needs of individual communities in the city's boroughs (N.Y. Times, 6/27/74). Others may follow the example set by the Metro North Association which has renovated the houses on the south side of 100th Street—diversification of buildings and population will ensue; even doctors might walk down the street and see their patients as people living within an environment whose features if taken into account may sometimes be modified to improve the patient's health more effectively than a prescription for a tranquilizer.

New York, N. Y.   BEATRICE BISHOP BERLE, M.D.
July 1974

80 PUERTO RICAN FAMILIES IN NEW YORK CITY

80 PUERTO RICAN FAMILIES IN NEW YORK CITY

HEALTH AND DISEASE STUDIED IN CONTEXT

By BEATRICE BISHOP BERLE, M.D.

 New York   1958
COLUMBIA UNIVERSITY PRESS

COPYRIGHT © 1958 COLUMBIA UNIVERSITY PRESS
PUBLISHED IN GREAT BRITAIN, CANADA, INDIA, AND PAKISTAN
BY THE OXFORD UNIVERSITY PRESS
LONDON, TORONTO, BOMBAY, AND KARACHI
LIBRARY OF CONGRESS CATALOG CARD NUMBER: 58-8226

Manufactured in the United States of America

FOREWORD

Physicians during the past century have made fetishes of the test tube, the electrometer, and most recently the IBM machine. As a matter of fact there is a rumor that the caduceus is to be replaced by a compactly arranged table of frequencies. Ordinarily the report of a health survey among a population sample retails the diagnostic tests employed and the incidence of organic pathology unmasked. Little or no effort is made to answer the question why, why such a geographic or ethnic group shows high or low incidence of disease.

This book is unique because it successfully flows against this modern current of medicine. It demonstrates the constant interplay of sickness and health with the cultural, physical, and emotional facets of the environment. It emphasizes on every page the factors which coordinate to create the pathological lesion. Diagnosis is given secondary importance to etiology, etiology in its broad social spectrum.

It is not a matter of accident that the author focuses her observations on the Puerto Rican slum dwellers of New York, since her extended travels and residence in Latin America have made her particularly qualified to analyze the health status of this underprivileged population.

This is a sobering book. For those living in the ivory-tower isolation of secure middle-class existence, it is shocking and revealing to read the vignettes of these eighty families. Dr. Berle's intimate, firsthand knowledge of virtually every one of the 420 people comprising these eighty families gives an authority to her conclusions which most treatises lack. The trite truism that life is a bitter, earnest struggle to which the weak surrender, and over which the strong triumph, takes on a new and vigorous meaning in these pages. Then, too, it is heartening to read of the deep, intelligent concern that so many people and agencies feel toward the weak and unfortunate.

Dr. Berle's study stresses the necessity of adequate preparation for migration so that it may result in successful adjustment. The importance of language facility, of education for accident prevention in transplanted rural peoples, and of the acquisition of premigration skills is documented in every chapter.

This is an important book. It is valuable for the student as well as the practitioner of medicine, sociology, theology, and government.

ALAN F. GUTTMACHER, M.D.
The Mount Sinai Hospital

ACKNOWLEDGMENTS

This study—as well as a parallel but independent anthropological study—was carried out under a grant made by the Foresight Foundation to the Department of Anthropology of Columbia University and to the Mount Sinai Hospital in New York City.

Professor Charles Wagley, Chairman of the Department of Anthropology at Columbia University, did much to smooth the differences which arise in the natural course of interdisciplinary research. Physicians and anthropologists are equally grateful for his broadmindedness and tolerance. I wish to express my respect for Elena Padilla, Ph.D., head of the anthropological team, and to say that from the association with her and her anthropologist colleagues—Joan Campbell, Vera Green, Joan P. Mencher, Edwin Seda, George Wee, and Muriel F. White—I learned much.

Special thanks are due to the many members of the medical, administrative, nursing, social work, and record room staffs of the Mount Sinai Hospital. Invariably courteous and helpful, they assisted us in solving large and small problems related to the obtaining of information concerning our Puerto Rican families and took on the treatment of these families when hospitalization and the services of specialists became necessary. The Department of Pediatrics of the Mount Sinai Hospital undertook the selection and supervision of the Fellow in Pediatrics assigned to this project, and advice given by Dr. Horace Hodes, chief of this department, proved very useful on numerous occasions. Dr. Alan F. Guttmacher, chief of the Department of Obstetrics and Gynecology of the Mount Sinai Hospital, was more than generous, and we are grateful for his wisdom and kindliness.

The responsibility for the examination of the majority of the children and the evaluation of their medical condition fell to Allegra Schiby, M.D., Fellow in Pediatrics of the Mount Sinai Hospital under the Foresight Foundation grant. Charles Goodrich, M.D., while Resident in Medicine on the Third Bellevue Medical Service, and David Baum, M.D., and Frank Moody, M.D., as undergraduate students in medicine, participated in the examination, treatment, and evaluation of the adults and in the summarizing of medical records. Without the record of their observations and their understanding approach to patients this book could not have been written. The author, however, is alone responsible for the interpretation of their findings and for the writing of the text.

Robert Hutchison, M.D., of the Division of Research and Statistics of the Health Insurance Plan of New York, was kind enough to help us in selecting the material suitable for statistical presentation. Mr. and Mrs. Nigel Chattey compiled the tables and figures which adorn the text.

Warm thanks go to my faithful secretary, Gertrude Washabaugh Pantano, whose patience and good humor never failed through long months of typing and retyping the many revisions of the text.

BEATRICE BISHOP BERLE, M.D.

New York City
November, 1957.

CONTENTS

x *Contents*

FIGURES

TABLES

PART ONE. *Methods and Materials*

While physiologists built their science by means of designed experiments, biologists built theirs by observing the experiments of Nature. Designed experiment divides phenomena into small sections of space and time. Naturalists, on the contrary, freely observe the course of life on a big scale.

Harold G. Wolff, "What Hope Does for Man"
Saturday Review, January 5, 1957.

I. THE PROJECT

During the past century the experimental method has yielded a rich harvest and has made possible the investigation of many problems in the laboratory where variables could be reduced to a minimum in a controlled environment.

Nevertheless, many phases of health and disease in human society still defy laboratory analysis and offer a challenge to the naturalist, to one who is interested in observing and recording the various items collected and assembling them into patterns that are significant. The current study was undertaken in this spirit by a group of physicians and social anthropologists. The physicians left the cloistered halls of the university hospital and of the laboratory to walk in the street and up tenement stairs with the social anthropologists, much as a naturalist might walk in the woods and record his observations on plant and animal life.

1. DESCRIPTION OF THE PROJECT

The field of study in this case is a census area corresponding to a health area which forms part of a larger health district in Manhattan. This area is inhabited by 13,575 people, 41.5 per cent of whom are American Negroes, 33.88 per cent Puerto Ricans, 10.7 per cent foreign-born whites, one half of these being Italians, and the remaining 14 per cent native-born whites. The Puerto Ricans consist of 4,610 individuals, of whom 78 per cent or 3,600 were born on the island, and 22 per cent or 1,010 were born in continental United States of Puerto Rican parents (1950 Census). A selected sample of eighty Puerto Rican households including 420 people became the focal point of the project for the physicians.

The area in which these people live is a slum, which, according to *The American College Dictionary,* is "a thickly populated, squalid part of a city, inhabited by the poorest people." The great majority of dwellings were built more than thirty-five years ago; many lack central heating and their plumbing facilities leave something to be desired. Since this project was undertaken buildings have been torn down to make way for municipal housing projects, and many people have moved out of the neighborhood while others have moved in. Estimates as to the actual number of people living in the area in the year 1955, the final year of field research, were not available through the U.S. Bureau of the Census. It is primarily a residential area serviced by small grocery, candy, clothing, and drug stores, store-front churches, and two public schools. Without taking into account housing projects reaching competition in 1956, the Census data of 1950 indicate that the differential range as to income, education, size of household, and type of employment is small and that all ethnic groups live under similar conditions of low income and marginal employment.

In February of 1953 the writer opened an office in a three-room apartment on the ground floor of a tenement building in the area with the intention of serving as a family physician to those people who lived within the health area and who applied for care at this office. It consists of a waiting room, a consulting room, and an examining room. Heat is supplied by a gas heater in the waiting room supplemented by an electric heater in the examining room. The office is equipped with a microscope and facilities for doing routine urinalyses and hemoglobin determination by the Sahli method. This office is still in operation and is open several times a week, when the patients who come are examined and treated for minor complaints as they would be in the office of a family physician. A charge of fifty cents is made to those who can pay, but no patient is ever refused examination because of lack of funds. Patients' fees are turned over to a private social agency which supplies the services of a visiting nurse and pays the office rent of $11.00 a month.

The physician who opened the office speaks Spanish and has followed the health problems of many of the families in this study for three years. The pediatrician, also Spanish speaking, worked out of the office for one year under a grant from the Foresight Foundation and examined practically all the children included in the study. Both men physicians associated with the project worked for a limited time. One was a senior medical student, and the other was in the third year of a medical residency. Neither spoke Spanish. All four physicians made home calls both to treat patients and to make firsthand observations on both sick and well individuals and families in the setting of their daily lives. When the physicians could not be reached, the sick person went to the out-patient departments of a near-by hospital or to another physician or called an ambulance. Many patients with conditions which could not be diagnosed or treated within these limited facilities were referred to the out-patient or in-patient services of near-by hospitals. In such cases, an effort was made to speak to the hospital physician who saw the patient and to read the hospital record so that the physicians working on this project kept abreast of medical developments in all members of a family during the period of observation.

This was a family oriented study. Unlike the usual hospital out-patient situation, where disease is studied in one member of a family and the others are seen only if the particular disease is considered to be familial or infectious, the entire household came under medical observation, and attention was focused on the setting in which illness occurred and on those factors which appeared to be related to its course. Every effort was made to obtain medical information on all members of the family. In those eighty Puerto Rican families which form the body of this report all possible sources of medical and social information were investigated for the members of a particular family in which such data were recorded.

The physicians wished to obtain a longitudinal picture of health in these Puerto Rican families living in a slum area rather than collect fragmentary data on disease entities. While surgical problems, obstetrical deliveries, and complex illnesses were treated in near-by hospitals, both the physicians and the social anthropologists who participated in the research were interested in observing the reaction of the patients to these procedures and the effect of a major illness in one member of a family on the health and daily lives of other members of the same family. Both research teams were also interested in observing the relations which these families had with the Department of Welfare, the schools, the churches, and other institutions in the community. Medical and social information were obtained by the physicians in the course of visits by patients to the doctor's office and in the course of the doctors' visits to homes. The approach of the physicians to the family was that of family physicians interested in securing the best possible care for any patient who applied to this office for treatment, by treating the patient when possible or by making a careful referral to the appropriate medical or social agency. As far as clinical research is concerned, this approach was variably satisfactory. For instance, exact and complete information on a particular family was lacking if the physician's initial association came through the treatment of one acute illness and no further contact was attempted until several months later, then only to discover that this family had moved and could not be traced. But where several members of a family were treated and face-to-face contacts between the family physician and his patients extended over a period of two to four years, a continuing rapport was established. In such cases more complete personal histories were obtained, and on the numerous occasions when these individuals were seen on the street, in their homes, in the office, observations on the spending habits, family relationships, neighborhood contacts, hopes and aspirations of the families under study could be made.

Thus the physician interested in formulating what constituted a special problem for a particular family was able to document the answer given in the office to the question "Does anything bother you" by direct observation of the behavior of parents and children on the street, at home, in the store. In other words, this study of health and disease in the eighty Puerto Rican families selected was conducted by family physicians in the environment in which the families were living. It was not conducted in a large medical center.

These were not physicians in white coats standing over a patient in a hospital gown lying in a hospital bed whose name and conditions of life they did not know. They were family doctors who saw the people in their homes, cooking supper, watching television, scolding and loving their children.

The physicians were associated in their study with a group of social anthropologists. The head of the anthropological team is a Puerto Rican with previous research experience on the island. The other five were candidates for master's or doctor's degrees in social anthropology and worked part time in the area on a particular phase of the project which became the subject of their theses. Altogether the anthropologists spent eighteen months studying the culture of the Puerto Rican population in this area and returned for follow-up observations over a period of three years. The usual techniques of interviewing and the participant observer supplemented by information from library and other sources were used by the group to construct what is known as the norms of behavior and ways of life for the particular society. The anthropological discipline involves the study of the social behavior of a group and deals with individuals as components of society and carriers of culture but not necessarily as unique individuals.

Physicians, on the other hand, may look upon individuals as hosts for a particular disease or, when psychologically oriented, focus their attention upon the psychodynamics of the member of the family who presents himself for treatment. In the present study the household became the meeting ground for both physicians and anthropologists. While anthropologists were abstracting norms of behavior for fathers, mothers, husbands, wives, and children in this society of

Puerto Rican migrants and of Puerto Ricans born in New York, all living in a New York slum, and observing the real behavior of these individuals in their environment, physicians might inquire from the anthropologist whether the behavior of a particular man or woman was consistent with the norm or expected behavior of a Puerto Rican father or mother in this slum environment. On the other hand, anthropologists might inquire from the physicians as to the medical basis for the complaints voiced by their informants. Thus both the physicians and the anthropologists strove to develop an understanding of the meaning of health and disease for Puerto Rican families living in a Manhattan slum area. Although many individuals and households from the several ethnic groups in the area became known to both teams and were treated in the doctor's office, the study was focused on the Puerto Rican group, and the medical report is concerned primarily with a selected sample of eighty Puerto Rican households.

Our own interest in the Puerto Rican group grew naturally out of awareness of the growing Puerto Rican population in New York City. According to the most reliable estimates, the Puerto Rican population of New York City more than doubled between 1950 and 1955. The U.S. Bureau of the Census reported that 245,880 Puerto Ricans lived in the five boroughs in 1950, and the Migration Division of the Department of Labor of the Commonwealth of Puerto Rico estimated that this figure had risen to 538,000 by the end of 1955. Besides, due to the growth of prepaid medical care insurance plans and the rising standard of living in a time of full employment, the group of medically indigent who apply for care to city hospitals has changed in character. In many institutions Puerto Ricans now predominate. Observing these men, women, and children sitting on clinic benches by the hour and witnessing the mutual bewilderment of patient and doctor who frequently did not share a common language, but even when they did, failed to communicate, it seemed to the writer that a study of the background and customs of Puerto Rican migrants living in a New York slum area might lead to greater understanding of these people by medical personnel and, consequently, more effective service.

While this study is concentrated on a small segment of the Puerto Rican population living in a slum area, it should also be regarded in the light of a pilot study in social medicine. Here medical doctors working in their capacity as family physicians, in collaboration with social anthropologists, learned to observe and evaluate *in situ* the influence of social factors in health and disease in a group of people under their care.

2. PROBLEMS OF METHOD

What is meant by health and what is meant by disease and how does one determine who is sick and who is well among the Puerto Rican inhabitants of a. Manhattan slum? These were questions that required definition by the medical team at the onset of the study.

Today, freedom from definable disease is not the only criterion for health; but a sense of well-being which permits individuals to function effectively is considered a desirable if not an essential characteristic of the healthy person. A sense of well-being and the ability to function are difficult to measure: ability to function effectively implies an interaction between the individual and his environment. Indeed a political scientist or an economist as well as a public health officer will argue that in some environments, such as a factory without safety devices, no human being should be expected to function effectively and that the environment, not the man, must be changed. In any event, both environmental factors and what constitutes ability to function require definition in terms of each particular study where health is being explored as an integral part of daily living. Disease is more easily definable in so far as it is limited to the diagnosis of recognized clinical entities by clinicians dealing with individual patients. In reporting the incidence of disease in a population, departments of health depend upon case-finding methods and upon reports from clinicians and hospitals. It is then possible to study the relationship between the incidence of disease and the demographic characteristics of a given population.

The study of health and disease as considered in the current project deals not only with the over-all public health picture but also with individuals in their daily lives, so that a combined application of clinical medicine, public health, and the social sciences—social anthropology, sociology, economics, and political science—is called for. For instance, the medical and anthropological teams wished to find out, among other matters, what were the particular social factors in this group of Puerto Ricans living in a Manhattan slum which appeared to affect the incidence, the natural history, and the management of episodes of illness in a family, and to study both the medical and social reverberations of the illness of one member of a family upon others in the same family in this particular environment.

While thinking of themselves as naturalists, the physicians were prepared to record any phenomena which came under their observations, but they were also interested in trying to record findings in terms that might permit comparison with other studies in environmental medicine. For this purpose the study of the association between health and social problems in the Arsenal Health District of Pittsburgh (Ciocco 1953) and the investigation of differences in general susceptibility to illness in a group of employees of the New York Telephone Company (Hinkle and Plummer 1952) were selected with the hope that data comparable to those obtained in these two projects might be secured in the Manhattan area.

The Arsenal Health study was conducted on the basis of a health questionnaire covering some 3,000 households and 10,000 individuals in an area whose population numbers about 80,000 people. The households were selected by approved probability sampling techniques. Among the 3,065 family units originally selected, 166 failed to cooperate in the first survey and could not be identified sufficiently to permit further characterization. In the second survey, carried on a year later, 251 families had moved away and 278 families did not respond. This involved an attrition of 695 families or 22.67 per cent of the 3,065 original families. For purposes of the Arsenal Health study, families were classified as having health problems who "(a) reported an illness during the month prior to the survey, (b) were hospitalized in the year prior to the survey, (c) reported an accident requiring hospitalization or physician's care in the year prior to the survey, (d) reported a chronic disease or physical impairment in the survey, (e) reported a death in the year prior to the survey." A social problem was defined in terms of a family being known to one or more social agencies which registers its cases with the Social Service Exchange of Pittsburgh. Twenty-two per cent of the families reported no health problem within the terms of the definition in either survey, 40 per cent had something to report in both surveys, and 38 per cent reported a hospitalization or some illness in one or the other of the surveys. Among families with reported illnesses, accidental injuries, and hospitalizations in both surveys, 12 per cent had social welfare problems currently in contrast to only 5 per cent of families with no reported illness, accident, or hospitalization in either survey. (Ciocco 1953.)

For both social welfare status and health status the author of the Arsenal study found that proportionately more families have problems when the families are large or the head of the household is advanced in age or is not in the labor force or has had little formal education.

Shortly after the opening of the doctor's office in the Manhattan area, the anthropological team, in cooperation with the medical team, attempted to apply a modified version of the Arsenal Health District questionnaire. This procedure was abandond after a few trials. In order to carry out an adequate sampling and administer a questionnaire consisting of structured questions as was done in the Arsenal Health District, certain characteristics would seem to be essential in the population to be studied. It should be possible to identify an individual by name and dwelling place. The individual must consent to be interviewed and must be able to answer direct questions. Finally, it is to be hoped that the same individual can be located again if a second survey is part of the original design of the study. This last criterion appears to be the most difficult to fulfill in the populations studied so far.

In the Manhattan area none of the three characteristics just described appeared to be present. It seems practically impossible to identify individuals by name and dwelling place through the usual means of names on mailboxes or obtaining names from the superintendent or janitor of the building. The names on the letter boxes in this area may either not exist or may be so defaced that they are illegiole. The janitor, when one comes to know him better, admits that he really does not know who lives in a given apartment because the rent is paid by the fellow whose name he knows and who used to live in that apartment, but this fellow has now moved to another apartment and has been replaced by a later migrant. The original tenant pays the rent and collects tribute from the subtenant; the whole procedure is illegal, so that difficulty in identifying a specific individual has advantages both for those who evade the law and for those who would find it embarrassing to enforce it.

Fear of opening the door to strangers in this neighborhood is realistic, and the pollster who knocks on the door (doorbells do not exist) is not welcome. After repeating his knock several times, he may be answered with the shout "Quien?" "Who?" When the would-be caller has identified himself by shouting "It's the doctor," a long, ominous silence follows, and the door may be opened only sufficiently to allow room for the snout of a snarling, barking dog. While doors are not opened to strangers in this neighborhood and it is not the custom to answer direct questions or to keep appointments, as soon as an individual becomes known, is "placed" as to "who he is" and "what he does" in the area, a considerable degree of confidence may be established. Thus *la doctora* became an accepted figure, as did those who were working on the project, and none of them was ever molested in any way. But this becoming known involved developing personal relationships with numbers of individuals and opening up avenues of approach other than those afforded by the structured questions of a questionnaire.

To summarize, the context of the Manhattan slum area with its particular mores made a reliable selection of an adequate sample of the population very difficult, and the limitations of a set method of questioning were more obvious than its advantages. Nevertheless, many of the items included in the Arsenal Health study questionnaire appeared to the clinicians to have a bearing on health and social problems in the Manhattan project. Such items were therefore incorporated into the schedule of information to be obtained through direct observation, medical histories taken in the office or at home, physical examinations, flexible interviews conducted by physicians and by anthropologists, and outside sources (that is, hospital records and Social Service Exchange).

While searching for a bench mark to serve as a guide for the definition of illness not only in terms of established clinical entities but in terms of capacity to function, it was found in a survey of employees of the New York Telephone Company that one third of the employed population was responsible for three fourths of the episodes of illness. (Hinkle and Plummer 1952.) Four fifths of the days of disability in any one year were attributable to this small group. In the New York Telephone Company, as in other large industrial concerns, an exact record of absences is kept on each individual worker, and a check by the medical department of the plant is required so that the definition of general susceptibility to illness in terms of performance at work can be documented by the records of twenty years as well as by interviews with the individuals themselves and with their supervisors.

When a population is studied from its home base rather than from its place of employment, it may well turn out that for 100 employed men living in a given area almost as many employers scattered over the five boroughs are involved. The analysis of attendance records, as was done in the New York Telephone Company, is therefore impractical. In the case of the Puerto Rican population, many individuals are marginally and irregularly employed due to conditions beyond their control. Therefore absences from work, even if they could be checked, would not furnish a fair criteria for determining susceptibility to illness.

In the usual American community, every child over the age of six and up to the age required by state law is expected to go to school. Schools keep records of attendance. Since 233 of the 420 Puerto Ricans in the current study are under fourteen years of age, it was thought that school attendance records checked against hospital records and the reports of parents would furnish a criterion for measuring the general susceptibility to illness in school children in terms of their ability to function, much as attendance records in the New York Telephone Company served as a guide for an employee's functional capacity.

But the assumptions that a sick child stays home from school and that a child who is not sick goes to school turned out to be untrue for the Puerto Rican group in the Manhattan slum area. Where a child had been hospitalized with rheumatic fever for three months (Family 31), the mother's testimony, the school, and the hospital records were all in agreement, but this was an exceptional situation. In another family (Family 78), according to the school record, three children under the age of ten were absent over fifty days each during the course of one school term. Our contact with the family came two years later, at which time the mother denied the children's having been ill at any time. No hospital record corresponding to the period of school absences could be found. On further investigation, it turned out that the absences took place a few months after the family migrated to New York, when the mother considered that the children did not have sufficient warm clothing to go out in the street.

Keeping the child at home for one or another family reason is not uncommon. Sometimes an older child will be kept out of school to mind the baby while the mother takes a younger child to a clinic or has an "appointment" of her own with a social agency. Truancy occurs at all ages, notably among teen-agers, but even an eight-year-old child (Family 14) came bouncing into the office one morning saying he did not have to go to school and could he play with our toys. The reverse is also true. Where an American middle-class mother will take a child's temperature and keep him home with a sniffle, a mother in this area is not likely to have a thermometer, the child may not appear "sick" to her, or she may be going to work and there may be no one with whom she can leave him. Such a child may remain in school until the teacher decides that he is sick, sends him to the school nurse or doctor, who sends him home with a note that he must see the doctor before returning to school.

This going to the doctor or clinic by a child perhaps re-
covering from a minor respiratory illness may be the occasion
for the absence of another "non-sick" sibling in the same
family. The well sibling may be kept at home to mind the
baby while the mother takes the child who was sick yester-
day to the clinic in order to comply with the request of the
school nurse or doctor. If the mother has difficulty in making herself understood in English or in communicating with
institutional authorities (Family 28 and others), she may
take a non-sick child with her on a clinic visit or for an
interview requested by a social agency in their office located
outside the area. In summary, the school attendance record
does not serve as an index of general susceptibility to illness
for children of school age in this area.

As far as we have been able to determine, the schools
themselves, while keeping records of daily attendance, do
not have cumulative records which would permit an estimate
of the average number of expected absences in the school
year in different grades. Nor has a careful study of the
reasons for absences been made by means of interviews with
parents at the time that absences occur; this might reveal
a pattern for the poor school attendance record in this area
and suggest means for its correction.

Although a structured questionnaire of the Arsenal Health
study type administered in a direct question and answer
form did not seem applicable to the Puerto Rican population
in this area and although no quantitative measure comparable to the one presented in the survey of New York Telephone Company employees for a functional appraisal of
illness was discovered for this particular environment, the
thesis proposed by the latter group to explain the greater

susceptibility to illness among some employees was of great interest to both teams of investigators in the current project.

Hinkle and Plummer concluded that the group of individuals chronically exposed to life stress is the group in whom most of the illnesses will occur and who will present the most difficult problems in interpersonal relations and administration. Life stress as defined by Wolff, the definition employed in this study, does not necessarily mean that an individual has been exposed to an extraordinary number of hardships, but an adverse life situation is one which is perceived as such by the individual involved. What constitutes stress for one individual is not necessarily stress in the eyes of his neighbor. (Wolff 1950.)

Among telephone employees the actual life experience of individuals in the well group did not differ materially from that of those in the sick group, if this life experience were to be calculated in terms of poverty and of the early death of one or both parents. But the well group were individuals "with no unalterable goals in life," and although capable of deep attachment to their relatives and friends these women had shown adaptability in the face of personal losses and changes in job situation. The sick group were not "readily deviated from their goals or their position in life," and it appeared that many of their bodily disturbances could be interpreted as an adaptive response to stressful situations in their environment. The association of stress and bodily disease has been demonstrated in clinical observations and also by means of recorded physiological changes in various organs of the body during a stress interview in the laboratory. (Wolff 1950.)

Two conditions are necessary preludes to this experimental

situation. First, the patient's complaints must be of such a nature that some of the physiological changes responsible for his symptom complex are subject to direct observation in the laboratory or may be measured by tests sufficiently sensitive and reliable to indicate a change during the stress interview. And second, the doctor must be sufficiently well acquainted with his patient to know what subjects are particularly stressful to him and must handle these during the interview in a manner that will bring out feelings of resentment, frustration, or helplessness in the patient. An observable or measurable physiological change under the conditions described is interpreted as a reaction to stress by that individual.

The concept that adversity is stressful in so far as it is perceived as such by the individual fits in well with the anthropologist's thesis (Padilla) that what constitutes a problem for an American middle-class housewife is not necessarily a problem for the Puerto Rican housewife living in a Manhattan slum, and vice versa. At this point the physicians looked to the anthropologists for an outlining of those factors in the Manhattan slum environment which might be particularly stressful to the lower-class Puerto Ricans population whose migration had been determined by a particular set of needs and aspirations, the fulfillment of which was bound to be hampered by many frustrations.

As a result of the anthropological study the physicians approached patients armed with some notions as to their background and were in a better position to explore whether episodes of illness, both observed and previously recorded, might be associated with a period of stress perceived by a lower-class Puerto Rican in a slum culture, and to interpret the meaning of illness for these particular people.

After taking into consideration the various methods and points of view discussed above, the following method for collecting and reporting data was agreed upon. The anthropologists used their observations, interviews, and questionnaires with many hundreds of individuals to construct a picture of the norms of behavior for the group of lower-class Puerto Ricans living in a Manhattan slum neighborhood. The physicians selected eighty families comprising 420 individuals as the basis for their report. All but three of the 420 individuals were born in Puerto Rico or were sons and daughters of Puerto Rican parents. All eighty families were living in tenements within a particular health area at the onset of the study. No family living in a housing project at the time that the study was undertaken is included in this group of eighty households. Fifteen families or 18.75 per cent of the group have moved to a housing project or to other neighboorhoods since the onset of the study and a follow-up report is included on those families who could be located and on whom a home call was made. For the purposes of this report families have been defined to include:

1. Members of the nuclear family in continuous residence.

2. Adult members of a nuclear family, their spouses and children who have been or may still be in temporary residence in the home of a parent and who in the opinion of the investigator play a role in the household.

3. Grandmothers, cousins, or others residing in the household temporarily or permanently.

4. Separated or divorced men who reside with and maintain a second family but who contribute to the support of the children and are recognized as having paternal authority and visiting privileges in the household under study.

The variable size and age composition of households has been recognized by other workers (Taback 1955), and the several types of individuals just described did constitute a family or household in this particular population.

The eighty families for study were selected in the following manner:

1. Fifty-one families came to the attention of anthropologists and physicians through various channels. While a majority of these came to the office seeking medical advice, the anthropologists became acquainted with many children at school and gained entrance to their homes, thus paving the way for the physician's visit or for an office referral. Still others were referred by private social agencies for medical care, and these were later visited in their homes by the anthropologists. These fifty-one families are comprised of people who for one reason or another were amenable to study and with whom a prolonged contact was possible, but the first contact with these families was not always because of illness in one of their members.

2. Just after the project had been undertaken, it became clear to all concerned that a further systematic exploration of the area was needed, and the anthroplogists made a new attempt at sampling by selecting every fifth Puerto Rican family in every fifth dwelling when it was possible to locate them and identify a member of the household. Where no one could be located after several calls or when the investigator was met by persistent refusal, the next Puerto Rican family who responded was selected. This might be number six or number seven and it is difficult to determine how many were missed. Those families who refused or who could not be located were not followed up.

Twenty-nine Puerto Rican families were brought under

observation by this means. Some of them were already known to the medical office, others were entirely new, but this second sample did not appear to differ significantly from the fifty-one families in the judgment sample in regard to age, family composition, medical records, or other characteristics.

A questionnaire constructed by the anthropologists to include questions designed to elicit more than a monosyllabic answer and to provide for a flexible interviewing technique was administered to at least one member of each of these twenty-nine families, and a medical study of these families was conducted by the physicians.

Taken together, the judgment sample of fifty-one families and the second sample of twenty-nine families constitute eighty families within the definition of a family as given above and include 420 individuals. The anthropologists have had some contact with all eighty families, either through the administration of their questionnaire to one or more members of the family or through participant observer contacts at home, at school, or on the street. A medical history including biographical material and a physical examination was made on all those individuals who consented. Observations on behavior and interpersonal relations over as much as four years in some cases were recorded. A chest X-ray, blood serology, and examinations of stools for ova and parasites were carried out by the local unit of the New York Health Department when indicated. Some of the individuals have been treated in their homes by the physicians during episodes of illness. The contacts by anthropologists in some instances have been prolonged and intimate to the extent that they are known in some households as being "de la familia" (that is, belonging to the family).

In the case of the twenty-nine families selected in the second sample by the anthropologists, individuals were encouraged to see the physicians by the promise of a free checkup. Some people, especially men, who did not consider that they had a medical problem were often difficult to reach. Where medical examinations were carried out in the home, rectal and vaginal examinations were omitted. In order to obtain as complete a medical record as possible on all members of the eighty families, a list of the names of the 420 individuals was given to the record room of the near-by voluntary hospital as well as to several municipal hospitals. The files were searched for these names, and the records were read and summarized by the physicians. Thus, all individuals who could be reached were examined by one of the physicians, but when an individual could not be reached and had had a physical examination within the past two years at a hospital, as an out-patient or an in-patient, that individual was counted as examined. All but twenty of the 420 individuals living in the eighty families were examined under the definition given above.

The medical data described were recorded for each member of a family in a family chart. In addition, information was recorded for all members of the family, when it was obtainable, concerning the date and circumstances of migration, family organization, amount of English spoken, number of years of formal schooling, skin color and appearance of hair, religion, housing, sources and amount of income, and whether or not the family was receiving public assistance. A summary of these data on each of the eighty families forms the Appendix of this volume, while the substance of the report consists of observations on the medical condition of these families as they appeared to be related to and interact with the various social and cultural factors described.

It will be noted that a diet study is not included in the case summaries. This omission may be attributed to the impossibility of evaluating the food intake of different members of a family with the limited personnel available for this project. Individual reports by patients were found to be unreliable when checked with clinical observations. In general, adult Puerto Rican migrants eat rice and beans, bananas, oranges, and pork products. Items from the American diet are added as soon as the family can afford them. Adolescent children who learn about American diets in school may refuse rice and beans. Scurvy and severe iron deficiency anemia were observed by us on several occasions in infants whose diet consisted only of milk until they were two years old. On the other hand, many mothers sacrifice themselves to buy baby foods for their children.

Summary. The following report is based on findings obtained by a group of clinicians working as family physicians out of a small office in a Manhattan slum neighborhood in conjunction with a group of social anthropologists. The data consist of medical and social information concerning a selected sample of eighty Puerto Rican families living in this particular neighborhood. Attention is focused on the relationship between social and environmental factors, the susceptibility to illness, and the management of such illness in this group. Problems of method encountered in this particular study are contrasted with those encountered in previous studies of this character.

II. GENERAL CHARACTERISTICS
OF THE EIGHTY FAMILIES

The U.S. Bureau of the Census defines a Puerto Rican as an individual whose birthplace is in Puerto Rico or an individual who has at least one parent whose birthplace was Puerto Rico. In this report the definition of a Puerto Rican has been extended to include a group of seven grandchildren of migrants. Thus, three generations and several stages of acculturation are represented: (1) migrants who came as adults or as children; (2) children of migrants who are young adults, adolescents, or small children today; (3) grandchildren of migrants who are the children of young adult Puerto Rican parents born in the neighborhood.

1. THE PATTERN OF MIGRATION

Migration from the island of Puerto Rico to continental United States has been proceeding at different rates since the beginning of the century, and the Puerto Rican migrant differs from the European immigrant not only in that he is already a citizen before migration but also in that he can visit his place of birth comparatively easily, and does so rather frequently, traveling back and forth between continental United States and Puerto Rico several times in the course of a few years. (See Padilla.)

The Puerto Rican migrants may be divided roughly into those who came before World War II and those who have come since. The latter group form by far the majority. The Migration Division of the Department of Labor of the Commonwealth of Puerto Rico reports that the average number of individuals migrating to continental United States between 1909 and 1940 ranged from 900 to 1,900 persons per year. This figure rose to an annual average of 18,000 for the decade 1941–1950, and an estimate of 49,000 a year is given for the years 1951–1955. Within these averages, there are wide annual variations which reflect changing job opportunities on the continent. For instance, it is estimated that there were only 21,000 Puerto Ricans migrating to the United States in 1954, as compared to 69,000 in 1953 and 45,000 in 1955.

Members of the eighty families under study reflect the dribbling character of the Puerto Rican migration and are representative of its general trend since 84 per cent of the group migrated after World War II. (See Figure 1.) The small percentage (4 per cent) of individuals migrating after 1952 in this particular group is accounted for, we believe, by the nature of the area. This is not an area of rooming houses but of apartments. In our observation, a number of families (Families 22, 45, 53) first lived in a rooming house before moving to an apartment in the area under study. For them it represented one step on the road of upward mobility.

In trying to set the eighty families against the background of other Puerto Ricans in the neighborhood, we can only say that the 420 individuals included in these families constitute approximately 10 per cent of the Puerto Rican population in the area as reported in the 1950 Census. Due to the many changes in this neighborhood during the past five years, involving the condemning and tearing down of old tenements

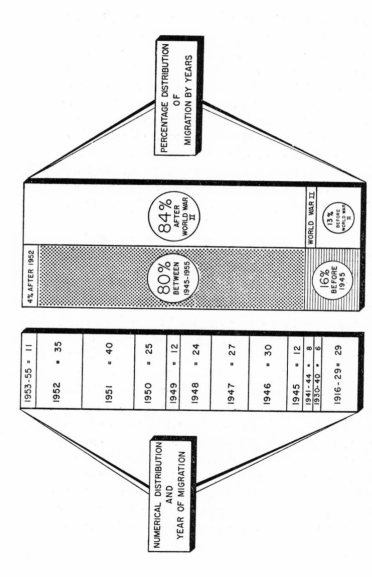

FIGURE 1. PATTERN OF MIGRATION OF 259 PUERTO RICANS BY YEARS THROUGH JANUARY 1, 1956

and the construction of housing projects, reliable estimates as
to the number of Puerto Ricans living in the same area in
1955 were not available. This area may also be considered
something of a backwater because it includes individuals
who migrated over twenty-five years ago (Families 50, 64,
66, 69), whose children were born in the area, married in
the area, and who have given birth to a second generation of
children born in this same neighborhood. These young cou-
ples, children of migrants, are in the process of moving out
of the area, but their close family ties and the prejudices
which exist against Hispanos (the term by which Puerto
Ricans designate themselves—see Padilla) and people of
darker skin color make such a move difficult at times.

2. AGE AND SEX DISTRIBUTION

The Puerto Ricans in New York City are young people in
comparison to the rest of the population. About one third of
the total New York City population were estimated to be
forty-five years old and over in the 1950 Census, whereas
only 13 per cent of Puerto Ricans fell into this category.
(Jaffe 1954.) Only 15 per cent of native Puerto Ricans in
the group under study were forty-five years old and over,
and no individuals born here of Puerto Rican parentage were
over forty-five. In fact, 82 per cent of the individuals of
Puerto Rican parentage in the group studied were under
fourteen years of age. (See Figure 2.)

The sex distribution of the Puerto Rican population in
New York City is of interest. Previous to 1950 the net migration from Puerto Rico contained a larger proportion of
women than men, but during the fiscal year 1953 about 58
per cent of all the net migrants were males. (Jaffe 1954.)

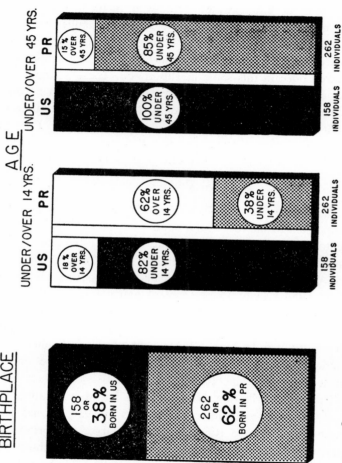

FIGURE 2. DISTRIBUTION OF THE 420 INDIVIDUALS BY BIRTHPLACE AND BY AGE

In the group under study, the number of adult women migrants is greater than the number of men—the reason being that our group contains a number of women who migrated with their children following separation from their mates in Puerto Rico. Also, since this is a family study, the unattached man who occupies a couch in his married brother's living room is only a fleeting figure.

Summary. The eighty Puerto Rican families in this study are comparable to other Puerto Rican migrants in New York City in regard to (1) migration pattern and (2) age and sex distribution. From the medical point of view, two characteristics are important; the migration pattern and the comparative youth of the group. In this respect one may expect that these individuals are a reservoir for diseases endemic in the area from which they came and that there will be a high prevalence of diseases of childhood and early adult life among them, in contrast to the degenerative diseases commonly associated with admissions to hospitals in areas where few Puerto Ricans live. Also, since the large majority have but recently moved to a Manhattan slum area, possibly from rural surroundings in a different climate and a different culture, one may expect a high degree of susceptibility to all types of illnesses among them, as has been noted for other recently urbanized populations. (Dubos 1952.)

3. HEIGHTS AND WEIGHTS

Weight gain is a criterion of health in the minds of many migrants, and those who migrated within the last ten years can usually tell how much they weighed on arrival in New York and are happy to report a substantial increase since that time. For women from 60 to 63 inches in height a weight of 140–150 pounds was not unusual in our group. Attempts on the part of the physician to bring the weight down might be interpreted by the patient as punishment and deprivation. As one stout woman put it when she marched into the physician's office on her return from a visit to the out-patient department of a city hospital where an 1800-calorie diet had been prescribed, "I did not come to New York to starve." Presumably the Puerto Rican woman who carries her bundles up three flights of stairs in a Manhatten tenement expends less energy—and consumes more calories—than she did climbing a hillside in Puerto Rico with a can of water on her head, and she is pleased with the change.

The increase in weight following migration in our observation is not so marked among men as it is among women. The fact that Puerto Rican males may be lighter in proportion to their height than non-Puerto Ricans and are not necessarily physically unfit for this reason is recognized by the United States Army.

Army Regulation 40-115 of 1948 contains a table for standard and minimum acceptable measurements of height, weight, and circumference of chest for Filipinos, Puerto Ricans, and individuals of Oriental descent. In this table the standard for weight and chest circumference in relation to height for Puerto Ricans, Filipinos, and those of Oriental descent is different from the standard for other draftees. For instance, a Puerto Rican draftee 60 inches tall, to be acceptable, may weigh between 101 and 114 pounds. His chest circumference may range from 18.50 inches to 31 inches. On the other hand, to be acceptable a non-Puerto Rican or non-Oriental draftee 60 inches tall must weigh between 105 and

116 pounds and must have a chest circumference of from 28.75 inches to 31.25 inches at expiration. A similar differential is observed throughout the scale.

But no similar special scale of body measurements for children of Puerto Rican parentage is available. The Department of Health of the Commonwealth of Puerto Rico knows of no recent studies on the growth and physical development of Puerto Rican children on the island, nor to the best of our knowledge have such studies of Puerto Rican children and children of Puerto Rican parentage been conducted on the continent.

The United States Children's Bureau under the direction of Helen Bary (Blanco 1946) conducted in 1923 a health survey and health education program among school children in Puerto Rico. In the course of this project over 3,000 boys and 3,000 girls between the ages of six and seventeen were weighed and measured. This group, though not selected by random sampling techniques, included children of various economic groups. Comparing the average heights and weights obtained on these children with the Wood Baldwin tables which form the base of many tables used in the United States, the Puerto Rican boys averaged 1 inch less in height and were 5 to 8 pounds lighter than the American boys. The girls were from 0.5 to 1 inch shorter than American girls but more nearly approached these in weight.

The children in the eighty families in this study were weighed and measured under standard conditions by the pediatrician or the family physician as a part of their medical examination. The weights and heights of these children, 93 boys (see Figures 3 and 4) and 92 girls (see Figures 5 and 6), as recorded following a single examination, have

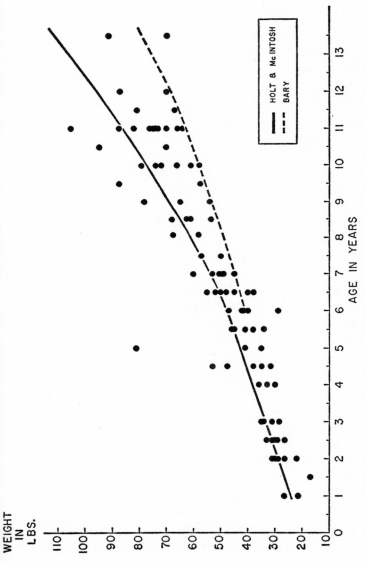

WEIGHT IN LBS.

AGE IN YEARS

HOLT & McINTOSH
BARY

FIGURE 3. WEIGHT OF 93 NEW YORK BOYS OF PUERTO RICAN PARENTAGE, 1–13 YEARS OF AGE, PLOTTED AGAINST MEDIAN WEIGHT OF WHITE AMERICAN BOYS (HOLT AND McINTOSH TABLE, 1953) AND OF PUERTO RICAN BOYS (BARY TABLE, 1923)

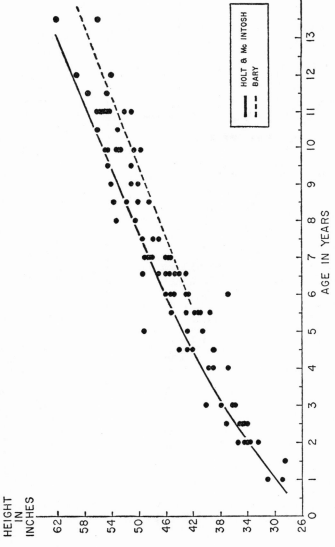

FIGURE 4. HEIGHT OF 93 NEW YORK BOYS OF PUERTO RICAN PARENTAGE, 1–13 YEARS OF AGE, PLOTTED AGAINST MEDIAN HEIGHT OF WHITE AMERICAN BOYS (HOLT AND MCINTOSH TABLE, 1953) AND OF PUERTO RICAN BOYS (BARY TABLE, 1923)

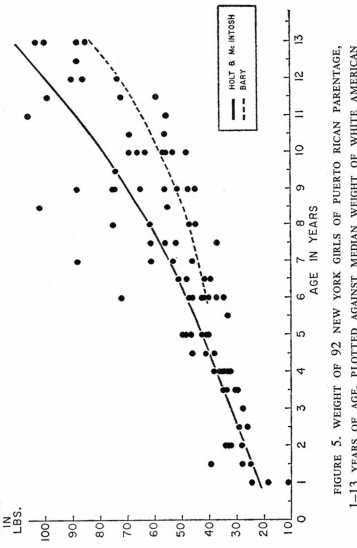

FIGURE 5. WEIGHT OF 92 NEW YORK GIRLS OF PUERTO RICAN PARENTAGE, 1–13 YEARS OF AGE, PLOTTED AGAINST MEDIAN WEIGHT OF WHITE AMERICAN GIRLS (HOLT AND MCINTOSH TABLE, 1953) AND OF PUERTO RICAN GIRLS (BARY TABLE, 1923)

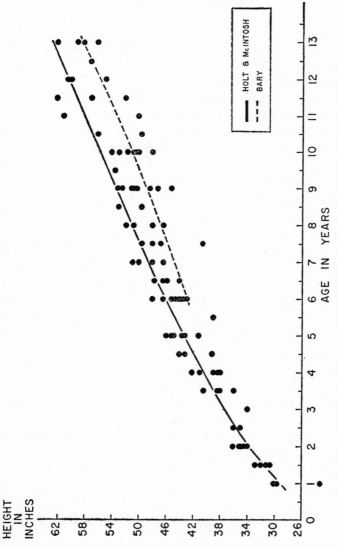

FIGURE 6. HEIGHT OF 92 NEW YORK GIRLS OF PUERTO RICAN PARENTAGE, 1–13 YEARS OF AGE, PLOTTED AGAINST MEDIAN HEIGHT OF WHITE AMERICAN GIRLS (HOLT AND MCINTOSH TABLE, 1953) AND OF PUERTO RICAN GIRLS (BARY TABLE, 1923)

been plotted as individual dots on the charts where the 10-, 50-, and 90-percentile figures of white American children (measured by the Harvard School of Public Health) and the Bary results are also recorded.

When the weights and heights for these Puerto Rican boys and girls are compared with the two scales, it becomes apparent that there is a wide range between individuals, but the greater number fall below the 50 percentile of the Harvard scale and above the average on the Bary scale. Also the Puerto Rican boys and girls above the age of ten do not appear to keep pace with their previous development. No X-ray studies were carried out on these particular children so that it is not possible to state in how many cases a retarded bone age was associated with small stature. A fair curve for the heights and weights of the children in this group, superimposed on the fair curve for the 50 percentile scale, corresponds more exactly to the latter for children between the ages of two and seven, suggesting that the rate of growth for these Puerto Rican children follows the same gradient as that of the American children when height and weight are considered together. (See Figures 7 and 8.) The results of the Harvard study and other similar projects have been used for the development of scales which appear in standard pediatric texts. (Holt and McIntosh 1953; Nelson 1954.)

White children of Northern European descent living in less privileged areas of Boston and its suburbs were the subjects of the Harvard study. (Nelson 1954.) While the concept of a range within which the height and weight of normal children falls has been emphasized rather than the one average figure, the scale is based on measurements taken on white children who have a genetic and nutritional background which differs from that of the Puerto Rican children. Therefore the fact that a majority of the Puerto Rican children measured in this study fall below the average in weight and height as plotted on an American scale does not help us in determining which children are "normal" within their own frame of reference. Yet, in the absence of a Puerto Rican scale, the American scale is taken as a frame of reference, and we have seen two children (Families 9 and 18) excluded from school at the age of six because they were "too small."

The Bary scale is composed of measurements made of Puerto Rican school children living on the island over thirty years ago. The fact that the measurements of the Puerto Rican children in this study who are either children of migrants or migrants themselves fall above the average in the Bary scale is interpreted as evidence of the improved conditions under which Puerto Rican children live as compared to thirty years ago.

More precise and extensive data are available for the birth weights of infants born of Puerto Rican parents in Manhattan. The birth weights of 847 white infants, 1,265 Negro infants, and 2,118 Puerto Rican infants born on the obstetrical wards of Mount Sinai Hospital between January, 1953 and July, 1956 were compared. (See Figure 9.) A smaller percentage of infants weighing less than 2,500 grams is found in the Puerto Rican group when this group is compared with the white and the Negro group. The difference between the percentage of premature Puerto Rican infants and the percentage of premature white infants is not statistically significant. The percentage of premature infants born of Puerto Rican parents is smaller than the percentage of premature infants born of Negro parents, and this difference is calcu-

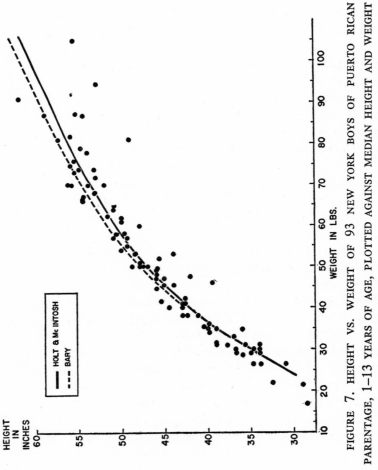

FIGURE 7. HEIGHT VS. WEIGHT OF 93 NEW YORK BOYS OF PUERTO RICAN PARENTAGE, 1–13 YEARS OF AGE, PLOTTED AGAINST MEDIAN HEIGHT AND WEIGHT OF WHITE AMERICAN BOYS (HOLT AND MCINTOSH TABLE, 1953) AND OF PUERTO RICAN BOYS (BARY TABLE, 1923)

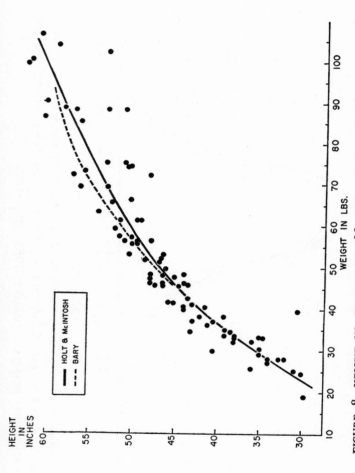

FIGURE 8. HEIGHT VS. WEIGHT OF 92 NEW YORK GIRLS OF PUERTO RICAN PARENTAGE, 1–13 YEARS OF AGE, PLOTTED AGAINST MEDIAN HEIGHT AND WEIGHT OF WHITE AMERICAN GIRLS (HOLT AND MCINTOSH TABLE, 1953) AND OF PUERTO RICAN GIRLS (BARY TABLE, 1923)

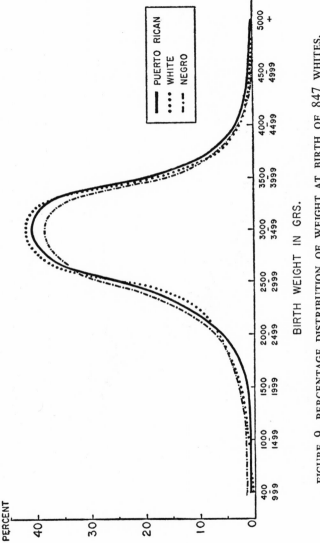

BIRTH WEIGHT IN GRS.

FIGURE 9. PERCENTAGE DISTRIBUTION OF WEIGHT AT BIRTH OF 847 WHITES, 1,265 NEGROES, AND 2,118 PUERTO RICANS, OBSTETRICAL WARD SERVICE, MOUNT SINAI HOSPITAL, JANUARY, 1953–JULY, 1956

lated as bëing significant at the .01 level for this particular group. The mean weights of white, Negro, and Puerto Rican infants in this group are 3,120, 3,030, and 3,150 grams respectively, as shown in Table 1, and these differences are not statistically significant.

TABLE I

Summary of Births on Wards at Mount Sinai Hospital January, 1953–July, 1956

	Number of Births	Per Cent of Infants Weighing Less than 2,500 Grams	Mean Weight at Birth in Grams
White	847	10.9	3,120
Negro	1,265	13.3	3,030
Puerto Rican	2,118	9.3	3,150

The higher incidence of prematurity among Negroes, when prematurity is defined in terms of infants whose birth weight is 2,500 grams or less, has already been noted, and the possibility that this might be related to a shorter period of gestation among Negro women has been suggested. (Anderson 1943.) We have no information on the length of gestation among Puerto Rican women. Poor nutrition is generally accepted as one of the factors contributing to prematurity. In the eyes of the clinician, the state of nutrition of most Puerto Rican women delivered on the wards of Mount Sinai Hospital appears inferior to that prevailing among white women on the same wards, so that finding no significant difference in the incidence of prematurity between the Puerto Rican and the white group comes as a surprise. The validity and the significance of this observation requires further investigation. As far as New York City is concerned at the present time, since the birth rate is higher among Puerto Ricans than it is among other groups, the total number of premature infants born of Puerto Rican parents in New York may be greater than that found in other sections of the population.

Another observation, although more than thirty years old, tends to confirm the impression that though Puerto Rican infants may start on an equal footing with other infants at birth, they tend to lose ground thereafter. In 1932 Dr. Harold Mitchell, working under the auspices of the American Child Association and the Department of Pediatrics of the Yale University School of Medicine, measured a group of infants who were attending well-baby clinics in Puerto Rico. Comparisons were made with observed averages for height and weight of white and Negro children in the United States and with children of Italian mothers in the United States.

The results indicated that Puerto Rican children were lighter in weight, shorter, and had slightly smaller heads than comparable children of the three continental groups, white, Negro, and Italian-American. The difference in height between Puerto Rican and American children from one to seven months old was two centimeters or less, from then on to the thirteenth or fourteenth month the difference was about three centimeters, and four centimeters thereafter. The difference from the sixth month onward is about 4 to 5 per cent. Differences in weight were more marked. In the early months differences were more slight, being from 3 to 5 per cent in girls in the second to the fourth month and 6 per cent for boys from the second to the third month. With increasing age the differences increased to a maximum for girls of 14 per cent at the thirty-second to thirty-third months, and 14 per cent for boys at the ninth to eleventh month. [Blanco 1946.]

Summary. The United States Army recognizes that Puerto Rican males may be lighter in weight than other draftees and measures them by a special scale.

Body measurements on large groups of Puerto Rican children have apparently not been made in recent years. Those made on the island over twenty years ago antedate recent advances in public health. Comparing the heights and weights of 93 boys and 92 girls in the eighty families in this study with scales based on the measurements of white children, the boys and girls of Puerto Rican parentage in general fall below the average for the white children.

There is need for the development of a scale of body measurements for children of Puerto Rican parentage since a comparison of the weights and heights of Puerto Rican children with those of white children does not provide the information necessary to detect deviations from a norm for these children which may be clinically significant.

A review of the birth weights for infants born to white, Negro, and Puerto Rican mothers on the wards of Mount Sinai Hospital for the period 1953–1956 indicates that the incidence of infants weighing less than 2,500 grams is significantly greater among Negroes than it is among Puerto Ricans. The validity of a comparison between the white and the Puerto Rican group is questionable due to the comparatively smaller size of the white sample.

4. COLOR OF SKIN

The standard ways of defining "race" are different in New York City and in Puerto Rico. In New York when a man or woman with Negroid characteristics marries a white person, the children are classed as Negroes. In Puerto Rico, a similar couple who have both white and dark children may move in white social circles. The Puerto Rican family in New York whose children have a wide range of skin color are considered Negroes by non-Puerto Ricans. The possibilities for upward mobility in such a family are limited by this fact, and this family also comes to consider its darker children as Negroes and therefore less favored. (See Padilla.)

Bearing these facts in mind, the clinicians looked at the color of the skin and the characteristics of hair and features so that they might be in a position to determine the manner in which skin color might be a factor of stress in terms of the individual concerned.

Clinical estimates of skin color were noted by the observer on the medical record and by the anthropologists in the course of their interviews. When several observers had records on the same individual, the estimates of color were usually compared and the agreement between different observers was substantial. Difference of opinion was generally confined to the description of the hair. Usually there was agreement on the color of skin and type of features. Skin color was described in our records as white, light olive, dark olive, light brown, or dark brown. Hair was described in our records as straight, wavy, curly or kinky, often with a note as to the coarseness or fineness. This latter observation was not always included. Features were described as Caucasoid or Negroid. These notations were made on the basis of clinical observations—no measurements were taken.

The manner in which a dark skin may stand in the way of one who desires to move out of the slum is illustrated by the following case. There was a period extending over several months when the family physicians could count on a visit from a pretty young woman with Negroid features, dark brown skin, and kinky hair (Family 62) at any time when the clinic office was open. This woman had come to New York from Puerto Rico as an infant and had lived in the neighborhood for over twenty years. She had recently been fired from her job as saleswoman because of an argument with her superior. She complained of "pounding headaches," dizziness, and a "stuffy nose." These symptoms came on after arguments with her mother, an authoritative woman with whom she and her two daughters lived. The apartment was immaculate and the grandmother never stopped cleaning. The young woman's marriage to a dark-skinned man ended in divorce shortly after the birth of their children, possibly because the couple, living alternately with her mother or his mother, had never succeeded in establishing a home of their own. She claimed that finding an apartment of their own had been impossible due to the fact that landlords objected to Hispanos, especially *trigueños,* "dark ones." Her daughter, a child of fourteen, who bore a strong physical resemblance to both her mother and grandmother, on being asked in the course of a physical examination what her ambitions were, said she wanted to be a teacher. The physician congratulated her, saying how useful a teacher who spoke both English and Spanish would be. The child, granddaughter of a woman who migrated over twenty years ago, replied quick as a flash, "But you see I am Hispano." In view of the grandmother's authoritarian personality, change might have been impossible in any event, but whenever the question of the daughter's moving away came up, it implied that this was impossible because they were *trigueños.*

An ambitious young man (Family 51) with curly, medium coarse hair, Caucasoid features, and light brown skin who suffered from chronic bronchial asthma came to the office during an attack. He had just been looking for an apartment in a middle-class neighborhood and had been unable to find one—this he felt sure was due to the fact that people did not want Hispanos. In another interview he told the physician that he had married the "whitest girl" (a bleached blonde) in the neighborhood and that henceforth he would send her out to find an apartment. Finally, an apartment was secured in Brooklyn which satisfied their desire to move away from the slum, but it was the wife who signed the lease.

Identification with the American-born Negro does occur, but we are not prepared to say how often. One such family was discovered (Family 24) in the random sample by the anthropologists. Unlike the young adults in Family 62, the brother and sister in Family 24, who had the physical characteristics of the Negro, spoke Spanish with an English accent, attended the Negro Baptist church, and spoke of themselves as Negroes. At the same time, since grandmothers, husbands, wives, and children of varying shades of skin color, texture of hair, and character of features are often found in the same family, it is hard to believe that estimating the exact shade of color is an important factor in the selection of a mate in all cases in this neighborhood. But color is an issue in the minds of most people. For instance, a light brown woman with Negroid features and kinky hair (Family 33) gave as one of her reasons for migration the fact that being darker than her siblings she could not hope to marry as well as they had in Puerto Rico. They were married to government employees and teachers. She actually married a man of light olive color, curly hair, and Caucasoid features whose earning capacity has turned out to be far below her expectations, so that she remains in the slum and has not achieved a social or economic position equal to that of her sisters in Puerto Rico.

Any comment on skin color may be a way of expressing disapproval. Two unmarried daughters in Family 64, who had light olive skin and Caucasoid features, became pregnant before finishing the eighth grade. The mother expressed her disgust with one of the boys involved by saying that he was a *moreno* (brown color), as was the grandchild. The darker skinned are apt to be blamed even if not identified. For instance, in Family 64, where every one has straight hair, light olive skin, and Caucasoid features, the mother brought the youngest child to the doctor to see if he had suffered an injury after being knocked down by another child who was surely a *moreno,* in this case she thought an American Negro. In this connection, and in the hope that future investigators will go into the question in greater detail, we wish to report the observation of an experienced social worker in the neighborhood. She noted that among the group of some twenty young drug addicts of Puerto Rican parentage with whom she had come in contact over a period of several years, the addict, except in one case, had always turned out to be the darkest member of his family.

Summary. The observations recorded here suggest that a note of the degree of whiteness of Puerto Rican individuals should be made by the physician to be used by him as a touchstone in his exploration as to whether and in what manner color may be a source of stress for the individual Puerto Rican family under his care.

5. EDUCATION

According to the 1950 Census, the median number of years of school completed by the Puerto Rican population twenty-five years of age and over, was about 7.2 years.

Among the total New York City population in this age group, the median number of years of school completed was 9.1.

In the group under discussion, information was available on the educational background of 141 migrants over fourteen years of age (see Table 2). Sixteen, or 11 per cent, of the 141 migrants had never been to school at all. Of these, five were grandmothers actively participating in the rearing of their grandchildren and the remainder were parents of school children. Of the 125 who had attended school, approximately one half had not completed grade school in Puerto Rico, and one third of the 125 had been or were attending high school.

TABLE 2

The Education of 141 Migrants

| | EDUCATED IN UNITED STATES | | EDUCATED IN PUERTO RICO | | |
	Male	*Female*	*Male*	*Female*	TOTAL
High school complete	6	2	5	1	14
High school incomplete	8	10	5	6	29
Grammar school complete	0	2	11	5	18
Grammar school incomplete	0	0	22	42	64
	14	14	43	54	125
No school	4	12			16
					141

There were no college graduates in this group. One individual of Puerto Rican parentage after graduating from high school in the neighborhood had attended the University of Puerto Rico for one year, but was unable to continue because of financial difficulties. A few individuals had taken special vocational training in electricity, tailoring, bookkeeping, etc. A few adults were attending night school to learn English.

Forty-three migrants and 19 individuals born in New York City had been or were attending high school. Only one girl completed high school in Puerto Rico while eight did so in New York. On arriving in New York City, migrants who are of school age are placed in the class corresponding to their chronological age. Three of the boys in this group who were between fourteen and fifteen years of age on arrival were so placed. They became delinquent and were sent to jail within two years. Data gathered from interviews with those boys who had returned from jail (Family 20) and with others who had had a similar experience suggest a possible sequence of events. Boys who migrate as adolescents and speak no English on arrival do not understand what goes on at school and consider the whole performance rather "babyish"; they become truants, fall in with gangs or with individuals already delinquent, try to steal cars or break into apartments, get caught, and land in jail. Girls who migrate as adolescents, in our observation, appear less prone to become delinquent at this point and may slide through school with or without learning English, or may marry young men migrants soon after arrival.

A study made in Puerto Rico suggests that those parents who have had four years of schooling or more are the ones who are prepared to make sacrifices to keep their children in school. (Tumin 1955.) In this small New York group, whether or not children remained at school seemed to be largely a matter of the individual determination of the parents, regardless of the years of schooling they themselves had enjoyed. In Family 19, for instance, where neither the mother nor the father had completed grade school in Puerto Rico, three adolescent children were attending high school; both they and their parents were determined that all nine children should receive high school diplomas. A similar situation obtained in Family 26 with six children.

These were exceptions to the general rule in this neighborhood, where most young people do not complete high school. The realization that certain job opportunities are closed to those who do not have high school diplomas comes later. At times young men took advantage of the G.I. bill of rights to return to high school. (Family 40.)

To the physician and public health worker, whether an individual is a reader or a nonreader is of greater importance than the number of years he has attended school. Our experience in this regard was sometimes surprising. A woman (Family 22) who claimed only three years of schooling in Puerto Rico leaned over the desk in the office and read the phrase "enfermo del pecho" (chest condition) on the medical record and denied that she had any such condition, while her fourteen-year-old daughter who had attended school in New York for three years was unable to read words such as "health" or "danger." Nonreaders in English are not confined to migrant Puerto Rican children in this neighborhood. Although it was not routine practice to test all high school children who came to the office, it was not unusual to find a child born in the neighborhood of Puerto Rican or Negro parents, not classified as mentally retarded by the school and attending the ninth or tenth grade, unable to read simple directions in a health pamphlet. The devising and carrying out of measures which would make it possible for every child not mentally retarded who attends a public school in New York City to acquire an elementary knowledge of spoken and written English is a goal still far from being realized.

Summary. The difficulties attendant upon the incorporation of a large group of Puerto Rican children into the New York City public school system have been briefly touched upon. Most important for the physician is the awareness that among adolescents who are recent migrants delinquent behavior may arise as a result of failure in school. Also, the physician should not assume that all those individuals who attend school are able to read health pamphlets or simple directions.

6. RELIGION

While Puerto Ricans in Puerto Rico are Catholic in the sense that all Spaniards are Catholic, and Roman Catholicism is the religion of people of Spanish heritage, it is estimated that about 20 per cent of the Puerto Rican population belong to Protestant churches and an unrecorded number are spiritualists. (Mills 1950.)

For every admission to a hospital in New York City, a notation is made somewhere on the chart as to the patient's religious affiliation. Where a space for this information is provided on the face sheet, the admission clerk puts a check in the appropriate box under the heading "Roman Catholic," "Protestant," "Jewish," "None." Such a notation may usually be found on the "pink slip" which accompanies a patient admitted by ambulance to a city hospital. Hospital personnel know that when an individual checked as a Roman Catholic is on the critical list a priest is to be called. The social worker called in to help a patient also looks over the information on religious affiliation: this helps her to determine whether the individual who needs her help may count on assistance from a social agency with an expressed preference for taking care of people of its own faith. In other words, a patient who enters a hospital is expected to acknowledge a religious affiliation, and hospital personnel are trained to consider this affiliation a fixed point and to act accordingly. Therefore, the practice and attitude of Puerto Ricans in this regard requires some elaboration.

For instance, a little girl in Family 15 was taken to the hospital, where she was registered as Protestant. She was subsequently taken to another hospital within the same month and there registered as Catholic. The father of the child said that in the first instance he had been accompanied by a nurse from a Protestant agency to whom he felt indebted; he therefore did not wish to hurt her feelings by saying he was not a Protestant, so the child was registered as Protestant. In the second hospital he was asked whether the child was Catholic, and he replied "yes." He himself had been brought up as a Baptist in Puerto Rico, but he kept a candle burning in front of the statue of the Virgin every night during the child's illness. His wife and he were married in a Catholic church at the insistence of his mother-in-law. His mother-in-law, in turn, is now one of the members of the council of a local Protestant church. "God is the same no matter where you find him," was his comment.

The mother in Family 13 was having difficulty with her nine-year-old daughter, who was staying away from school. The matter had been brought up to the Children's Court by the Youth Board, and the mother was referred to a Catholic agency for guidance since the child had been baptized a Catholic. She hoped the child would be sent to a Catholic boarding school eventually, as the Catholics "were very strict." She herself attended the Pentecostal church, and the little girl enjóyed going to a Baptist Sunday School with the children whom she had met at a Baptist summer camp. A similar situation obtained in Family 43 after they moved away from the neighborhood. The mother was looking for a Catholic parochial school for her eldest son because she considered instruction inadequate in the public schools. At the same time she hoped to find a Protestant church for her husband because she believed the Protestant attitude towards male philandering was "more strict" than the Catholic.

These examples suggest that for Puerto_ Ricans in this neighborhood association with_one particular religious group does not necessarily exclude them from other groups. Also, their interest in different religious organizations appears to be prompted by a desire to find a group which meets their needs as they see them rather than by any consideration of differences in religious doctrine. The Pentecostalists are an exception and concern themselves with the literal interpretation of the Bible.

Five of the eighty families in this group attended the Pentecostal church, and one presented a special problem to the family physician. The mother (Family 35) was starting her fourteenth pregnancy when she came to the physician's attention. Arrangements were made for prenatal care at Mount Sinai Hospital, and the possibility of a tubal ligation was discussed with the family. The woman said she would be willing if her husband consented. Several conversations were held between husband and physician, while leaning on the battered mudguard of an old car parked in front of the house or sitting in the home. There the husband brought out the Bible and read eloquently the Lord's command that man should multiply and also referred to the sin of Onan (Genesis 38:9). Therefore, he was unwilling to sign the permission for tubal ligation. His wife was admitted in the sixth month of her pregnancy with vaginal bleeding, which continued for several days. The presumptive diagnosis at the time was a placenta previa. The family physician visited the mother in the hospital. She was in a room with two other women. The possibility was discussed of tying her tubes should an abdominal intervention be necessary. She was rather noncommittal, but the other two women, also Puerto Ricans, who had been listening intently, chimed in like a Greek chorus to say that they would have their tubes tied under these circumstances. The hospital physicians called for the father and explained to him the risks of additional pregnancies for his wife. He would not sign a permission for tubal ligation at that time, but agreed that if a Cesarean section became necessary and the child were not delivered from below, he would then give his consent. The bleeding stopped and the mother went home. She returned a month later when a child weighing 5 pounds, 4 ounces, was delivered through the vaginal route. The final diagnosis was low implantation of the placenta. The child went home on the twenty-fifth day but has since been hospitalized for pneumonia during its first year of life. The woman is now forty. There is no indication that any form of contraception will be used, but the husband has promised the physicians to practice complete abstinence. A similar difficulty with patients who belong to the Pentecostal church has been experienced by other workers in the field of contraception. A social worker at Mount Sinai Hospital called upon the family physician for help in the case of a young woman member of the Pentecostal church who refused to accept contraceptive advice although this had been recommended by the resident physician on imperative medical grounds. A fellow patient, a Catholic, who had been acting as interpreter, turned to the social worker completely helpless, saying "what do you expect—she is a Protestant."

Even among individuals reared in New York City the family physician discovered some who believed in spiritualism and consulted *espiritistas* on occasion. As Padilla points out, the espiritista or medium is one who is believed to be in communication with *seres,* spirits in the next world, and who is able to affect cures of illnesses which were caused by these spirits. These types of illness, as an espiritista explained in the course of a visit to the family physician's office for the treatment of diarrhea, are not amenable to treatment by physicians. They arise from a current which passes from the spirit of an individual who is dead or from an individual who is angry with another one to the body and spirit of the afflicted. The espiritista is informed through her voices or spirits of the nature of the malady and of the spell which has been cast upon the sick individual. It is then necessary to cast off this spell, and this may be done by brewing certain potions which are prescribed by the espiritista. The sicknesses produced by the spirits may include "tuberculosis," but are more apt to involve bad dispositions, provoking fighting between spouses, spells (*ataques*), and nervous ailments of various kinds.

Summary. The examples cited indicate that the line between religious denominations is not as hard and fast among

this group of Puerto Ricans as it may be among other population groups. Nevertheless, the Puerto Rican family's particular beliefs affect their attitude toward medicine, and in certain instances the espiritista or spiritualist is one who may
have more influence than the physician in this particular
group.

PART TWO. *Environmental Factors:*
Stress and Disease

III. MIGRATION

The physician who walks in the slums of New York City, or is driven there to make a house call in the course of his assignment to the home care service of a city hospital, on seeing the broken windowpanes in dirty hallways, garbage-littered vacant lots, and crowds of people on the streets may indeed ask "Why did these people come here?" He may ask the question even more insistently if after long days and nights on duty in a city hospital he is fortunate enough to fly across the Caribbean to spend a few golden days in San Juan in mid-February and deserts the beach long enough to visit new factories, new housing developments, and clean though poor areas where light and air abound in comparison to the murk of a New York tenement. But if he drives further into the country and walks about in a rural area on the outskirts of a sugar plantation in the dead season when it is not cane-cutting time, he will begin to understand that for people who are hungry and have no work, beautiful scenery is not sufficient to sustain life. For an unemployed cane cutter a dismal New York tenement may represent a ticket in the lottery of a more abundant life. And, in fact, Puerto Rican migrants in time, like European immigrants before them, earn more money, get a better education, and live in better neighborhoods.

Although during the past eight years, under the leadership of Governor Luis Múñoz Marín, many new factories have been built and increasing opportunities for employment have been created on the island of Puerto Rico, migration is still an economic necessity. As a result of a decreasing death rate (7.7 per thousand in 1950) and a reproduction rate which continues high (38.7 per thousand in 1950), births exceed deaths by about 65,000 per year. (Commonwealth of Puerto Rico, Department of Labor, Migration Division, March, 1956.)

Compared to continental United States, Puerto Rico has a high rate of growth in its population of labor force age. Even with the accelerated industrial development which is taking place in Puerto Rico itself, it is estimated that an annual migration of 30,000 to 35,000 Puerto Ricans to continental United States may be expected for the next few years. (Weiss and Jaffe, 1955.) In New York City, Puerto Ricans are found in all walks of life: there are Puerto Rican teachers in the school system; skilled workmen; owners of small grocery stores and managers of supermarkets. The personnel director of the Waldorf-Astoria Hotel states that the hotel could not run without its Puerto Rican workers. (New York *Times,* May 31, 1957, p. 39.)

Underlying the economic necessity for migration are many social factors which influence the selection of those individuals who migrate. The migrant population divides itself into those who have lived here for many years, those who were born and raised here (*nacidos y criados*), and the more recent migrants. Among the more recent migrants there are numbers of able-bodied, unmarried young men and unmarried young women. These young people have come to earn a living, and for the most part they are both employed and employable. When an already constituted nuclear family (see page 73) migrates, the father is apt to come first, to be followed by his wife and some children, while others may come later. This dribling of individual migrants is demonstrated in Figure 1, which indicates migration of individuals by years. Another group of recent migrants include women (*mujeres*). These may be divided into three classes: those young women who have lost their virginity and, finding marriage more difficult on this account, came to the continent for another chance; other women who are divorced and hope to find employment more easily on the continent; and finally, women who are husbandless with a number of children. Women of this last class may be either unwed, divorced, or widowed. Another small but distinct category includes those individuals who are considered by their families to be either seriously ill or unmanageable in their home environment. In this last group, the individual's fare north may have been paid by his relatives in the hope that he may find medical care and another opportunity on the continent. Sixty-two per cent of the 420 individuals were born in Puerto Rico and the remaining 38 per cent in the United States. (Figure 2.)

The eighty Puerto Rican families under discussion include individuals from all of these groups. It has already been noted that 84 per cent of the 259 individual migrants came after World War II and 16 per cent before 1945. (See Figure 1.) Two individuals migrated before 1920. Since the study is primarily concerned with families, the able-bodied, unmarried young man or young woman of working age appears only as a transient visitor using a couch in the home of his brother or sister and moving on. But the families of some recent migrants consist of individuals who came here to work when they were single, stayed with a relative or friend, married, settled in the area, and are now raising their own children.

It is not possible to get a clear picture of the problems of pre-World War II migrants at the time of their arrival in the city. Municipal hospital records of twenty years ago are not easily uncovered, and the individuals concerned are living in the present and their problems center about the next generation, as will be shown later.

The actual dangers attendant upon migration today will be considered first. These in some cases are very real indeed, as the following examples will show.

A pretty little girl now eleven years old (Family 13) spent two months in a hospital three months after her arrival in the United States. She was hit by a car in the street where she was playing and her skull was fractured. She was readmitted six months later to another hospital with a diagnosis of postcompression syndrome. At the present time the physical examination is negative, but the child complains of dizziness, is unhappy at school, and speaks little English compared to her younger brother, who may be classified as almost bilingual.

Another child, now thirteen (Family 17), migrated to the area in 1948. A few months later, he was hit with a stick by another child with a resulting corneal ulcer. His vision is permanently impaired and he has difficulty in keeping up with his school work. The same year, that is, less than one year after migration, he and two other children in the same family, the three being six, five, and three years old at the time, were separated from their parents and hospitalized at Willard Parker because their mother was unable to take care of them when they had measles.

Sometimes a family never recovers from the accidents which occur in the first year following migration. A dark olive, tall man (Family 28) often may be seen in the street, walking with drooping shoulders and a discouraged expression. A regular visitor to an out-patient clinic, he suffers from seizures and labyrinthine disease. There is no history in the clinic chart as to how these seizures started. The man speaks little English. He informed us that he was well and worked as a manual laborer in Puerto Rico until migration in 1948. He left because he could find no work and no food during the dead season in the cane fields. He migrated in 1948 and found a house on Long Island where he obtained employment in a gang of men picking potatoes. One night the house caught fire, he fell through a floor, hit his head, and was unable to rescue his three children, who were burned to death. The seizures date from the time of this accident, and while these are controlled with medication he suffers from vertigo. His wife has borne him three children since that time, but he is unemployable due to his age, his lack of skills, and his illness. His wife is a patient at an out-patient department in another hospital where she complains of dizziness, palpitations, and nervousness. This hospital, also unaware of the family's previous history, treated the woman for obesity with amphetamine without appreciable results. The children are all feeding problems, and the family seen together on the street present a picture of dejection and misery. They appear to represent those who fell to the ground on reaching for the first rung of the ladder and know that they cannot climb again.

The number of cases is insufficient to determine statistically what percentage of migrants may be expected to suffer a disabling accident immediately following migration. But in reviewing the reported street accidents among this small group it appears that the majority did occur during the first year, and it is reasonable to assume that it takes a certain time for both parents and children to work out defenses against the physical hazards of life in New York.

On the other hand, the family which leaves Puerto Rico ceases in large measure to be exposed to chronic reinfection by intestinal parasites, but the risk of contagious diseases is not minimized. As far as small children are concerned, this applies particularly to pertussis, which may run through a rooming house and affect all the children in the house. Another sibling in the same family will be spared owing to the fact that he did not migrate until the following year, when his family had moved to better quarters. Sometimes intimacies develop between comparative strangers. Children may be left in the care of a neighbor while both parents are working in an effort to pay their rent and feed their families. This neighbor may have tuberculosis and infect a child, whose infection may not become apparent for some time. Formerly the discovery of tuberculosis in small children was invariably followed by hospitalization for several years (Family 45), but this particular traumatic experience is less frequent since the introduction of antibiotics and the treatment of many tuberculosis patients on an ambulatory basis.

The tragedies resulting from tenement fires and the deleterious effects of prolonged hospitalization on small children have been described, but for Puerto Rican migrants a traumatic accident or an illness occurring immediately following migration appears to be a serious setback from which the child or more particularly the breadwinner may never be able to recover. Such accidents are at present one of the risks inherent in migration, but modern society is endeavoring to reduce accidents through safety campaigns and control contagious diseases through immunizations. However, information concerning the medical and social problems which may be associated with a family's experience previous to migration or with disappointments and frustrations following migration is fragmentary, and no concerted effort has been made to deal with these difficulties.

In Puerto Rico a man who is now fifty-two years of age (Family 20) was a foreman on a sugar plantation. In addition to this he owned and ran one of the small *bodegas* or local stores in the town, and he had acquired some land on which he and his sons grew part of the food needed to feed the large family of ten children. Ten years ago he found himself growing weaker and weaker and was unable to handle his responsibilities. Finally, as his wife describes it, he was found asleep under a tree, unable to be aroused. At the local hospital the diagnosis of diabetes was made. Over the next few years, he seemed unable to get a grip on his former responsibilities, the older boys started to gamble, the bodega got into financial difficulties and had to be sold. The two oldest boys came to New York in 1948 on the invitation of their maternal grandmother. One of these boys has been more or less steadily employed, is married, and has a family; the other is in jail for stealing a car.

Two years after the arrival of the boys, the mother came to New York with three children, and six months later the father and the remaining children arrived. Three more children have been born since migration. The father's diabetes is under control, and he regularly attends the out-patient department of a hospital. Having been a foreman and a small businessman before migration, he thought that he should be employed in a manner commensurate with his previous skills and experience. Such an opportunity has not developed, and he has been unemployed for the major part of the five years since migration. In Puerto Rico he provided food for the family from his store and garden, and his sisters-in-law helped his wife with the children and the housekeeping so that she rarely needed to go out. In New York, some of the children sleep in the grandmother's apartment in the same building, and the mother herself sleeps a greater part of the day just as she did in Puerto Rico. "In the day, there are too many people, too much noise. I cannot do my work," she says. During the first year the mother applied to a social agency for financial help. Two of the children were referred by the social worker to an out-patient department for the treatment of club feet, but seeing no immediate results they discontinued attendance. Also during the first year following migration the eldest daughter committed suicide, apparently as a result of the disapproval expressed by her brothers for her lover. Two adolescent children were dismissed from school following outbursts of violent behavior, one of which involved hitting the teacher. A younger child who had been hospitalized because of suspected rheumatic fever was often seen running up to be embraced by a visiting nurse or friend on the street at a time when she should have been in school. Although neither the hospital record nor several examinations performed in the family clinic office revealed evidence of rheumatic activity, both the mother and father told everyone that the child had rheumatic fever and need not go to school.

This family, we believe, is an example of one in which the combination of the illness of the breadwinner and the disorganized behavior of the children led to a difficult situation in Puerto Rico which the family hoped to escape from or to remedy through migration. However, in the new environment their problems and society's reaction to them have become greatly intensified.

Family 5 offers a striking contrast to Family 20. The father became partially blind in the left eye before migration as a result of an injury sustained at work in a machine shop. Nevertheless he continued to work and has been steadily employed since he migrated as a single man ten years ago. His wife also migrated as a single girl and was employed in a factory until her marriage. She still accepts calls for work in rush seasons, when her mother, who lives in the same building, takes care of the two children. The family as a whole reports few illnesses; the wife had pneumonia during her second pregnancy. There are no apparent behavior disorders in any of its members, and the father has been observed repapering the rooms of their apartment in the evening after work. He sometimes takes his wife and children out on Sunday. After several visits to the home by different observers, each concluded independently that this was a cohesive family whose members appeared to be working successfully toward the goal of a better standard of living for themselves.

Progress in the sense of raising one's standard of living is one of the reasons frequently advanced for migration.

Coming to New York is the great adventure, "es el sueño"—
it is the dream. But the reality does not always turn out to
be like the dream, as the case of Family 33 illustrates.

The mother dresses better than most people in the neighborhood. She purchases her clothes from a friend in the
garment industry, where she was formerly employed. Her
children are better kept and better dressed than most. She
migrated in 1944 and expresses herself well in English. Her
medical record and those of her children and husband include
more visits to the out-patient department than any other
family save one in this study. A chronic peptic ulcer was recently demonstrated by X-ray in the father. The mother has
had several episodes of acute bursitis over a period of two
years. The complaints listed in the out-patient department
include dryness of the mouth, difficulty in swallowing, and
backache, for which a lumbar tap was performed and an X-
ray taken; the findings were within normal limits. The children have been treated for tonsillitis, anorexia, and asthmatic
attacks, and the youngest child was admitted for pneumonia
on two occasions. This woman is light brown with wavy hair
and Negroid features. Through her father's family in Puerto
Rico she is connected with people of lighter color and higher
social position than her own, that is, schoolteachers and
white-collar government employees. One of these helped her
get a minor clerical position in Puerto Rico after she had
completed one year of high school. She thought she would be
able to "progress" further if she came to New York. For
the first five years after migration she was employed in the
garment industry. She then married a Puerto Rican who had
migrated at the age of eight. This man continues to shift
from job to job, and now eight years following their mar-

riage his earnings as a kitchen helper do not average more than $55.00 a week. She sees no prospect of progress in the sense of moving to a better neighborhood or being able to associate with people who have had more education. Besides, the husband has turned out to be a very dependent individual who makes many demands, is highly critical of her cooking, and asserts himself from time to time by a show of physical violence. She has taken to wearing dark glasses habitually so that an occasional repetitive black eye will not be visible and give rise to questions on the street from curious neighbors.

Summary. The manner in which illness and disability may occur in lower-class Puerto Ricans as a direct result of the dangers encountered following migration to a Manhattan slum has been pointed out. An analysis of the pre-migration history of a few cases suggests that where illness or behavior disorders are important motivating forces in the migration of a family, the family is not apt to resolve its problems through migration, and that social reverberations of these problems are intensified in the new environment. It is also suggested that one may expect to encounter a greater number of medical problems in a family where the individuals are not "progressing" after migration in the manner in which they had hoped, in contrast to those who believe that they are on the way to achieving their goals.

IV. FAMILY ORGANIZATION

A middle-class American, be he physician or layman, would probably define a "family" as a group composed of a father, a mother, and their children. Within this framework of the American nuclear family certain relationships are implied. It is assumed, for instance, that the man and woman who are moving into a new house in suburbia have a marriage certificate granted by the state, that they were probably married in church, and that they are the natural parents as well as the legal guardians of the children who live with them. It is also generally understood that these children were born at an appropriate interval after the wedding ceremony was performed. In middle-class America, one who finds his marital partner intolerable may seek relief through legal separation or divorce, the grounds for which differ from one community to another. If such a separation or divorce occurs, provisions for the care and support of the children are worked out; a legal remarriage is possible and may be entered into when certain conditions have been complied with and when remarriage does not violate the individual's religious convictions. Further, this couple moving into a new house do not expect to have a mother-in-law living with them, nor do they expect to shelter their own brothers and sisters or aunts and uncles. The "folks" may come for a brief visit at Christmas or come to "take over" when the next baby is due, but they should not be a permanent part of the household.

These contemporary middle-class American concepts are reviewed here in order that the physician, being aware of his own frame of reference, may understand lower-class Puerto Rican family structure more readily in so far as such understanding may relate to the practice of medicine.

This middle-class American "ideal" of the family is not always shared, or at least is hardly realized, by Puerto Ricans in New York.

For purposes of this study the physicians adopted a classification prepared by the anthropologists to describe family organization as it appeared in this particular slum. This classification takes into consideration four types of family:

1. The nuclear family—a stable couple with their own child or children.

2. A stable couple with their own child or children and also a child or children of a previous union of one or both parents.

3. A woman with a child or children and without a stable male partner.

4. The extended family, which may involve any of the above three types, plus a grandmother and married or unmarried brothers and sisters living in the same apartment, in the same building, or in the immediate neighborhood, all these individuals being bound in a complex and intimate network of relationships.

Observations on the manner in which the family organization may be a significant factor in the practice of medicine among Puerto Rican patients are reported here.

1. *The nuclear family.* Family 43, consisting of father,

mother, and six children, has been rising in the social scale since migration from a slum in Ponce to a Manhattan slum area five years ago. The mother came first with the children and stayed with her godfather: she was angry because of her husband's unfaithfulness. The husband repented and joined her at her godfather's home a few months later. They then "bought" an apartment of their own for $210.00. This consisted of three rooms and a bath and had central heating of sorts. For this they paid $21.10 a month. After spending two years there they moved to a better area in Brooklyn, where they "bought" a six-room apartment for $1,200.00, including three fairly good beds. They now pay $50.00 a month for these six large rooms four flights up in a moderately well-kept apartment house.

The father is now thirty-five years old. He was born the eldest of six in a rural district in Puerto Rico where his father owned a small plot of land and also worked cutting cane. He went through the eighth grade and was interested in mechanics, not farming. After obtaining some mechanical training during his service in the National Guard in Puerto Rico, he moved from his home town to a slum in Ponce, where he worked in a big shop, becoming a skilled machine-tool operator. He obtained a job in his field the first week after landing in New York. He has never been unemployed and averages about $80.00 a week. He owns a 1948 Oldsmobile sedan. He speaks English fluently, his complexion is light olive, his hair black and curly. He has never been a patient in a hospital in New York and disclaims any illness except for occasional minor injuries at work.

The mother is thirty years old and was born in the same region as her husband, the family living in social and economic circumstances similar to his. She went through the fifth grade and was legally married at the age of sixteen to the father of her children, her first child being born when she was seventeen. She has not worked outside the home. Her English is not as fluent as her husband's but she can make herself understood in the chain store. Her complexion is light brown, a brown more evenly distributed than that achieved by an enthusiastic sun bather; her hair is black and curly. Her only hospitalization except for a normal delivery two years after migration has been in a private hospital in Manhattan where she paid $225.00 for a tubal ligation. She told the family physician that this was the only way to make sure that she would have no more children. A routine chest X-ray taken a year ago was reported as normal; physical examination was remarkable only for the excellent tissue turgor and firm abdominal muscles in a woman who had borne six children in nine years.

The six children are all of light to dark olive complexion with wavy hair and Caucasoid features. The three eldest were born at home in the country, the fourth and fifth at home in Ponce, and the sixth in a voluntary hospital in New York City with a reported birth weight of 7½ pounds. The older children were vaccinated for smallpox in Puerto Rico but have received no other immunizations; the two youngest have had their full complement of shots at the local unit of the City Health Department. All but the youngest fall below the level of normal standards for weight and height for children in the United States. Except for the detection of a functional heart murmur in the fourth child and skin lesions suggestive of vitamin deficiency in the fifth, physical examination in the family doctor's office seemed to indicate that they were all normal children. The two oldest had pertussis and measles in Puerto Rico and have been seen in the out-patient department of a near-by hospital on two occasions for minor complaints over the past two years. The fourth and fifth have each been treated once for otitis media in the same hospital, and Trichuris ova were found in their stools. Intra-dermal tests for tuberculosis were negative for all children. The sixth child, who was born in New York, developed acute gastroenteritis at six months of age and spent two months in a municipal hospital. Paratyphoid B was identified as the causative organism. Two years later she was treated in the out-patient clinic for Giardia lamblia with a hemoglobin of 7.3 grams, which rose to 12 grams under treatment. "Always trouble with that one," says the mother. "But now that we have moved away from the area and everything is much cleaner, she is not sick." Both parents consider that they and their family are eating better and living better in New York than they did in Puerto Rico.

They are not sure that their children are getting an education, as the eldest, though she speaks English fluently and receives satisfactory marks in the sixth grade, cannot read. They are also concerned about the fact that here in New York "if the father hits the boy he goes to school and tells the teacher and an inspector comes to the father and takes him to court." But, the father goes on, "I always had work and when you have work you have everything." "Nos sacrificamos" is one of the mother's favorite expressions. By this she means that her husband learned a trade by dint of hard work and that they saved in order to pay for their apartment and the tubal ligation. Their future aspirations include a house of their own and a new car.

The nuclear family among Puerto Rican migrants may consist of a man and woman—and their children—who do not possess a marriage certificate and do not consider that they are "living in sin." A consensual union per se is not necessarily a source of stress to the individual nor does this arrangement mean that the individuals concerned are less faithful to each other or more irresponsible than those living in the next apartment who possess a legal document (Padilla). In cases where the union has been established for some years, it is possible that one or the other partner was married in Puerto Rico, but did not obtain a divorce and so could not remarry legally.

On a bench in the waiting room of the medical clinic of a city hospital sits a neatly dressed, anxious-looking woman with obvious dyspnea. As the doctor passes by, audible wheezes are heard. The record states that this woman was discharged from the ward a week ago. She had been admitted in status asthmaticus. She responded well to treatment and was discharged at the end of five days. Two days later she was readmitted for the same complaint. The intern, seeking to link up the asthmatic attack with a life situation, commented that this woman was living in a basement apartment with a man to whom she had borne three children out of wedlock and that the man was alcoholic and unemployed. "Unless these conditions are remedied," the intern said, "little can be done to improve this woman's asthma." Indeed during the week following her second discharge, in spite of being provided with adequate medication for the treatment of her symptoms, she returned three times to the emergency ward. At this point the clinic physician took up the intern's points one by one in order to place them in the context of her illness and of her life experience. She and her family had been living for the past year in a damp three-room basement apartment with no private bath and the paint peeling off the walls. Previous to this she had lived in a better Puerto Rican neighborhood in the Bronx and had rarely suffered from asthma. The family had come down the social scale.

She did not have a marriage certificate. She and her mate had lived together for the past ten years, but they were not legally married because he had previously been legally married to another woman in Puerto Rico and had not obtained a divorce. This situation had not disturbed her until the investigator from the Department of Welfare informed her that the physician's recommendation for improved housing for the family could not be carried out since they did not have a marriage certificate and were therefore not eligible for a municipal housing project.

The couple had migrated eight years earlier with one child; the other two had been born in New York. The man had been employed regularly in a small restaurant until he fell eighteen months ago. His drinking, although constant and of long standing, had not been a problem until he lost his job. She had done light factory work intermittently until a year ago when she developed asthma following prolonged exposure to dust. As both parents became ill, they were obliged to move to less desirable quarters and applied for public assistance, which was granted. The man had a long-standing dorsal scoliosis, and while the orthopedic service of the hospital recommended a brace, the orthopedists were not prepared to say that the condition of his back was substantially altered for the worse by his fall a year and a half ago. His drinking became more severe and he was depressed and irritable, paralyzed by his sense of inadequacy. When the woman was asked if she could work, she replied she was sick. She was then questioned as to whether she would work if she were well. "That is what he cannot tolerate," she answered. "But you worked before." "Yes, but only part time and he was the main support of the family."

For her to become the principal support of the family meant destroying the last vestige of this man's self-respect. If both of them were ill, they could accept public assistance with dignity. When the suggestion was made that efforts be made to rehabilitate him, she accepted the doctor's suggestion with enthusiasm. But since this scene took place in a city hospital clinic, and not in the family doctor's office, the difficulties in the way of carrying on the coordinated treatment of an entire family in this setting have not been surmounted. At the time of writing the family has been lost to general medicine because of appointments in various specialty clinics where a different physician sees the patient on each visit.

Family 26 is a similar case. The father had supported his wife and six children until the time of his accident one year after migration. The family was now receiving public assistance, and both the man and the woman expressed resentment at being no longer self-supporting. But when the possibility of the woman's going to work was suggested, she replied that her husband had always supported her, had never allowed her to work, and would not permit her to do so now. Indeed, her working, she believed, would destroy what little self-respect her husband still maintained, and it was preferable to accept public assistance until the following June, when the eldest son graduated from high school and could help to support the family.

In the first example (Family 43) of a nuclear family the

father was a skilled machine-tool operator and earned a good living. The family was advancing in a manner consistent with the American pattern of upward mobility, aided by the preferred Puerto Rican method of controlling family size through a tubal ligation (see Chapter VIII, Fertility and Sterilization). The family health record was good except in the case of the sixth child, who had had one of the now infrequent cases of paratyphoid B in New York City.

In the last two case vignettes, the clinic family and Family 26, the family structure was similar in that the father had always been the major provider and his position as head of the house was undisputed. But neither of these two men were skilled and though both had made some upward economic progress since migration, accidents and illness followed by prolonged unemployment had made the families dependent upon public assistance.

These observations and others of a similar nature suggest that in the context of the Puerto Rican lower-class nuclear family, where disabling illness occurs in the father, the mother's potential role as chief breadwinner of the family is considered more threatening to family integrity and masculine self-respect than acceptance of public assistance.

2. *A stable couple with their own child or children and also a child or children of a previous union of one or both parents.* This type of family does not appear to be substantially different from the nuclear family of parents with their own children. Confusion may arise as a result of one of the children's bearing the name of his natural father who is not his mother's current husband, but it does not follow that the child is treated as a stepchild or that he may not have contacts with his own father if the latter is in New York. (See Padilla.)

One of the ways in which this type of family develops is of special interest.

This woman came to our attention through Mount Sinai Hospital. She had come to New York with her three children after she had been abandoned by an alcoholic husband from whom she had obtained a divorce. Previous to the dissolution of this marriage her tubes had been ligated in Puerto Rico, for she wanted no more children. At the end of two years in New York she and her children were befriended by a recent migrant with no children of his own. He was regularly employed and was prepared to undertake her support and that of the children provided he could have a child of his own. At her request, the gynecological department at Mount Sinai Hospital undertook a successful tubal repair, and she bore a child to this man, who married her and is now supporting her and all her children.

Where both the man and the woman have two sets of children, a variety of problems may be encountered. The man and woman in Family 59 have lived together for nine years and have four children of their own. In addition, he has three children by a previous legal marriage to whose support he contributes, and she has two children by a previous marriage who live with her mother in Puerto Rico. No divorce was obtained by either party. This particular woman is filled with guilt concerning her irregular marital situation and regards the mental deficiency of her eldest daughter born of this illegal union as a castigation from heaven.

3. *A woman with a child or children and without a stable male partner.* In some lower-class Puerto Rican families, the mother may assume the main responsibility for the care and support of her children, as her mother did before her. She expects some contribution from the child's father. Though he

lives regularly elsewhere, and she may have another sexual companion, he is known as the father of the child and has the privilege of visiting his child.

Family 8 is an example of one in which a Puerto Rican woman, who migrated ten years ago, is raising children of different fathers. She is a large brown woman of thirty with kinky hair and Negroid features. She stands firmly on two sturdy legs in which no trace of varicose veins could be detected in the course of a medical examination. Her breasts are full, her shoulders round, and she weighs about 190 pounds. There are four children in their two-room apartment, born of three different fathers. This woman has never been legally married. Her current sexual partner is twenty-five years old, of medium build, light olive, with Caucasian features. He is not the father of any of the four children and has lived in the household for approximately two years, contributing some $25.00 a week for his board. She went as far as the sixth grade in Puerto Rico, leaving school to help her mother support her younger brothers and sisters since there was no steady man in the house. At the age of nineteen she became pregnant; her first child was born in Puerto Rico. She left her man following a quarrel, took up with another man, became pregnant again, and came to the United States, where the second child was delivered nine years ago. The father of the second child died in an accident in Puerto Rico. The father of the first child found her in the United States and contributed to the support of his child. She again became pregnant by him, but unfortunately the third child was a daughter when he wanted a son and he then disappeared. Six years later she became pregnant a fourth time, by another man, who supports his child.

She denies that she has ever applied for public assistance. She has never been to the hospital for herself or for her children except for normal deliveries, and there is no record of the family in the Department of Welfare. She denies any illnesses nor could any pathology be found on physical examination.

She is employed the greater part of the time in a factory. When she is not at home the children are upstairs with her mother or in their own apartment under the guard of the eldest daughter, a slender, brown girl with chronic conjunctivitis, kinky hair, and Negroid features. This thirteen-year-old girl does the cooking when her mother is out, and when the doctor knocked, she came from the stove to the door with a large knife in her hand, a warning to intruders.

On another occasion, the medical examination was completed at home while the mother was cooking dinner. As the smallest child moved towards the stove, the mother firmly shouted "no toque," do not touch. The child obeyed and, the mother now seated, he climbed on to her ample lap and was encircled in her arms.

The apartment consists of two rooms and a toilet. Heat is furnished by the kitchen stove and a portable kerosene stove. A curtain separates the bedroom from the kitchen. The children sleep in two folding beds in the kitchen, while the man and woman occupy the double bed in the bedroom.

The attendance record of the three children of school age reveals an average absence of ten days per child a year. This record, compared with those of other children in this group, is exceptionally good. The school physician and the family physicians noted dental caries in two of the children, a congenital hernia in the oldest boy, and a harsh systolic murmur in the pulmonic area in the third child. The school record bears the note "mother uncooperative, recommendations not followed out." The mother reports she is "too busy to spend time attending clinics." After the necessity for surgery had been explained to the mother by the family physician, she took the oldest boy to the municipal hospital, where a herniorrhaphy was performed. Recommendations for treatment of dental caries were made, but the mother considered that she could not take any more time off from work, and the dental clinic would not accept the children for treatment if they were not accompanied by a parent. The dental caries remain untreated.

In Family 14 also there are children of more than one father. The mother was raised in the neighborhood. Recently a broken kitchen utensil was thrown or dropped out of a fourth-floor window into a vacant lot and hit her on the head, resulting in a scalp laceration for which she was treated in the emergency ward of a municipal hospital. "Something is always happening to me," she said disgustedly. She is a dark olive, stocky woman of thirty with an unhappy expression. She was brought to the area at the age of six months by her widowed mother after her father had died of tuberculosis in Puerto Rico. Her mother, now age fifty-six, never went to school and understands no English, but was employed steadily in a commercial laundry for many years. She completed the first year of high school and then worked in the garment trade up to the time that she gave birth to her first child, whose father was a high school friend of Puerto Rican parentage. This boy left her and now provides uncertain support for his son by order of the Domestic Relations Court during those intervals when he can be located or is not in jail under sentence as a peddler of drugs. Later, this woman became legally married to a Puerto Rican migrant and had two children by him. This man deserted her shortly after the birth of their second child. "We did not get on, he never took me out," was the woman's only comment. The youngest child, age six, a dark olive, curly-haired girl, was admitted to the hospital at the age of one month with pneumonia. She has had pneumonia three times altogether, as well as a fractured ankle resulting from a fall downstairs the day following her return from one of numerous visits to an out-patient department for the treatment of tonsillitis. She has an anterior synechia in the right eye, the result of being poked in the eye with a pointed object by an unknown child in the street several years ago.

When this child is brought to the family doctor's office her mother pushes her down on the examining table with the comment "always sick, always in trouble." All three children are seen on the street frequently. Their grandmother, who stopped working after the first grandchild was born nine years ago in order to help take care of them, shouts summonses in Spanish out of a third-story window. The children pay no heed, and sometimes rush into the office when they should be in school, hungry for affection and attention. For the major part of the past six years, the family has received public assistance, and the mother, who complains bitterly of the wickedness of men, still hopes to find a man who will support her and her children. The major portion of her time during frequent lay-offs is spent in visits to the Department of Welfare and the Domestic Relations Court.

In Family 8 the mother migrated to the United States ten years ago and lives in the same building with her own mother, who assists her in the general care of the children. The pattern of successive sexual unions in the case of these women goes back for more than two generations. The mother, as did the grandmother, expects to assume responsibility for the children and does not expect to get married.

The mother in Family 14, brought up in the United States since she was an infant, acquired a partial high school education in the neighborhood. Although her own mother did not make the transition into the American world, this woman brought up in the slum neighborhood seems to have wanted to make a marriage involving companionship between husband and wife and mutual responsibility for the children. She has not achieved this. With three children of two different fathers, both having deserted her, and with no reliable means of support but with the expectation that such support should be forthcoming, she has an attitude of resentment towards her children and of bitter disillusionment towards men in general. The result in so far as the children are concerned is one of family disorganization. Both our own observations and the hospital records indicate that the children run around the street inadequately clad and inadequately supervised.

In Family 8, on the other hand, the woman apparently assumed that her successive partners would not be permanent but would provide some support for the children. She has maintained a strong sense of family cohesion and interdependence and responsibility of one member for another. There has not been a high incidence of illness in members of this family. Those illnesses which have occurred have been disregarded when an approach was made through the usual institutional means of the school or out-patient department, because the woman did not consider them serious and thought it more important to stay at work and keep the children in school rather than attend out-patient department clinics. In contrast, the incidence of illness in the third child in Family 14 is high, and there is evidence to suggest that some of these episodes of illness have occurred as a result of parental neglect.

No doubt the personalities of the mother in Family 8 and the mother in Family 14 account for many of the differences between the two families. But viewing these families in the context of the Puerto Rican Manhattan slum environment, we suggest that the determined and warm-hearted woman in Family 8 is an example of a recent migrant from a matriarchal Puerto Rican family following her mother's pattern. She entered into successive sexual unions, expecting and receiving some support from the fathers of her children, while assuming full responsibility for the care of these children. The mother in Family 14, on the other hand, reared in New York, her mates not having fulfilled her hopes for a man who would be faithful, companionable, and support her and her children, is now a disappointed woman with three children, deserted in turn by her first lover and her legal husband. The unsuccessful transition into the American world in this case has been a source of great stress and has been associated with a high incidence of illness in this family.

4. *The extended family.* Both Family 8 and Family 14 are extended families in that three generations live in close proximity and are interdependent. Young people of Puerto Rican parentage born and raised in this area have been observed

to delay a move to a better neighborhood even when it became financially possible (Families 40, 46, 68), saying that they did not wish to move far away from their parents.

The way in which relationships in an extended Puerto Rican family may be relevant to the practice of medicine is shown by the following example.

The door to this home (Family 66) is seldom locked. At dusk on a winter afternoon the smell of frying food pervades the public hall. Inside the apartment a number of people, relatives—not always the same ones—are sitting around a kitchen table or on the sofa watching television and eating from plates piled high with brown rice and pieces of fried beef and pork.

The principal breadwinner in this family is over sixty years old and has a moderate degree of hypertension. He does not speak a word of English and can neither read nor write. He works as a porter, but his earning capacity has not increased as the firm for which he has worked for the past seven years is becoming more and more mechanized, and the higher pay goes to younger men who have had more education and are able to handle machines. He came to New York about fifteen years ago and married a widow with four children whom he had known in Puerto Rico. They have three children of their own who have had few recorded illnesses. This woman has never been hospitalized except for the normal delivery of these three younger children. Ten years ago, when her husband was temporarily unemployed, she induced an abortion. Recently she suffered from a major respiratory infection and was treated at home. Medical examination revealed no positive physical findings other than obesity. She is 5 feet 2 inches and weighs 160 pounds.

Her four children by her first husband are now adults

and married. All of them have had from two to three years of high school in New York. These young people have married individuals of Puerto Rican descent also born and raised in the area, except one daughter, who married a recent Puerto Rican migrant. The oldest son (Family 40) is a well-built, healthy appearing young man of twenty-five who lives in the neighborhood with his wife and children. His employment as a mechanic in a garage is not always steady, but he hopes to become a licensed electrician after completing a night school course. A few visits made to the local hospital and to the family physician for the complaint of epigastric pain have not revealed demonstrable pathology. His two children have had the usual childhood diseases and are considered normal by the pediatrician. From time to time he is laid off and his wife goes to work, much to his distress, but his mother is happy to take care of his children at such time.

The oldest daughter (Family 1) has an apartment in a housing project on Staten Island, but she is seldom at home since she likes to spend the day with her son at her mother's house. This three-year-old boy is a feeding problem, always whining and clinging to his mother's skirts. He is taken frequently to the family physician for the treatment of minor respiratory infections. Her husband is irregularly employed and receives a weekly disability allowance of $14.00 for a leg injury sustained while in the service. He believes his problems would not have been so great had his wife agreed to join him overseas when he was in service. At that time she remarked to the physician that she could not leave her own mother because her child was always sick. Now her own mother comments "I don't like it when my son-in-law beats my kid when he is drunk but a woman should stay with her husband." Another married daughter (Family 15) lives one flight below her mother in the same building, and the youngest of the four children by her first husband, a daughter who married a few months ago at the age of seventeen, occupies one of the four rooms in her mother's apartment.

The mother's home is a center not only for her adult married children and their children and her own second batch of children but also for her own brothers and sisters. The divorced wife of one of her brothers ate at her table for many months until she was admitted to a hospital for the treatment of tuberculosis. When this woman was admitted to the municipal hospital, she was asked where she lived. She replied that she lived alone, as indeed she did, since she occupied a room alone in a rooming house near by. The question was not asked as to where she took her meals, nor did she volunteer the information. It was only three months later, in the course of a routine checkup at the Child Health Station, that a positive Mantoux reaction was obtained in one of the matriarch's grandchildren. The contact was then traced back to the aunt by marriage, who took her meals in the grandmother's house. This child became quite ill but was successfully and consistently treated. The rest of the family, having been checked by the Health Department, are considered "very cooperative" by the authorities.

Two years previous to this episode the matriarch's brother became ill with a malignant lesion and was declared incurable by the physicians in a voluntary hospital. He was a widower and his own children had moved out of the neighborhood. His sister took him into her home, moving him into the room which is now occupied by her youngest daughter and her husband, and for six months she provided terminal care for him with the help of the family physician and the visiting nurse. Her daughters assisted in the care of their uncle, having previously responded to a call for blood when transfusions were necessary at the time that he was hospitalized.

The picture of the extended family presented here suggests that failure to inquire into the ramifications of family relationships may result in delay in the discovery of contacts where contagious diseases are concerned. On the other hand, an evaluation of the potential strength of an extended family may provide an environment especially suited for the tender loving care of a sick person.

Summary. Four types of family organization prevail among the eighty Puerto Rican families in this study: (1) the nuclear family, a stable couple with their own child or children; (2) a stable couple with their own child or children and also a child or children of a previous union of one or both parents; (3) a woman with a child or children and without a stable male partner; (4) the extended family, which may involve any of the above three types, plus a grandmother and married or unmarried brothers and sisters living in the same apartment, in the same building, or in the immediate neighborhood.

The interrelationship between the individuals involved varies in individual cases, and an understanding of the potential strength and weaknesses in these relationships makes it possible for medical personnel to define therapeutic goals more realistically when dealing with a particular family.

V. HOUSING

This is not, as was noted previously, an area of rooming houses. It is an area of old tenement buildings, four or five stories high, with four, six, or eight apartments to a floor, and no elevators. The apartments consist of two, three, and four rooms. Each apartment is equipped with a separate toilet. This toilet is not counted as a room in the enumeration which follows. The term room is used to describe an enclosed space separated from the next enclosed space by an incomplete partition or by a door that can be closed. Every room under this definition does not necessarily have a window. The kitchen is counted as one room, so that where a family of six or seven live in a three-room apartment, if the kitchen is not used to sleep in there are more than three people sleeping in one room. The bedroom may be just large enough for one double bed, a bureau, a makeshift closet, and space for one person to pass between these objects without stepping on the bed. The living room can usually accommodate a bed sofa, a television set, a table, two straight chairs or one overstuffed chair, and standing room for four or five people.

The kitchen is the room which usually opens into the public hall. It almost always contains a gas stove with oven, and most families also have an electric refrigerator of uncertain vintage and sometimes doubtful functioning. In fifty-seven families the bath is in the kitchen. Under these circumstances, if one is a member of a large family, taking a bath or washing one's feet every night is not easy.

As Figure 10 shows nine families have no central heating and no separate bath. This means that the rooms are heated by a kerosene stove or a gas stove supplementary to the kitchen stove or by the kitchen stove alone. The lack of central heating may raise the cost of shelter to $60.00 or $70.00 a month during the winter since the monthly rent of from $11.00 to $35.00 paid to the landlord in some cases represents only a small part of the cost of housing. Most likely the family who migrated less than five years ago "bought" their apartment for $500.00 or more from the previous tenant, an earlier migrant who has moved to better quarters. Since this "selling" of apartments is illegal, the previous tenant appears around the first of the month to pay the landlord, having collected the rent and the installment on the purchase price from the actual tenant.

In this group of eighty families, five families moved to housing projects in the course of the study. One qualified as the family of a recently returned veteran and the remaining four had "health problems" which prompted social agencies to recommend them for special consideration by the City Housing Authority. Among the remaining seventy-five whose housing condition is reported on the chart, two moved out of town in 1956 to an unimproved area in New Jersey, and nine have found better neighborhoods in other parts of Manhattan, the Bronx, and Brooklyn. Their places have been taken by more recent migrants, except in those cases where the building is being torn down to make room for a housing project. The reasons given for moving by those who found new quarters on their own are chiefly social—they wanted

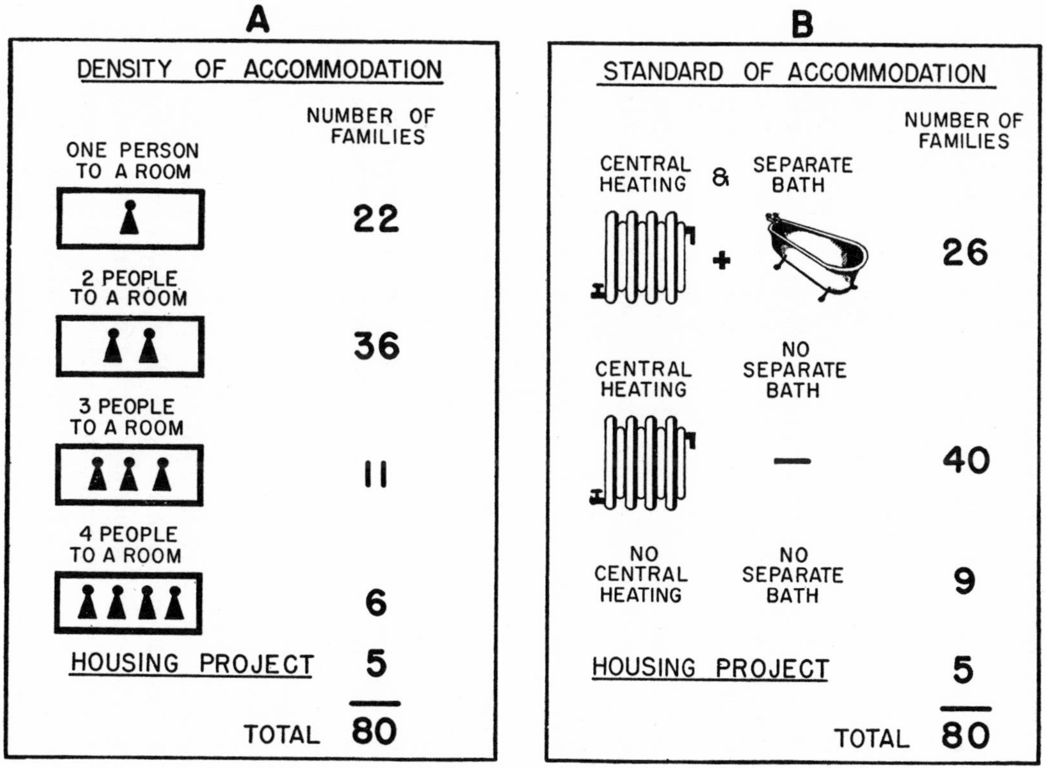

FIGURE 10. HOUSING CONDITION OF 80 FAMILIES AS OF DECEMBER, 1955

to get away from the drug addicts, the *mal criados,* badly behaved adults and children, in the neighborhood.

The reaction to dilapidated walls, falling ceilings, dirty hallways, and cockroaches varies from family to family. Some individuals, finding that the possibility of moving lies very far in the future, lay new linoleum and buy new furniture and kitchen appliances on the installment plan so that when the door to the public hall is closed they are indeed in their own castle (Family 5). Others are helpless or too poor to contend with the situation and protest only when they bring the baby to the doctor to have him treated for cockroach bites on the arms and buttocks (Family 18). For still others the conditions described are a source of stress in the same sense that they would be for a middle-class suburbanite. The mother in Family 42 suffers from migraine headaches, and over the course of a year she used to drop in to the doctor's office at least once a week asking for help in relieving her headaches and for information on what to do about the defective plumbing and the rat holes that had not been stopped up. In spite of the fact that her husband was hospitalized for a chronic disease, that she had six children, and that she had no known source of income beyond that provided by the Department of Welfare in the form of aid to dependent children, she succeeded on her own initiative in finding another apartment in a better neighborhood. When the family physician called on her in her new quarters, she expressed great satisfaction with the change and said that she no longer felt the need of medical attention to relieve her headaches.

Figure 10 indicates that in twenty-two families there was one person to a room. These were families with no children at home or only one child. In such cases the child would sleep in the bedroom with the parents or on a couch in the living room. In cases where a two- or three-room apartment was shared by six people, sleeping arrangements involved two or three children in one bed or one or more children sharing a bed with an adult. These sleeping arrangements may be compared roughly with the closed-bay barracks in the armed forces where four men sleep in an enclosed space.

Summarizing the extensive studies which have been carried out in the armed services, an investigator for the United States Army Air Force (Bernstein 1957) points out that the space allowance per man, the number of men per barracks room, the number of men present at any one time, and the length of service of each man have all been found to bear some relationship to the number of respiratory infections occurring in armed forces personnel. Bernstein's own study involves a comparison in the incidence of respiratory infections among air force personnel living in open-bay and closed-bay barracks. He reports that the over-all risk of upper respiratory infections was greater in open bay barracks, where there are no partitions between bunks, than in closed-bay barracks, where partitions are placed between every four bunks. Among the recruits as a whole those who had most recently taken up residence in the barracks were most susceptible.

The physicians observed that the number of reported respiratory infections was greater where three or four persons slept in one room and there was no central heating than where families had more ample living space. A decline in the rate of respiratory infections was reported by two families (42 and 48) after they had moved to less crowded quarters. And while the impossibility of counting with any degree of accuracy the number of respiratory infections occurring in these families has been pointed out, it appears reasonable to suggest that in the slum as in army barracks crowding and new recruits, that is, new migrants arriving from Puerto Rico, are significant factors where a high incidence of respiratory infections exists. One may add that where crowding is an indication for moving to a city housing project, a move may be delayed for a long time since the number of apartments available for large families is comparatively limited. Also, a family consisting of a man and woman who have several children and who have lived in consensual union for many years but cannot produce a certificate of marriage is not eligible for admission to a city housing project.

So far we have been describing the physical characteristics of the tenements in which these Puerto Rican families live. Obviously this is an area of substandard housing, and it has long been known that the incidence of tuberculosis, mental disease, juvenile delinquency, and other afflictions is highest in the slum areas of a city, although the factors responsible for this correlation are not clear.

Since the improvement in sanitation has led to the elimination of water-borne diseases even in the worst slums, it is felt that a multitude of other human ills can be cured through better plumbing. Therefore, when a high incidence of minor disease or one serious illness is found in a family living in a slum, a recommendation for moving to a housing project is included in the general plan of treatment. Doctors and social workers plead with the City Housing Authority that the family with a child who has rheumatic fever or tuberculosis be granted preference in admission to a housing project.

While not minimizing the desirability of light and air and increased privacy and play and living space for all people, observations on several families whose move to a housing project was recommended by medical personnel for reasons of health suggest that the improvements in health to be expected after better housing has been secured for a particular family depend upon many variables.

The father in Family 31 is over fifty years old. In Puerto Rico he worked as a foreman on a construction job. Since coming to the United States ten years ago he has been employed only for a few months, having been discharged as a dishwasher because both the union and the employers considered that an old hand injury presented too great a hazard. He has been admitted several times to Bellevue following episodes of explosive behavior in which he threatened to harm himself and other members of his family. Cooperative in the hospital, he was released after a few days with the final diagnosis of passive aggressive, schizoid personality. One of the children had one episode of rheumatic fever shortly after migration, and another child was hospitalized for tuberculosis three years ago. Several months after the family moved to the housing project, the father was described as much quieter and more contented in his new surroundings, where he could take a daily walk in less crowded streets and the children had a bedroom of their own.

Quite a different outcome was observed in the case of Family 53, where seven individuals lived in two rooms and where the combined admissions to Mount Sinai Hospital totaled 56 hospital days over a two-year period (excluding admissions for normal deliveries), in addition to 150 visits to the out-patient department. Two months after the family had moved to a housing project in Brooklyn the mother was seen in the out-patient department by one of the doctors, who asked cheerfully, "How are things now?" "Igual" (the same), she replied sadly. "It takes me one hour by subway to come to the hospital now, and I have been there every day this week with one of the children. Before I just walked around the corner." "Is your husband working?" "Oh, no, how could he, I need someone to look after the children when I come to the hospital." The Social Service Department of the hospital was considering the possibility of requesting the City Housing Authority to move this family once more in order to establish them in another project within walking distance of the hospital.

Another family not included in this series came to our attention through the behavior problem of one of the children. The child improved greatly under the care of a private child guidance agency, and the move to a housing project in Staten Island was effected as part of the treatment plan. Six months later the father dropped into the family physician's office, beating his breast and wishing to be examined. He was found to be a muscular man in his late fifties with no history of major illness and in whom no abnormalities could be found on physical examination. "You say I am not sick," he wailed, "but no one will give me a job; the fashion here is to give work only to the young." (He had been an agricultural worker in Puerto Rico and knew nothing about handling machines.) From his point of view the situation was greatly aggravated since moving because in the housing project where he now lived, his son who was about to graduate from junior high school needed a suit if he were not to be "ashamed." In the Manhattan slum where he lived formerly he had many friends who were also supported by the Department of Welfare and who understood that one could not afford to buy a suit for graduation.

While we share the hopes of city planners that slums may be eliminated and that new ones will not arise to take their place, the examples cited suggest that for individual families a move to a city housing project is not necessarily a panacea. The effect on the family's health may not be apparent, while the break in a set of human associations which were an important source of emotional support to the family creates new problems.

Although this study has been confined to Puerto Rican families living in tenements, the writer attended a number of families, white, Negro, and Puerto Rican, living in neighboring housing projects. A strong clinical impression developed that people in municipal housing projects are no less sick than those living in the tenements. Indeed it could not be otherwise. The examples cited indicate that in New York City, the family that does not have too many children (less than five) and can muster a list of affidavits from health and social agencies testifying to the multiplicity of its problems takes precedence over others in being admitted to a municipal housing project. A recommendation for a move to a housing project has been until very recently one of the unchallenged therapeutic tools of social medicine. But the fact that new bricks and mortar and good plumbing are not in themselves a panacea to all ills is becoming apparent.

A study made in New York for the Citizens Housing and Planning Council indicates that many eligible tenants are refusing public housing because problem families have given it a "bad name." This study recommends that special measures be instituted for the treatment of problem families now living in housing projects and for the education of problem families not now considered ready to become desirable neighbors in a project. (New York *Times,* May 6, 1957, p. 31.) Further, the Department of Welfare has issued a new order prohibiting the assignment of relief clients, except in emergency cases, to any project in which 20 per cent or more of the apartments are occupied by families whose rent is paid by the Department of Welfare. In some projects the relief population is as high as 34 per cent.

Assignments will now be spread among other projects, some of which have less than 10 per cent of their tenants on relief. Warren Moscow, executive director of the New York City Housing Authority, believes that with an annual turnover of 10 per cent among all families in public housing, it "should not take very long" to reach a balance in which families on relief would be evenly distributed among all subsidized projects. (New York *Times,* February 14, 1957, p. 29.)

Summary. The eighty Puerto Rican families in this study live in old tenements from which fourteen families have moved out since 1955, either on their own initiative or with the help of social agencies. Since a pure water, milk, and food supply are available to all people in the City of New York, the exact relationship between poor housing and poor health in this group is not clear, but our observations suggest that for the Puerto Rican families we have known in this neighborhood, the social and familial aspects of housing are equally if not more important than the physical aspects.

Recent quantitative studies by the Citizens Housing and Planning Council and the Department of Welfare corroborate the validity of the observations made on this small Puerto Rican group and suggest that a move to a municipal housing project is not a panacea. An understanding of those elements in the housing environment per se which bear directly on community mental health will be greatly enhanced as the results of longitudinal studies involving a group of families moving from "bad" to "good" housing become available. (Wilner 1956.)

VI. LANGUAGE AND COMMUNICATION

English is taught in school in Puerto Rico, and some migrants have a knowledge of the language on arrival in New York. In our experience most men and all children of elementary school age learn to make themselves understood in English within two years after migration. The adolescent migrant, as we have already pointed out, is less likely to learn English (Families 13 and 20) in junior high school and easily becomes a truant. Both men and women who are employed in concerns where the majority of employees are Puerto Ricans suffer some delay in learning English.

Women who live in a Puerto Rican neighborhood, spend their lives at home with small children, and shop at the bodega across the street have little or no opportunity to learn or to speak English. This applies particularly to older women who never had the opportunity to go to school in Puerto Rico and whose cruising radius, both physical and social, is limited.

In this respect the Puerto Rican migrant is no different from the European immigrant, and any physician working in a municipal hospital can recall encountering more than one Italian or Central European immigrant who, though she had lived in New York over thirty years, could not tell the doctor about her symptoms without the help of a younger interpreter.

Spanish is the language in which mothers address their

small children, even those mothers who have been to high school in the United States, so that a preschool child who is not allowed to play on the street may not speak or understand English. This was the case with the little girl in Family 15 when she was admitted to the hospital at the age of two and a half. In some instances (Family 68) a reaction against the older generation may lead young people of Puerto Rican parentage to put small children in a nursery school to learn English.

But the fact that a Puerto Rican patient speaks English or that a doctor or nurse speaks Spanish with those who do not know English does not always mean that an understanding has taken place. The premise from which the physician or the nurse starts may be entirely different from that of the Puerto Rican patient, and neither may be aware of what lies in the mind of the other. For instance, it is taken for granted by medical personnel working in the out-patient department of any hospital that various examinations may be required before another visit is made to the physician and that these examinations will be arranged by appointment. The patient is given a number of slips of paper which tell him where he is supposed to be, at what time, and for what purpose. Thus, a chest X-ray, blood chemistries, a blood count, a urinalysis, a stool examination—the minimum requirements for a routine medical "work-up"—will involve visits to several parts of the hospital on separate days and contacts with a number of different individuals, none of whom know the patient and whom the patient does not know. Eventually the patient may get back to the starting point, the clinic where he was first examined, but the likelihood that the same doctor will attend him is not great. After the unknown doctor has thumbed through the multicolored slips pasted in the chart, he may hand the patient more slips for additional appointments, write a prescription, or have the patient return "to be followed." Such a patient, who came to have his pain or his anxiety relieved and to whom the concept of a "work-up" has not been explained, may come to the family doctor's office enumerating the many visits made to the out-patient department, adding a final bitter comment—"no me hacen na," they don't do anything for me.

Where more than one institution is involved, the situation becomes very complicated indeed, as the following illustration shows. The father in Family 20 has many problems. He has been attending a night school in the neighborhood with a view to learning English. At the time of the incident reported here, eight of the twelve living children were located in five different institutions, some committed through court order, others having been placed in boarding schools by a social agency. He showed the family doctor a printed form which he had received in the mail from a state training school. He read the first paragraph haltingly but correctly in English. It was a request for the baptismal certificate of the child who had been committed to this school. "Do you have it?" "No," he replied. "Anyhow, don't you see," he pointed to the next paragraph joyfully, "if I do not send it, they will send the child home and that is what I want." Actually, the next paragraph stated that if the certificate were not sent the child could not be prepared for his first communion.

This man was resentful of the dispersal of his family by various agencies and could only react to a request made by an agency in terms of a refusal, hoping that this would result in the release of the child. On another visit, the doctor found that one of the boys had just been discharged from a state training school where he had spent a year and learned to speak English quite well. Being under sixteen, it was still necessary for the boy to attend continuation school. The father had taken his son to the school in the neighborhood, but in order to be admitted, it was necessary for the father to obtain a "paper" from the central office of the Board of Education in Brooklyn. He showed an appointment slip for the next morning, but he also had an appointment at the United States Employment Bureau in upper Manhattan and one in lower Manhattan with the worker in the social agency—all three for the same day. He laid the three slips of paper on the kitchen table and shrugged his shoulders. "Yo tengo, too many appointments," he concluded. An attempt was made to help this man by calling the family agency but there was a "new worker on the case" who did not know this man and said he should come downtown for an "appointment" next week. Three weeks later, the boy was seen on the street; he was not in school—his father had not been able to find the office in Brooklyn.

These are the circumstances under which an interpreter-intermediary flourishes and acquires both prestige and cash. He knows his way around in the subway and has acquired experience in working his clients through a maze of appointment slips and impersonal officials behind grilled windows, but even the intermediary, be he adult or child, does not always interpret correctly what lies in the minds of either party, as the following instance shows.

Late on a winter afternoon a telephone call came from a patient asking if the family doctor would come at once to her apartment to see a sick child. The doctor went up two flights

Language and Communication

in the building across the street to find a young ⌐
a six months old baby and a fourteen-year-old g⌐
tor started to examine the baby and found a rectal tem⌐
ture of 101 degrees and enlarged cryptic tonsils. "That is
just what the other doctor said," the fourteen-year-old girl
volunteered. "The other doctor—why did you call me if another doctor is taking care of the child?" The fourteen-year-
old girl, a cousin of the mother, who was a new migrant, had
acted as interpreter and intermediary, taking her charges to
the emergency room of a neighboring hospital, where an injection had been given. At this point, the misunderstanding
was complete. The family doctor was furious to have been
called to see a child who had already received treatment at
the hands of another doctor, and the fourteen-year-old girl
was bewildered, since in her role of intermediary and interpreter she was bound to bring all the neighborhood resources
into action to reassure the frightened young mother who
thought her baby "muy grave" (seriously ill), and they had returned from the hospital not understanding that this was not
the case.

The examples cited involve attempts at communication between Puerto Rican migrants and metropolitan institutions.
In New York everyone is expected to deal with institutions
in which functionaries are interchangeable. In rural Puerto
Rico, as in other small communities, communication takes
place face to face between individuals—the teacher, the po-
liceman, the nurse may be someone's cousin. The Department of Health, the Board of Education, the City Housing
Authority, the municipal hospital in New York are no one's
cousins.

Communication by means of face-to-face contacts through

informal channels between Puerto Rican migrants sometimes produces results which are surprising to the outside observer and which run contrary to the premises on which social agencies operate.

An unmarried girl, in the course of a prolonged hospitalization for subacute bacterial endocarditis on the ward of a municipal hospital, was discovered to be three months pregnant. When the diagnosis of pregnancy could no longer be denied, the girl was very unhappy for several days. She said the father of the child, legally married to another woman, would refuse all responsibility for it. A week later she appeared much more cheerful and said that the matter was now settled as a cousin had been to visit her and, being childless, would be glad to take over the child at birth. The patient is unaware of the formalities involved in legal adoption and expects to carry out this plan as a private arrangement without help from organized social agencies.

Among the eighty families, there were two instances (Families 23 and 35) in which children were given at birth to friends or relatives because the families felt they were unable to support the child. The family physician learned this in the course of taking a routine medical history some time after the transfer of the child had taken place. Both mothers expressed some regret that they had lost a child but were also pleased that he had a good home and was better off than their own remaining children. On another occasion the family physician found the foster parent and child visiting the natural mother (Family 35), and the introductions were made with courtesy and no implication that this procedure was out of order.

A situation of this type has been presented with great

feeling in a recent off-Broadway play, *Me Candido,* in which a waif is taken into the home of a family who already have six children. He confounds the authorities by saying he has three fathers and does not know his name. The boy does not remember his natural father, his mother is dead, and his maternal uncle who brought him to the continent also died. He does not know himself by any other name but Candido and has no birth certificate. From the point of view of the authorities, an institution is the solution to this problem, a solution violently opposed by the boy himself and the three fathers, three men in the neighborhood who wish to assume responsibility for his care. In the end the authorities relent and the boy is adopted into the family and the neighborhood.

The fact that the Puerto Rican migrant and the authorities operate from different premises requires further examination.

The man in Family 11 is a short stocky man with a relatively large head and a shock of dark curly hair. On the street he is generally dressed in a suit and white or light shirt and tie, wears a felt hat, and often carries a briefcase, thus giving the impression of being a businessman. He speaks English fluently and forcefully. He is one who knows his way around and often accompanies a less knowledgeable compatriot to an "appointment." His wife is a short, pale, moderately obese little woman whose clothes and grooming are not on a par with her husband's. When doctors or field workers visit the home, he carries on the conversation and she serves coffee at his command. She does not sit down with the guests and has little to say even when a question is addressed to her in Spanish, although she is responsive when interviewed in his absence. The two children physically resemble their mother.

He was born in Puerto Rico in 1925, one of nine children. His father had a twelve-acre farm on which he cultivated tobacco and other small crops and kept some cattle which were slaughtered and sold in town. Starting at an early age, the children worked on the farm and helped the father with the distribution of meat in the town butcheries. "My father depended on me," is his comment. Although poor, the father's business apparently carried the family through without major deprivations. He was considered "a good boy, because my father whipped me every day." * He adds that his father was kind and would take the children to the beach. His father's death is described as the "unhappiest event in my life." He does not have much to say about his mother. When he was about fifteen, he impregnated a girl. Both his parents and hers insisted upon a "forced" marriage, and he brought the girl to his parent's home, while he continued in school to finish out the year. This marriage was subsequently dissolved by divorce in Puerto Rico, and the girl has since died. The child born of this union is being raised by his parents in Puerto Rico.

Soon after coming to the United States six years ago, he married his present wife, whose husband had died of tuberculosis, leaving her with two small children. For a time he walked the street with a bandage over his left eye, telling anyone who asked that he had had an operation on his eye and that another one would be needed. The operation was for the removal of a pterygium. There is a small pterygium in the temporal region of the right eye which does not encroach

---

* The anthropologists observe that punishment in this context is considered preventive, corrective, and necessary in order to teach the child what is right.

upon his field of vision and which in the opinion of the ophthalmology department at the clinic which he had been attending does not need to be removed at the present time or perhaps not at all. The man says that when he was working as a machinist several years ago he became suddenly blinded and that he has had difficulty with his vision ever since. According to the ophthalmology department his vision was 20/30 before the removal of the pterygium. There were no corneal ulcerations and the visual fields were normal. These observations suggest that he may have had an episode of hysterical blindness.

At a later date he worked in a packing house as a shipping clerk. This meant that he was responsible for checking merchandise in and out. One day his boss asked him to help with the unloading of a perishable cargo which had recently arrived. The man reports that in the ensuing discussion he set forth that he had not been hired as a porter and quit the job. Since then he has been looking around for a clerical situation. In the meantime his wife has had a variety of obstetrical problems, and as a result of his wife's illness and his unemployment the family has been receiving public assistance. Arrangements were made through Mount Sinai Hospital for the Cesarean delivery of the current pregnancy.

Since his wife had four successive fetal deaths, two of them in Mount Sinai Hospital, and a cholecystectomy in the early part of the current pregnancy, everyone was very much concerned that this should not happen again, and she was surrounded with the special attention of several agencies. Aware of this problem, the Department of Welfare sought to find a housekeeper for the family, but not finding one, decided that it would be simpler until the termination of the pregnancy for the man to assist her in the care of the children and of the house in order that she might be able to obtain the extra periods of rest recommended by the department of obstetrics. During this period the father, walking up and down the four flights of stairs to their apartment, has faithfully done the shopping and shepherded the children several times a day to and from school. For this he has earned the commendation of the various authorities concerned, the hospital, the school, the church. He and his wife have been attending a near-by Protestant church, where instruction has been given in the reading of the Bible, and after a period of several months he was received as a member of the congregation and later became a member of the parish council.

On the instigation of the man himself, letters were written to the City Housing Authority by the Social Service Department of the hospital, the church, and the various social agencies to whom the family had been known through the years, recommending that this family be granted priority in moving to a municipal housing project on account of the woman's health. Shortly after the woman had been successfully delivered of a daughter by Cesarean section, the family moved to a four-room apartment in a new city housing project in the Bronx.

Six months after this move was accomplished, the family physician visited this family in their new quarters. The man complained that his eyes were still bothering him and that he was expecting to have another operation on the recommendation of the Department of Welfare. The family physician tested his vision, using a Spanish newspaper, and did not consider that the pterygium had progressed or that his vision had deteriorated since the last examination.

He was also going to the dental clinic of the Department of Welfare. Furthermore, since this was a new neighborhood and his wife did not know her way around, it was necessary for him to continue taking the children to school to make sure that they did not get run over as they crossed a wide avenue with heavy traffic. The impending operation, the dental work, and his role as father and interpreter-intermediary, both for his family and others in the neighborhood, made it impossible for him to get a job at present. He concluded with an expression of disappointment in the church he had joined in his previous neighborhood because "I passed an examination and they did not give me a job."

After making a thorough review of the record set down here, physicians suggest the following interpretation. Pathological study of the placenta following the two fetal deaths which occurred at Mount Sinai Hospital revealed extensive calcific deposits and hyalinization of the placenta which appeared to be responsible for the previous intra-partum deaths. Therefore, this woman was given special care and attention during the prenatal period and delivery by Cesarean section a few weeks before term. This program was carried out jointly by Mount Sinai Hospital, the Department of Welfare, and the family physician. A live child resulted.

During the prenatal period, the father earned social approval from the authorities by his cooperation. No pressure was put upon him during this time to work, the assumption being that he would find a job after his wife's major health problem had been solved.

As was pointed out, this man had a spotty employment history and aspired to become a white-collar worker. The particular church which he joined requires that an individual learn something of the articles of the faith before becoming a member of the congregation. This he did and he was given additional responsibility of being a member of a church committee.

From the church's point of view this was splendid but did not involve a paid job in the organization. If he aspired to a white-color job, it was expected that he would take a job and go to school at night until he had acquired the skills necessary for such a position. But from this man's point of view, one who can do clerical work has risen in the social scale, and this higher status is demonstrated by refusing to do manual labor. Thus, a request by an employer to perform a menial task is to be resisted.

There was the trouble with his eyes and a doctor had operated on him. This meant that his eye condition was serious, that he could not see properly, and so he could not work, thus his status as a potential clerical worker was maintained. The move to a housing project encouraged the continuation of this pattern. He was now being examined in another hospital, where his past history was not known. Also it would take some time before his dentures were complete so that the final referral to the employment clinic of a municipal hospital by the Department of Welfare was still in the future.

This Puerto Rican migrant, whose parents demonstrated little affection towards him, learned to be subservient to those in authority while being combative with his contemporaries and predatory towards females. In his present home environment, he is apparently secure. His wife is subservient and does not question his authority; neither do the stepchildren. While she was ill, he did everything that the authorities expected of him and also achieved a status among his compatriots through his ability as an interpreter-intermediary. He is working to achieve the same position in his new environment, and as long as he is ill, he cannot work and his unachieved aspiration for a higher social status is maintained.

It is not possible to say whether this man's history could have been different. In retrospect it appears that he had achieved being a "good boy" during his wife's illness by cooperating with those in authority and that through this pattern of behavior he acquired greater social recognition than he had ever enjoyed.

It was not quite clear how he was going to maintain himself in this position. The church, he thought, would give him a job but had not done so. The Department of Welfare expected him to look for a job, but not until he was well. "Well," from the point of view of the Department of Welfare, meant the correction of physical defects, eyes and teeth. As long as some one thought he was sick, he was able to maintain his unachieved aspiration to become a clerical worker with self-respect.

Summary. Physicians and their associates are accustomed to communicate with each other through institutional channels involving written forms and interchangeable personnel. In contrast, the means of communication of Puerto Rican migrants involve face-to-face contacts and intermediaries who are thought to have influence and know their way around. Medical personnel and Puerto Rican families were observed to operate at times from entirely different premises, and this lack of reciprocal understanding was a source of frustration to both groups.

VII. WELFARE

The Department of Welfare of the City of New York, as a matter of principle, does not keep or publish statistics which distinguish families on relief by ethnic group, color, or religious affiliation. But in answer to requests for information by the public and the press, a member of the Department of Welfare permits himself from time to time to make an "educated guess" in these matters.

The number of Puerto Ricans receiving public assistance apparently varies considerably from year to year. Before the outbreak of the Korean war in June, 1950, there were 353,000 persons receiving public assistance in New York City, and 35,000, or 10 per cent, were thought to be Puerto Ricans. (Robison 1954.)

In April, 1950, according to data furnished by the United States Bureau of the Census, there were 245,880 Puerto Ricans living in New York City, so that if the Department of Welfare estimate was correct, 14.1 per cent of these were receiving aid.

Less than three years later the New York *Times* of February 25, 1953, reported that according to Welfare Commissioner Henry L. McCarthy's guess-estimate of the date, 20,000, or roughly 7.2 per cent, of the 276,000 persons receiving public assistance were Puerto Ricans. The Puerto Rican population of New York City was estimated at 382,900 persons as of December 31, 1952, an increase of 37.5 per cent over the 1950 figure. Therefore at the beginning of the calendar year 1953, 5.2 per cent of the estimated Puerto Rican population of the city were thought to be receiving public assistance. According to data obtained by Daniel Burnham of the *Wall Street Journal* from Henry J. Rosner, assistant to Commissioner McCarthy, there were 280,000 persons receiving public assistance in May, 1956, an increase of 4,000 persons, or 1.4 per cent over the 1953 figure. The guess-estimate was that between 55,000 and 60,000 of these, or 19.6 to 21.4 per cent, were Puerto Ricans. The number of Puerto Ricans estimated to be living in New York City at the end of 1955 was 538,000, more than twice the number counted by the 1950 Census.

Those Puerto Ricans thought to be receiving public assistance in May, 1956, therefore constituted between 10.5 and 11.1 per cent of the total Puerto Rican population of New York City as it was estimated in December, 1955. A similar figure is quoted as of May, 1957, when Welfare Commissioner McCarthy estimated that "about 11 per cent of the city's Puerto Ricans may be on relief." (New York *Times,* June 2, 1957.)

These figures are presented in order to set the individual families observed in this study against the background of the growing Puerto Rican population of New York City and those persons receiving public assistance. The figures from the Department of Welfare are expressed in terms of the number of individuals receiving public assistance, while the figures in this study refer to the number of families in which more than one individual may be receiving aid.

Of special interest in connection with the present study

is the "educated guess" of the Department of Welfare that 50 per cent of all persons receiving public assistance are children, and that 28 per cent of these children are Puerto Ricans.

Also, 15 per cent of all cases on the relief rolls are supplementary assistance cases, and 50 per cent of these are Puerto Ricans. Supplementary assistance is granted in those cases in which a man's earning capacity is insufficient to meet even the minimal needs of a large family, even though he may be steadily employed. For instance, Family 19 receives supplementary assistance because the father, who is fifty-three, earns only $54.00 in take-home pay and has a wife and nine children to support. Since he is unskilled and over fifty years old, the possibilities of increasing his earning power are not great. There were five families in our series with more than six children who received such assistance. (See Table 3.) The health record in the families receiving supplementary assistance follows the pattern observed in other large families. No family in this group with less than six children received supplementary assistance if the father was steadily employed.

In summarizing the major causes which lead Puerto Ricans to apply for public assistance, the Department of Welfare lists (1) dependent children, (2) low incomes and large families, and (3) illness. These same reasons, according to the anthropological team working in the area we are discussing, justify seeking and accepting public assistance in individual cases.

In forty-nine, or 61 per cent, of the Puerto Rican families in this study there was no record for any individual in that household in the files of the Department of Welfare. One or more individuals in the remaining thirty-one families had a record with the department and in twenty-six families the case was active as of January 1, 1956.

Table 3 presents in summary form data concerning the men in both those families who are on record as receiving public assistance from the Department of Welfare and those for whom no record was found.

In one third of the families receiving aid, there was no man contributing to the support of the woman, who might be raising from one to six children of school or preschool age. From a review of the history of these ten fatherless families it appears that this situation came about in several ways. Four of them involved desertion by the fathers (Families 14, 45, 49, 79); three of these were recent migrants, one was a man of Puerto Rican parentage. These men had left their women pregnant or with small children and had returned to Puerto Rico or could not be located in New York.

There were four women (Families 21, 22, 42, 52) in this group who left Puerto Rico with their small children in order to escape alcoholic and brutal men. These four women have received aid for their dependent children for most of the period since migration. The health record of these families is not the same in all cases. In two families (42 and 52) the hospitalization utilization rate, the number of recorded illnesses, and the absences of children from school are among the lowest in the entire group. Both these mothers expressed satisfaction at being rid of their men and receiving instead the protection and care of the government. (See Padilla.) But the hope of becoming self-supporting or of finding another man who will support the children is not entirely absent. One woman (Family 21) with three years of high school education in Puerto Rico wished to "progress," to be employed, after

TABLE 3

Categories of Families According to Status of Father

	Receiving Public Assistance		No Record with Department of Welfare		Total
No father in residence					
Children under 10	10		4		
No children under 10	0		3		
		10		7	17
Families with six children or more					
Father sick employed	0		0		
Father well employed	5		4		
Father sick unemployed	3		0		
Father well unemployed	0		0		
		8		4	12
Families with less than six children					
Father sick employed	1		5		
Father well employed	0		26		
Father sick unemployed	5		0		
Father well unemployed	2		0		
		8		31	39
Families with no children at home					
Man sick employed	0		3		
Man well employed	0		2		
Man sick unemployed	2		2		
Man well unemployed	0		0		
		2		7	9
Extra member of family (child of other marriage, grandmother)	3		0		
		3		0	3
		31		49	80

arriving in New York. In Puerto Rico she had borne an imbecile child with a club foot and reluctantly consented to have her placed in an institution on the recommendation of a hospital in New York. She soon became pregnant by another man, who, she hoped, would support her, but he deserted her. Shortly after birth, severe congenital heart disease was diagnosed in the infant born of this union. The mother, now jobless, manless, and dependent on public assistance, waits in hospital corridors while physicians determine whether or not the child is a suitable candidate for cardiac surgery.

Yet the hope that there may appear another man who will support the family is not altogether groundless. Recently a woman (Family 22) came rushing into the office hoping that a diagnosis of pregnancy could be established. She squeezed a pale watery liquid from her nipples in an attempt to convince the physician that even though a tubal ligation had been performed in Puerto Rico fourteen years ago, following two Cesarean sections because of a contracted pelvis, pregnancy was still possible. According to her story, she had met a man who had given her money so that she might be free of public assistance and promised to marry her and support her children if he could have a child of his own.

The few cases cited do not justify any conclusion, and one may not say that they are or are not typical of the "family break up" which accounts for one third of the cases which receive public assistance. Nevertheless, these particular illustrations and the clinical observations made in the course of serving in the medical division of an out-patient department in a city hospital lead one to suspect that whereas formerly a Puerto Rican woman had no option but to suffer abuse from her man and tolerate infidelity as a price for the support of her children, if he were inclined to exact this price, she now knows that there are alternatives. If she can manage to get to the continent with her children, she may find gainful employment, she may get another man, or she may obtain public assistance to support her children. The man also has learned that society has provided alternatives and that extramarital affairs which were formerly regarded as a proof of his masculinity but did not relieve him of the duty to support his children may in fact not only relieve him of that duty but also deprive him of his family.

Where public assistance is granted on the basis of illness, the responsibility for declaring that a man is too sick to work rests with the physician.

The connection between being sick and receiving public assistance is well understood by the Puerto Rican migrant and was expressed in a simple way by a woman of forty who presented herself to the author in the medical out-patient department of a city hospital. She was holding her right arm and complaining of pain—a previous medical examiner had found no reason for the complaint and sent her on to a Spanish-speaking physician. The physical examination was repeated and again no reason for the complaint could be demonstrated. She then explained that she had not worked for four months, having found the work in a canning factory too heavy. "My arm gave way," she said, "and my investigator told me that with such a pain I could get taken care of in any hospital." She then admitted that she had come alone to New York less than a year ago, was illiterate, spoke no English, and did not wish to go back to her old job. She was examined, reassured, referred to a class in basic English, and urged to consult her priest or neighbors in order to find some one "con quien andar" (with whom to go) to seek light factory work. (See Padilla.) At a subsequent appointment with the same physician she complained of pain in her side. The physician reassured her and repeated the same recommendations, urging her to seek work. She then requested, without further urging, that her social security papers declaring her able to work be filled out.

After several fruitless visits to an out-patient department over a period of several weeks, an individual of this type may be sent to the employability clinic of a municipal hospital by the Department of Welfare. Following examinations in this clinic a written report of the objective findings along with the physician's opinion regarding employability goes to the Department of Welfare. By the time the medical report reaches its destination it is possible that the patient's case is in the hands of an investigator different from the one who made the original referral. In any event a period of several months may elapse between the time the patient presents himself with a complaint to a medical out-patient department and a report of employability is made. But during this period the patient will be examined by a number of physicians who "have not told him anything." He feels rejected, unrelieved, and his symptoms have become increasingly important to him.

Of the thirty-one families (out of eighty) in this study who received public assistance, eleven were granted such aid on the grounds that the man of the family was incapacitated by illness. Six of these eleven men had been injured at work either before or since migration. (See Table 4.) On the other hand, there were seven families with chronic illness or physical defect in the man for whom there is no record of receiving public assistance. Two of these seven men had been injured at work, one before and one after migration. (See Table 5.)

TABLE 4

Eleven Families Receiving Public Assistance on the Grounds of the Father's Illness

Family Number	Medical Diagnosis	Disturbance of Thought, Mood, and Behavior	Injury at Work
1	Paresis left peroneal following trauma	Yes	Yes
2	Chronic bronchial asthma; bilateral pulmonary tuberculosis (arrested); benign prostatic hypertrophy	Yes	No
3	Partial blindness	Yes	Yes
11	Bilateral pterygia; carious teeth	Yes	?
12	Chronic bronchial asthma; rheumatoid arthritis, mild	Yes	Yes
20	Diabetes controlled	Yes	No
26	Herniated intervertebral disc	Yes	Yes
28	Traumatic epilepsy and labyrinthine disease	No	No
31	Osteoarthritis lumbo-sacral spine, mild; index finger amputated	Yes	Yes
41	Low back pain syndrome	Yes	Yes
53	Bronchial asthma; ill-defined gastrointestinal complaints	Yes	No

TABLE 5

*Seven Families with Chronic Illness or Physical
Defect in Man and No Record with the
Department of Welfare*

Family Number	Medical Diagnosis	Disturbance of Thought, Mood, and Behavior	Injury at Work
4	Tuberculosis, moderately advanced (?), refused treatment	No	No
5	Synechia left eye	No	No
7	Synechia right eye; carious teeth	No	Yes
17	Emphysema	Yes	No
30	Synechia left eye; ill-defined gastrointestinal complaints	No	Yes
33	Chronic peptic ulcer	Yes	No
60	Rheumatoid osteoarthritis, severe	No	No

An injury, slight though it may have been, was one of the elements which contributed to the subsequent disability and made the acceptance of public assistance justified, necessary, and inevitable in the eyes of the eleven individuals in Table 4. (See Padilla.) The manner in which the three factors—(1) injury at work, (2) a medical condition which may or may not be related to the work accident, and (3) a disturbance of thought, mood, and behavior—interact and how long-term dependency on public funds results for a particular family may perhaps be best illustrated by the following case.

The man in Family 26, who is described in the anthropological volume under the name of Rios, had been self-supporting all his life and was proud of his versatility and ability to find work. When he migrated to the continent at the age of forty-five, he had no particular skill but great hopes and aspirations to "progress." After he had fallen and injured his back at work and did not improve with conservative treatment, surgery was recommended but was delayed for four months while the surgeon waited for authorization from the Workmen's Compensation Board to perform the operation. During this period the patient was examined by many physicians representing the insurance company and the Board. These examinations confirmed him in the belief that he was too sick to work and was entitled to sick benefits.

On the day following the operation, he walked out of the hospital against advice, under the delusion that a patient in the next bed was making improper advances towards him. Since that time the Department of Welfare has sent him for repeated examinations to different specialists to determine his employability. He has not been under the continuing care of any one physician nor has he been seen by the Rehabilitation Bureau. He returns from each of these examinations bewildered and frustrated, saying that the doctors are not doing him any good. Indeed, they tell him he is not sick, but they are not making him well. His argument goes somewhat like this: "I have worked since I was a young boy. Look at me now, I am weak, my muscles are small, I cannot pick up a pin from the floor. I have terrible pains in my head. I paid insurance, they should pay me when I am sick and have to live on welfare." Arachnoiditis and conversion hysteria are the final diagnosis in his case, and since the pattern of illness and dependency have been established for over three years the prospects for rehabilitation are poor.

Another man (Family 31) had worked in a sugar mill in Puerto Rico all his life. He had lost the index finger of his right hand many years ago. When he came to New York in middle life, he obtained a job as a dishwasher but was dismissed after a few weeks on the grounds that because of his missing finger he presented a potential compensation risk which neither the union nor the employer wished to undertake. He was unable to obtain other employment. Formerly, in Puerto Rico, he had been somewhat irascible but drank heavily only on Saturday nights during the cane-cutting season. Now he was drunk more frequently and shouted at his family so loudly and abusively that the neighbors prevailed upon his wife to call an ambulance to take him to the psychopathic ward of a city hospital. There he was cooperative and quiet and was discharged after a few days with the diagnosis of passive dependent personality. On subsequent examination made in the employability clinic of a city hospital, he was pronounced employable. He did not find work, but his behavior has improved greatly since he has been living in a housing project on Staten Island under less crowded conditions.

In an attempt to draw an inference from these several observations, we would like to point out that a man over the age of forty with no special skill, speaking little or no English, who migrates with the hope of "progressing," has few job opportunities open to him in New York. Seasonal or even steady employment as a dishwasher is not the fulfillment of his dreams. Slipping on the proverbial banana peel permits him to be cared for without losing his self-respect and may relieve him from the responsibility of continuing to strive for a goal which would satisfy his aspirations but is beyond his capacities and his opportunities.

When the forty-nine families having no record with the Department of Welfare are compared with the thirty-one who received aid, significant differences are noted. Though there were seven families with no record and no steadily employed man in residence (see Table 3), the mother in three families was able to work since the children were older and were also able to contribute to the family support. In three others the visiting father, who might be living elsewhere, contributed to the support of the children who were living with their mother. (See Padilla.)

Several men in the self-supporting families of Table 5 had physical defects objectively comparable to those encountered in the "sick men" of Table 4 receiving public assistance, but with this difference—these defects were not considered incapacitating by the individuals concerned and were not complicated by major disturbances of thought, mood, and behavior as in the case of those men described above. The one individual with a severe personality disturbance in this group was unemployed and would have been receiving public assistance had he not been supported by his son.

Summary. It has been estimated that as of May, 1957, about 11 per cent of New York City's Puerto Rican population of over 500,000 were receiving public assistance. Of the eighty families in this study, thirty-one, or 38.75 per cent, are on record with the Department of Welfare as having received public assistance for one or more individuals in the family. For forty-nine families, or 61.25 per cent, there was no record in the Department of Welfare.

The major causes which lead Puerto Ricans to apply for public assistance are (1) dependent children, (2) low incomes and large families, and (3) illness. When public assistance is granted on the basis of illness, the responsibility for declaring that a man is too sick to work rests with the physician.

Three factors—(1) injury at work, (2) a medical condition which may or may not be related to the work accident, and (3) a disturbance of thought, mood, and behavior—often determine the length of dependency on public funds.

VIII. FERTILITY AND STERILIZATION *

In the eighty Puerto Rican families under study there were eighty-six women who gave a history of having had sexual intercourse. Eight of these were young women born in New York of Puerto Rican parents. Three women had never been pregnant and their mates gave a history of gonorrhea. Seventy-five were born in Puerto Rico and had migrated to Manhattan, some as long as thirty years ago, others as recently as two years ago, their ages ranging from sixty-seven to twenty-one. Six grandmothers living with their adult children are included in this group of seventy-five native Puerto Rican women.

The fertility record of these seventy-five women is shown in Table 6. This indicates an average of five pregnancies per woman and an average of 3.85 live children per woman. The median was 4.5 live children per woman, and eighteen women had borne six children or more. The following observations are reported as illustrations of the attitude of some Puerto Rican women towards childbearing.

One of the first patients who came to the family physician's office was a girl fourteen years of age at the time, the third

* Some of the material in this chapter has already been published in my article "Sterilization and Birth-Control Practices in a Selected Sample of Puerto Ricans Living in a Manhattan Slum," *Fertility and Sterility*, Vol. 8, No. 3 (May–June, 1957), 267–81.

TABLE 6

*Fertility Record of 75 Puerto Rican Women
of Ages 21–67*

	Number
Para	331
Grava	371
Spontaneous abortion	30
Induced abortion	5
Stillbirths	7
Twin pregnancies	5
Living children (1955)	289
Fetal deaths	4

child in Family 64. She was a depressed, unkempt, dirty child with hair streaming down her face, dressed in ill-fitting blue jeans tucked into muddy rubber boots. During the examination she was uncommunicative and appeared very unhappy. Her tonsils were found to be cryptic and enlarged and the right ear drum was bulging. Appropriate medication was prescribed and she recovered in a few days. She was not seen again for a period of over one year, when her mother brought her in for prenatal care. Examination revealed a uterus symmetrically enlarged to the size consistent with a three-months pregnancy. On this occasion the child presented a complete contrast to the waif seen the year previously. Her hair was combed, she wore a dress, shoes, and clean socks. A discreet amount of lipstick outlined a smiling mouth. Altogether she appeared radiant, as young pregnant women are reported to be by poets and artists. She was referred to Mount Sinai Hospital for prenatal care and went through an uneventful pregnancy and uncomplicated delivery. Psychological examinations done at the hospital revealed a child of dull normal intelligence with no particular psychopathology. An interview with the hospital psychiatrist confirmed the family physician's clinical impression that this was a child reared in a poor, disorganized home by an indifferent mother and an even more indifferent father and that the love and attention of her boy friend provided a new and unique experience in an otherwise drab life.

When questioned by physicians and others she consistently affirmed that she wanted the baby and denied any intentions of inducing an abortion. The fact that she was under sixteen years of age meant that she could not marry without special permission of the court. This was not granted, although the request was made by the parents of both young people. Her mother felt considerable shame over the whole affair, but the girl seemed unconcerned over the lack of legal sanction. Following a custom prevalent in certain parts of the island of Puerto Rico, the young couple remained under the protection of the boy's parents and lived in their home. Unfortunately, they moved to Ohio soon after the baby's birth so that we have only a word-of-mouth report, as of December, 1956, to the effect that the young couple are now legally married, have three more children, and are still living with his parents. The young man is not steadily employed.

The fact that pregnancy and a new baby may afford satisfaction under adverse life circumstances was observed also in Family 20. This woman had already borne twelve children. When she became pregnant for the thirteenth time two of her older sons were in jail for stealing a car, one daughter had committed suicide at sixteen, five years previously, two children had been committed to state training schools, and four had been placed in boarding schools by a social agency. The remaining two children were at home, a sixteen-year-old girl, considered lazy by her parents, who had been expelled from school for hitting a teacher, and a fourteen-year-old boy who, though discharged a few months previously with a good record from a state training school, was not employed and was not attending continuation school since arrangements for this had not been made.

Over the three years of our acquaintance the father had repeatedly expressed his helplessness in regard to his children's behavior and his despair over the family's being scattered. The mother, asked if she used contraceptives, replied in the negative; since her husband was now impotent such precautions were not necessary. When, some time later, the family physician met the parents and the thirteenth child, age one month, on the street, both parents were all smiles. The baby was dressed in a new yellow bonnet and sweater and covered with a white blanket. The mother expressed delight over the child's good looks and good health. The father also was pleased and told the doctor proudly that this baby proved he was not impotent. The mother concurred. Any oblique suggestion that this child might turn out to be a problem like the rest was rejected. This new baby represented a new hope, a new creation.

On the other hand, problems arising from too many children and too little money are keenly appreciated in many cases. In this particular group (Families 1, 3, 15, 40, 46, 51, 63, 68), all eight women were married, native New Yorkers of Puerto Rican parentage between the ages of twenty and thirty. All had attended high school in New York, five for an average of two years, three had graduated. These women had an average of three children, or a median of 2.5, while their mothers had an average of 6.7 children, or a median of 6.5. The mothers of these particular women, who are now in their late forties, are native Puerto Ricans who had not been sterilized and denied the use of contraceptives. (See Table 7.) One of them admitted to an abortion induced over ten years ago at a time that her husband was unemployed.

Among the native New Yorkers, one had five children (Family 63), two of them born as a result of failure to use the diaphragm correctly, although she had been carefully instructed by competent authorities in its use. Six others were currently using prescribed mechanical means of contraception with apparent success and satisfaction and were emphatic in their statement that two or three was the maximum number of children any of them wished to bear. In fact none of the six had more than two children. When the possibility of future pregnancies was discussed with one woman (Family 68), she shuddered and launched into a history of the misfortunes that had befallen her mother (para 6, grava 6) as a result of having too many children.

Eight induced abortions were reported by four of these women. These unwanted pregnancies were attributed to contraceptive failure or to carelessness in not using contraception. One woman (Family 46) admitted to three induced abortions and declared that were she to become pregnant again she would take the next plane to Puerto Rico in order to obtain tubal ligation.

In comparing the fertility record of these eight native New Yorkers of Puerto Rican parentage with twelve native Puerto Rican women who are also under thirty (Table 7), we find that the native Puerto Ricans average 4.4 children per family, or a median of 3.5, that is, in effect one more child per family than their American-born sisters. While the native New Yorkers have expressed a fervent desire to limit their families

TABLE 7

Fertility Record of 8 New York Women under 30 of Puerto Rican Parentage Compared with That of Their Mothers and of Young Native Puerto Rican Women

	Daughters under 30 (8)	Mothers (7)	Native Puerto Rican Women under 30 (12)
Para	18	47	53
Grava	24	48	62
Spontaneous abortion	0	0	6
Induced abortion	6	1	3
Stillbirths	0	0	8
Sterilized	0	0	5

and have been instructed in accepted means of contraception, their previous record of contraceptive failure or failure to use contraceptives suggests that their reproductive careers may not yet have come to an end.

Five of the twelve native Puerto Rican women in this group who are under thirty have already had their tubes ligated. The three operated on in New York had six live children each and were sterilized post partum on the grounds of medical complications during their last pregnancy. Of the two operated on in Puerto Rico, one had four children and the other three. For them this was enough; the one with four children returned to Puerto Rico four years after migration for the delivery of her fourth child and to obtain post-partum tubal ligation.

When the obstetrical history of seventy-five native Puerto Rican women who have borne children is analyzed (see

Table 8), we find that twenty have been sterilized. These seventy-five women are currently between the ages of twenty-one and sixty-seven. Of the twenty sterilized, ten were operated on before they were thirty. In the United States at a few hospitals multiparity justifying routine post-partum sterilization is strictly fixed in terms of a woman's having borne six live children when she is less than thirty years old. Complications sometimes justifying sterilization on medical grounds include previous Cesarean sections, recurrent toxemia, severe varicose veins, and uterine prolapse. In the reports of the Department of Health of the Commonwealth of Puerto Rico, medical indications for sterilization in public maternity hospitals are similarly defined. But a woman who wishes to obtain a tubal ligation after the birth of two or three children is able to do so in a private clinic.

The fact that four women returned to Puerto Rico from New York for the express purpose of having this operation performed following delivery of their third or fourth child and that a twenty-seven-year-old woman (Family 43) paid $225.00 to a private physician operating in a proprietary New York hospital to tie her tubes after the delivery of her sixth child is evidence that the motivation for limiting family size through tubal ligation is a powerful one.

As the family physician became more conversant with the Puerto Rican point of view on tubal ligation, the subject of *la operación,* as it is known, was brought up routinely in the course of taking medical histories from Puerto Rican women. The term was familiar to all of them and entered into the calculations of women who were thinking of limiting the size of their families much the same way as mechanical means of contraception form a part of the mental furniture

TABLE 8

Twenty Sterilizations in 75 Native Puerto Rican Women

Family Number	Age	Grava	Para	Living Children	Stated Reason	Where	When
22	21	2	3	1	Contracted pelvis Multiple sections	P.R.	Pre-migration
32	21	3	3	3	Enough children	P.R.	6 yrs. post-migration
74	23	3	3	3	Enough children	P.R.	13 yrs. post-migration
16	23	3	3	2	Enough children	P.R.	Pre-migration
59	25	6	10	6	Varicose veins	M.H. NYC	7 yrs. post-migration
67	25	4	4	4	Enough children	P.R.	Pre-migration
73	27	3	3	3	Convulsions	Vol. H. NYC	25 yrs. post-migration
43	27	6	6	6	Enough children	Pr.H. NYC	2 yrs. post-migration
18	28	6	13	6	Multiparity	MSH	4 yrs. post-migration
62	29	3	2	2	? Pelvic inflammatory disease	P.R.	Pre-migration
36	30	7	7	7	Multiparity	MSH	7 yrs. post-migration
78	30	5	5	5	Enough children	P.R.	Pre-migration

TABLE 8 (*Continued*)

Family Number	Age	Grava	Para	Living Children	Stated Reason	Where	When
23	30	8	6	6	Multiparity Placenta previa	MSH	5 yrs. post-migration
61	31	4	4	4	Enough children	P.R.	4 yrs. post-migration
55	31	8	7	7	Multiparity Multiple sections	M.H. NYC	4 yrs. post-migration
76	33	5	5	5	Varicose veins	MSH	5 yrs. post-migration
33	33	3	3	3	Enough children	P.R.	6 yrs. post-migration
53	34	8	8	5	Hysterectomy, cystocele retro-cele, secondary menorrhagia	MSH	6 yrs. post-migration
2	48	10	6	2	Hysterectomy prolapse	P.R.	Pre-migration
31	54	8	8	4	Hysterectomy, cystocele retro-cele	MSH	2 yrs. post-migration

Age: At time operation was performed
M.H.: Municipal Hospital

M.S.H.: Mount Sinai Hospital
Pr.H.: Private Hospital
Vol. H.: Voluntary Hospital

of the average middle-class American woman. The anthropologists also found from their questionnaire that both men and women migrants consider *la operación* as the accepted and only sure means to limit families. This opinion was expressed to physicians and anthropologists alike by individuals, regardless of its possible application to their particular case. (Padilla.)

Failure in the use of the usual mechanical means of contraception by Puerto Ricans living on the island, in spite of the free distribution of materials by the prematernal clinics of the Department of Health, has been attributed by Stycos to the lack of communication between spouses on sexual matters. (Stycos 1954 and 1955.) Figures on the large group of women to whom vaginal inserts have been distributed through the out-patient department of Mount Sinai Hospital are not yet available, so that we do not know whether Puerto Rican women on the continent and those of Puerto Rican parentage are more or less reliable than other groups of American women in the use of this particular method.

La operación, on the other hand, is something which can be talked about, and the matter of future pregnancies is settled once for all. (Stycos 1955.) The cases cited from our group indicate that the attitude toward and the interest in tubal ligation carries over on the continent and that women return to the island expressly for the purpose of having the *la operación* performed. This attitude prevails regardless of religious affiliation, except in the case of Pentecostalists (see Chapter II, section on religion).

The history of sterilization in Puerto Rico is an interesting one. In the middle thirties the Puerto Rican Reconstruction Administration (successor to the Puerto Rican Relief Administration) made contracts with the Church of the Brethren, Quakers, and Mennonnites to operate some of the homesteading projects which the Federal government had started on the island. (Hanson 1955.) These projects included a school and a hospital. One of these, the Castaner project, was conducted by the Church of the Brethren, which reported the sterilization in the course of one year of 300 women, who had an average of 6.6 children each. The Congress of the United States protested against the performance of sterilization on Federal property. (Hanson 1955.) During World War II the property was sold to the Church of the Brethren by the government. Dr. Franklin K. Cassel, who served with the Brethren Service Commission and was in charge of the maternal and child health program in the Castaner project from the spring of 1943 to the fall of 1945, reports:

Only post-partum tubal litigations were done where medical indications and the health of the mother and her family made it advisable for such a procedure to be carried out. . . . Indeed we did a considerable number of these operations because of the relatively low standard of health and sizable number of large families. At one time our medical program was under fire by the Catholic authorities, who complained to the Insular Department of Health, who in turn investigated this phase of our work. After reviewing our statistics and observing first-hand the situation, they issued on official report recommending our health program and requesting a continuation of this good work. [Personal communication.]

The extent to which sterilization is practiced on the island is a matter of speculation, and the most sophisticated guesses available are presented in Table 9. In the seventy-five native Puerto Rican women in our group, 26.6 per cent had been sterilized. Half of the sterilizations were performed in women less than thirty.

A different aspect of the sterilization problem is illustrated in the case of a woman whose tubes have been prematurely ligated and who wishes to become pregnant. Four cases of

TABLE 9

Summary of Records and Observations on the
Number of Women Sterilized in Puerto Rico

Source	Sample	Proportion Sterilized
Hatt [1]	6,000 representative households, island-wide in 1947	6.6% of all ever married 8.3% upper income group 2.7% lower income group 11.3% marital unions between 1930 and 1939
Belavel, quoted by Stycos [2] and Sutter [3]	All women delivered in hospitals during calendar year 1949	17.8% to 19.3%
Stycos [4,5]	Random sample of 2,667 females interviewed in pre-maternal clinics in 1954	38% of those with more than 6 children 20% of total number
Puerto Rico Department of Health [6]	Municipal hospital patients, 1952–53:	
	Mayaguez—1,225 deliveries	18 sterilizations or 1.5%
	Rio Piedras—3,154 deliveries	119 sterilizations or 3.80%
	Caguas—999 deliveries	0 sterilizations
Grace [7]	U.S. Army base hospital (spot check in 1955 of 60 successive medical admissions of young women-wives of Puerto Rican army personnel)	20%

[1] Paul K. Hatt, *Backgrounds of Human Fertility in Puerto Rico* (Princeton, Princeton University Press, 1952), p. 445.

[2] J. Mayone Stycos, *Family and Fertility in Puerto Rico* (New York, Columbia University Press, 1955), p. 224.

[3] Jean Sutter, "Le mouvement dans le monde en faveur de la limitation des familles," *Population, Revue de l'Institut National d'Etudes Démographiques,* 10e année (avril–juin, 1955), pp. 277–94.

this type (none of them from our eighty families) were seen in the gynecological clinic of Mount Sinai Hospital during 1955.

Two were young women who had never been pregnant. Each reported that her tubes had been ligated when she was eighteen at the insistence of her husband, who did not want children. Now, five years later, these women were divorced, and remarriage depended on the possibility of becoming pregnant. Bilateral tuboplasty was performed on one patient with resulting patency of tubes, as tested by insufflation immediately following the operation. However, on reexamination four months later, the tubes were no longer patent. In the case of the second patient, an ovarian cyst was found at operation, and both tubes had been surgically removed at the time of the first laparotomy, suggesting that they may have been diseased, thus casting some doubt on the patient's account of the reason for surgery.

The other two patients, both in their early twenties, had borne two and four children respectively and now wished more. A multiple myomectomy and bilateral salpingoplasty was performed on the patient with two children with no resulting pregnancy, although one tube was patent by insufflation.

On the recommendation of the department of psychiatry, a successful tuboplasty was performed on the woman who

[4] J. Mayone Stycos, "Female Sterilization in Puerto Rico," *Eugenics Quarterly,* I, 3 (1954).

[5] J. Mayone Stycos, "The Pattern of Birth Control in Puerto Rico," *Eugenics Quarterly,* I, 3 (1954), 176–81.

[6] Puerto Rico Department of Health, *Annual Report, 1952–1953,* p. 96.

[7] Major William J. Grace, U.S. Army Medical Corps, personal communication.

had borne four children. She conceived six months post-operatively and her fifth child was delivered successfully. When seen at home, this woman reported that her first husband did not support her and their four children, ran around with other women, and was a drunkard. She did not wish to bear any more children by him, and her tubes had been tied in a Puerto Rican municipal hospital four years ago following the delivery of her fourth child. The couple separated. She and her four children came to New York, where she has been receiving help from the Department of Welfare. Complaints of dysmenorrhea and constant lower quadrant pain, as well as the desire to bear a child by the man who wished to marry her and support her if he could have a child of his own, brought her to the hospital. Now, that she has had the child she is sure that she does not want any more pregnancies, but in order to avoid a third laparotomy she says she will use "birth control."

This last case illustrates, aside from economic considerations, the ambivalence of women in this particular society with regard to surgical sterilization. The woman who is sterilized is telling her man that she wants no more children by him. On the other hand, another man who might approach her is relieved of the responsibility for her support since she cannot bear him a child. The woman we have just mentioned had terminated her marriage with an alcoholic, brutal husband and came to the United States. For her the chance of making a new home was bound up with her ability to bear a child to another man, and for this she underwent a second operation.

Induced abortion is a subject on which little information was obtained, largely for fear that individuals in the area might misinterpret the family physician's interest in the subject. Women came in at times wishing to be examined to determine whether or not they were pregnant. When a diagnosis of pregnancy was made and referral for prenatal care suggested, they might disappear and report a month later that they started to abort and were admitted bleeding to a city hospital, where curettage was performed. In such a case, instrumentation is denied by the patient but is strongly suspected by the physician.

Summary. A significant difference in the attitude toward fertility and in the actual number of children borne was found to exist between Puerto Rican women and their American-born daughters in this group.

Among native Puerto Ricans tubal ligation was the preferred form of family limitation, and some individuals returned to Puerto Rico many years after migration to have this operation performed. In this regard, the observations made for this group are consistent with those of previous investigators. Difficulty of communication between spouses in regard to sexual matters and lack of experience with long-range planning are suggested as possible motives for the apparent unacceptability of other methods for the control of conception among native Puerto Ricans.

Four cases are cited where tubal reconstruction was undertaken in New York at the request of women who regretted their inability to conceive following a tubal ligation performed in Puerto Rico with their consent.

IX. TUBERCULOSIS

"Tuberculosis, it has been said, is a disease of incomplete civilization." (Dubos 1952.) In the past, an increase in new cases of tuberculosis has been noted in a population during the period in which it was undergoing rapid industrialization and urbanization. The Puerto Rican migrant to New York City is no exception in this regard.

The death rate for tuberculosis in the island of Puerto Rico since 1940 has been following the general downward trend. In 1940, 260.2 deaths from tuberculosis per 100,000 population are reported for the island, and the preliminary estimate for 1955 is 32.6 deaths per 100,000 population. During approximately the same period, the death rates from tuberculosis in New York City per 100,000 population are reported as 49 in 1940 and 14 in 1954. Although the general trend for new cases reported in New York City has also been downward, some upward fluctuations occurred in 1948 and 1949, so that the new case rate in 1952 and 1953 was not lower than that reported for 1945.

The New York City Health Department differentiates among various groups in reporting new cases of tuberculosis. Fewer new cases were reported in 1954 among members of the Negro, white, and yellow races as compared with 1953. Among Puerto Ricans, on the other hand, there was an increase of new cases totaling 783 in 1954, compared with 725 in 1953. (Lowell 1955 and 1956.) The Puerto Rican cases accounted for 12 per cent of all new cases reported in the same year. This increase in the number of new cases reported for Puerto Ricans in 1954 occurred in a year when the net migration was lower than it had been at any time since 1945.

The number of individuals who come from Puerto Rico in order to be treated for tuberculosis already diagnosed and partially treated on the island cannot be ascertained with any degree of certainty since the New York City Health Department has no figures bearing on this point. One of the physicians working in a chest clinic in one of the districts with a high concentration of Puerto Ricans "guessed" that between 3 and 5 per cent of the new cases admitted in the course of a year were individuals who had come from Puerto Rico with previously diagnosed tuberculosis and applied for treatment in that particular district of New York City. Three tuberculous individuals who had migrated to the continent in hopes that miracles could be performed in New York hospitals that are not possible elsewhere were seen in the family physician's office during the period of observation.

But it is likely that conditions of life prevailing among recent migrants in New York City are the factors most responsible for the high incidence of tuberculosis among Puerto Rican migrants. As Dubos points out, "Whereas the germ theory of disease gave a rational basis to the development of high effective sanitary measures, no similar body of scientific doctrine has come to guide the anti-tuberculosis movement in its efforts to render man more capable of dealing with the bacilli once contagion has taken place."

The observations of Dubos are substantiated in a quantitative study made in the state of Washington, in which a significantly greater number of cases of tuberculosis was found among individuals living under marginal unstable social conditions as compared with the general population. (Holmes 1956.)

In Manhattan the distribution of Puerto Rican cases showed the highest concentration in the East Harlem Health District, followed by Riverside, the Lower East Side, and Lower West Side. In the Bronx, Mott Haven Health Center District had the largest number, followed by another concentration in Morrisania. In Brooklyn the Red Hook-Gowanus section recorded the largest number of Puerto Rican cases. (Lowell 1955.)

The prevalence of tuberculosis throughout New York City is reported as the number of total known cases per 1,000 population in the Department of Health Register on a given day. The range is from 0 to 8 cases.

Among the seventy-seven health districts in Manhattan, the prevalence was 8 cases per 1,000 population in eleven districts and 6 to 7.9 per 1,000 population in another eleven districts. The present study was made in one of the areas where 6 to 7.9 cases per 1,000 population were reported for 1954. (Lowell 1955.) Since this is a study of disease in context, the environmental factors which appeared to contribute to the development of the disease in individual cases and the manner in which the disease was regarded and handled by the families concerned were the points of focus for both the medical and anthropological teams.

The Puerto Rican population of this slum area, as we saw them in the office, were well aware of tuberculosis. They were more apt to speak of an individual as being "enfermo del pecho" (suffering from chest disease) rather than use the word tuberculosis. An inquiry made in the course of a routine medical history as to whether an individual had ever been himself "enfermo del pecho," or had relatives who were so afflicted, was always understood and answered with a violent denial, or with a detailed account of so and so in the family who was said to have died from the disease but with whom the informant had not been closely associated. This type of answer suggests some awareness of the contagious features of the disease while indicating great fear of its consequences, a fear to be met by denial of the existence of the disease. Tuberculosis was also considered shameful and thought to result from privation and ill treatment. A neighbor, for instance, remarked that so and so acquired tuberculosis as a consequence of beatings inflicted by her husband. Another woman (Family 61) expressed the belief that evil spirits might be responsible for tuberculosis in certain cases. An individual (Family 18) who had been hospitalized for a long time and was considered to be incurable was referred to as "inutil," useless.

Six families in which nine patients had been or were under treatment for tuberculosis were observed. All nine patients were registered with the Department of Health. Denial of the existence of the disease was a feature in four of the patients, and in this denial they were supported by their family (Families 2, 4, 22, 73). When a positive sputum was discovered in the father of Family 4 in the course of hospital admission for pneumonia, he was transferred to a city hospital for further study and treatment. No other positive sputum was obtained, and he left against advice at the end of two weeks. On repeated visits made by the Health Department nurse, he was never found at home and the family stated that he had left for Puerto Rico. This man was examined by one of the family physicians, but no history of tuberculosis was obtained in spite of leading questions by the physician, who knew this history through another source. The rest of the family, however, did submit to chest X-rays, which were found to be normal.

Another woman (Family 22) in one interview told the physician that she had been hospitalized for tuberculosis. Looking over the physician's shoulder on a subsequent visit to the office, she saw written in Spanish on the chart "enferma del pecho." She became very angry and denied that she had ever been "enferma del pecho" or had any illness other than pneumonia. According to the Department of Health record, she had been hospitalized on three occasions over a period of three years and each time left against advice. At the time of our contact, her case was considered arrested by the Department of Health. Since medication had been supplied for use at home and the threat of hospitalization was removed, she returned for X-rays at the prescribed intervals. These pills were a source of great satisfaction; along with her false teeth, they were a "gift of the government," and she displayed both with equal pride to visitors in her home. She based her refusal to remain in the hospital in former years on the fact that she had no one to care for her daughter, who suffers from severe chronic bronchial asthma, but in whom, up to the present time, no evidence of tuberculosis has been found.

This woman was the fifth of twelve children in a poor cane cutter's family. Seven of her siblings had died in infancy. At the age of fifteen, she married a man who beat her and whom she divorced after the birth of twins by Cesarean section. Both these children died in infancy. According to her story, her second husband, the father of her daughter was no better than the first, so she left him and came to New York with her child. While denying that she has tuberculosis, she considers herself sick, and the support furnished by the Department of Welfare spells independence for her. "No man is my boss," she declares. "I am supported by the government and I live very well." Still, her feelings must be somewhat mixed, for she was entertaining a marriage prospect recently.

It is probable that the denial of tuberculosis is associated not only with a fear of the disease and its consequences but also with the dread of prolonged hospitalization, involving as it does separation from the family. To fear the consequences of hospitalization for small children is not altogether unjustified, as the following cases will show.

Active primary tuberculosis was demonstrated in a little girl of three (Family 15) after she had shown a positive patch test in the well baby clinic of the Department of Health. Immediate hospitalization was recommended, and the mother took the child to a municipal hospital where strict isolation techniques were practiced. This child, who had never been alone and had spent her life among chattering aunts and uncles only a few years older than herself, was placed in a cubicle which her mother was not allowed to enter. The child cried incessantly and would not eat. At the end of four days, the mother could stand it no longer and took the child out against advice, saying firmly, "I believe I can take care of this child better than any one else." With the help of the family physician, admission to a voluntary hospital with a more liberal policy was arranged. The situation was discussed with the family: a plan was worked out by which the child could be treated at home on a combination of restricted activity and antibiotics. Her younger sibling was cared for by the grandmother for a few months so as to reduce the degree of exposure and permit the mother to devote herself to the patient's care. All members of the immediate and extended family have been examined, and now, one year later, the patient's tuberculosis is considered healed by the out-patient department under whose care she has been.

A little boy (Family 45) of two was admitted to a hospital from a furnished room which he shared with his mother and two brothers. His admission temperature was 105.4, and a diagnosis of left upper lobe pneumonia was made, which was later demonstrated to be tuberculous. The nurses' notes report that for the first four days he cried, but played quietly in bed thereafter. At the end of a month he was transferred to a special hospital for tuberculosis, where he remained for eight months, and then to a third hospital, where he spent two years. His brother, one year younger, also contracted tuberculosis and was hospitalized for twelve months.

When the family first came to our attention, the child, who was then eight years old, had been discharged from the hospital two years previously and his case was considered arrested. He had been somewhat of a behavior problem during his last year in the hospital, and it was noted that he walked poorly at the age of three. Now he was found to be retarded in school and exhibited violent explosive behavior, which led the school to request a psychiatric examination. No psychiatric appointment was available for the next three months. In the meantime, a minister from one of the storefront churches in the neighborhood became interested in the child, encouraged him to visit, and treated him like a son.

The boy's behavior gradually improved, and when the time came around for the psychiatric appointment neither the school nor the mother considered it necessary.

It seems that while the child was in the hospital the parents separated. The father visited the child frequently and was always promising to take him out in a beautiful new car. When the child was finally discharged, the father had returned to Puerto Rico and had no further contact with his family. The child could not understand what had happened. He blamed his mother and had frequent temper tantrums. He became increasingly difficult to control until this accidental relationship with the minister developed and seemed to meet his needs. Unfortunately, since the family has been moved by the Department of Welfare to a housing project and they were not at home when visited, we do not know whether the child, separated once more from a father figure, has become a behavior problem again.

In this case, hospitalization of a small child for the treatment of tuberculosis over a period of almost three years while the family was breaking up was followed by a severe emotional disturbance. Tuberculosis was contracted by the child as a result of close contact with a woman who subsequently died of the disease. The family met her in a rooming house where they spent the first few months after migration, four people in one room, sharing a kitchen and toilet facilities with three other families. Both parents, in their desire to "progress," went to work, leaving the children in charge of this woman.

This is not an unusual story among recent migrants. The situation in Family 15 was somewhat different. This child's grandmother is the central figure in a large family, including her own siblings, their spouses, and many children. Her door is never locked, and there is always an extra plate on the table for some relative who drops in. In this particular instance, the divorced wife of her brother who had died recently lived alone in a room in the neighborhood. This woman had been in poor health for some time and took most of her meals in the grandmother's home, helping other members of the family with sewing and other household duties. At times she stayed overnight with the little girl's parents in the same building. When this woman was hospitalized for tuberculosis she stated, when being interviewed about possible contacts, that she lived alone, as indeed she did. A second question asking with whom she ate her meals might have brought out the customs of the extended Puerto Rican family, but it was not asked, so that the child's tuberculosis was not suspected until revealed some months later by means of the routine patch test.

Summary. The incidence of tuberculosis among Puerto Rican migrants in New York City is known to be high in relation to that prevailing in white and Negro sections of the population. The experience with the selected group of families in this study indicates great fear of the disease, which is met by a denial of its existence. It is probable that the home treatment of tuberculosis will diminish the need to deny the existence of the disease, since this fear is in part dread of prolonged hospitalization.

The cases described indicate the need for a knowledge of the conditions under which Puerto Rican migrants live, their family organization, and their individual problems as an aid to case-finding and in the treatment of individuals.

X. DISTURBANCES OF FEELING STATE, THOUGHT, AND BEHAVIOR

In accordance with the pattern set by Hinkle and Plummer (1952) in their study of the general susceptibility to illness among employees of the New York Telephone Company, the expression "major disturbances of feeling state, thought, and behavior" is used to include all of the major psychoneuroses and psychoses. Episodes of anxiety, tension, depression, and asthenia are considered as minor disturbances of feeling state, thought, and behavior.

The discussion of this subject as it relates to the eighty Puerto Rican families is not intended to be an epidemiological study of the incidence of mental disease and of neuroses in this population group. Our report consists of a summary of observations made by the family physician on individuals who exhibited various forms of behavior considered inappropriate by health, school, and police authorities in the context of family and community life, although not always so considered by the families themselves. The manner in which these aberrant reactions were handled also forms a part of this discussion.

Although no special study of drug addiction was undertaken, anyone who lives or works in this neighborhood knows that this is a well-recognized behavior disorder and that it is not confined to the Puerto Rican population. Drug addicts suffering from infectious hepatitis acquired through common use of injection paraphernalia or from skin infections, at the sight of infection came to the office occasionally for medical treatment, and the family physician was in a position to confirm some of the observations made by the anthropological team. (Padilla.) Many of the confirmed drug addicts are known by sight to the majority of the population on the block. The addicts congregate on particular stoops and are treated as social outcasts by nonaddicts. When a drug addict who has been institutionalized for treatment returns to the neighborhood after an absence of several months, he may swear to his wife, the priest, and the family physician that he will never touch the stuff again, but his old companions are sitting on the same stoop, ready to lure him back should he so much as turn his eyes in their direction.

More prevalent than drug addiction in this population, easier to handle and less destructive, is a form of nervous reaction which goes under the name of *ataque*.

"Do you have ataques?" became a routine question for the family physician working in the neighborhood. The practice of asking this question has been carried over into the examination of Puerto Ricans in hospital out-patient departments. So far no patient has failed to respond to this question, replying in the negative or relating circumstances under which an ataque might have taken place.

The clinical phenomenon which Puerto Ricans call an ataque was witnessed many times by Dr. William Grace of New York Hospital while serving in the Rodriguez Army

Hospital in San Juan, Puerto Rico, and he describes the disorder as follows:

Men and women appear to be equally susceptible. The episode begins quite suddenly, without warning either to spectators or without any warning for the patient; there may be a short cry or scream just before the patient falls. Usually the presenting symptom is falling to the ground or sliding off a chair. In doing this the patients often injure themselves.

Most often at this point the patient is flaccid but this is not always so, and some are rigid. The patient stares out into space, is uncommunicative, does not respond to questions, but may follow directions or move purposefully, such as touching a bleeding part, resisting removal of clothing, or fighting against a venipuncture. At this point the abrupt alternation of a state of unresponsiveness with a state of responsiveness is not unusual.

Shortly after the fall to the ground, or at the same moment, the patient begins moving his arms and legs, usually the movements of both arms and both legs are coordinated. These movements are often purposeful, such as beating the fists on the floor, striking out at persons nearby, or banging the head on the floor.

Foaming at the mouth is common, but no instance of incontinence or tongue biting was seen. The attack usually ceases abruptly, the individual then resuming whatever he was doing before, apparently without ill effect. During the ataque no special change in pulse, blood pressure or neurological signs was noted. The usual ataque lasts for 5 to 10 minutes, but may go on for hours. One instance was observed where the patient continued in this state for 4 days.*

The clinical picture described is well recognized by the population, and reports of individuals having *ataques nerviosos* appear from time to time in the Puerto Rican news-

* Personal communication.

papers in connection with accounts of automobile accidents.
Dr. Grace witnessed many ataques among close relatives at
the bedside of a dying man in the hospital; in the course
of funeral processions, where the mourner who had an ataque
would be carried by others not so affected; on the receipt
of bad news, for instance, when a man received orders to
go overseas or parents learned that a child was seriously ill
and required hospitalization.

Dr. Grace suggests that this type of reaction is widespread
among the Puerto Rican population in the lower socio-
economic group and represents a popular and conventional
reaction to overwhelming catastrophe. The same interpretation for this phenomenon is proposed by the anthropological
team working on this project. Indeed, it is conceivable that
a mother who did not have an ataque at the funeral of her
husband might be considered woefully deficient in expressing
appropriate sentiments of grief. Individuals in the eighty
families also reported the occurrence of ataques in themselves or in their relatives under the situations described.

In New York an individual who has an ataque may be
very puzzling to the house officer of a hospital, who may not
be acquainted with this pattern of behavior. Dr. Grace was
called recently to the emergency room of a hospital where a
Puerto Rican woman was lying unconscious on the floor.
With her husband and two children looking on, the intern
was wondering whether to start investigating the possibility
of a brain tumor. It turned out that the woman had just
learned that a diagnosis of tuberculosis has been made on
her daughter. Her vital signs were normal, and she recovered
spontaneously within half an hour.

Ataques also occur under circumstances which to the

patient represent a situation not necessarily catastrophic but beyond his ability to handle. Dr. Grace reports witnessing a severe ataque in a young man hospitalized for pneumonia. This was a *Jibaro,* a man from the hills who had never been away from home before. He had been in the army only two days. The first day in the hospital he was frightened— too frightened to ask for directions to the bathroom. When his bladder became painfully full, the ataque started. It ceased when, after examining him, the physician reassured him and told him he could empty his bladder into a urinal.

A similar situation was observed in the mother of nine children (Family 19) who developed an ataque at work in a factory. She had gone to work in order to get off the relief rolls. In the factory she was thinking of the harm that might come to the younger children if they went out on the street while she was away from home. She slipped to the floor unconscious and an ambulance was called. She had recovered consciousness by the time she reached the hospital. On the day following this episode she was seen at home by the family physician. Her vital signs were normal, and she complained only of fatigue and numbness in the right arm. After discussing the matter with the investigator of the Department of Welfare, it was decided that she should continue to receive supplementary aid for her children until her eldest son graduated from high school the following spring and could assist the father in the support of the family. Another visit was made to the home three months later, and she denied having further ataques.

In summary, ataques appear to be a form of hysterical syncope which occurs in lower-class Puerto Ricans, both on the island and on the continent, in response to catastrophic or intractable life situations. They may occur "once in a life-time" or they become a continuing pattern of reaction in particular individuals. In the latter instance, further investigation is indicated and may result in the finding of an abnormal electroencephalogram compatible with the diagnosis of a seizure disorder, in which case the institution of anticonvulsant therapy is indicated.

Whether the electroencephalogram be normal or abnormal, a review of the circumstances under which ataques occur in a particular individual suggests that ataques, like other fits, are sometimes rage equivalents, and efforts directed towards helping these patients to deal more constructively with their life situation are often rewarding.

Another problem which confronts the physician and the social worker who practice in a slum area is the management of children who have been classified as mental defectives. While a high incidence of mental deficiency has been found to exist in lower socio-economic groups compared to other sections of the population, except where the degree of mental deficiency is at the imbecile level, individuals are not apt to be institutionalized unless orthopedic, neurological, or behavior problems are also present. (Lemkau 1957.)

The Puerto Rican population under study affords ample confirmation of these observations. There were twelve children of school age in the eighty families with sufficient degree of mental retardation to warrant the recommendation that they be placed in special classes at school. These twelve children belonged to seven families.

In some families the mentally retarded child did not pose a problem. This was apt to be so in families in which the parents themselves were not of a high order of intelligence but maintained a strong feeling of family cohesiveness within which the children had a degree of security but were not asked to fulfill a role beyond their capacity (Family 35). This was especially true when a girl (Family 38) helped in the care of a younger child. The fact that she obeyed her mother put her in the class of a "good girl" (see Padilla), and her inability to learn to read was not a problem in the eyes of her mother.

In another situation a mentally retarded child (Family 31) turned out not only to be docile in the home but to have a talent for dancing and at the age of eleven performed for small private parties. Since the father was incapacitated and did not work, this child, far from being a problem, represented for her mother the only tangible sign of "progreso" in the new land.

The sending of retarded children to state training schools took place in disorganized families where disorders of feeling state, thought, and behavior were present in other members as well as in the defective child. The dilemmas presented to the parents by children of this type and the conflicting views with which they are regarded by medical authorities are exemplified in the following case.

An eight-year-old boy (Family 18) was admitted to the children's ward of the psychiatric division of a city hospital after he had run away from home a number of times, was picked up by the police, and returned home only to run away again. He gave as his reason for running away the fact that he disliked the old woman from whom his parents sublet the two basement rooms where the family lived. During his six weeks stay in the hospital he was found to be a gentle, quiet, cooperative, alert child who had considerable trouble understanding English but was well behaved in the hospital school. There were no significant physical findings beyond a notation of "undersize." The electroencephalogram was normal for his age. He earned a performance I.Q. of 72 on the Bellevue Wechsler children's scale and a mental age of 6.6 on the Goodenough draw-a-man test. On the Bender Gestalt test he showed marked difficulty in drawing angles, and his performance on this test was interpreted as evidence of difficulty in conceptual thinking due to organic deficit.

He was discharged to his home with the expectation that he would be placed in a class at school conducted by a Spanish-speaking teacher. Actually, he spent a part of the following year with relatives who lived under circumstances more favorable than those prevailing in his own family. But when returned to his own home, he started to run away again and was picked up by the police. Following an examination in the same city hospital, where the results were substantially the same as those obtained the previous year, he was committed to a state training school for mental defectives, where he remained for one year.

On his return, he was seen by the family physician, who noted a great improvement in his ability to speak English. He was sent to be tested at another hospital, where special studies are being carried on to determine the effect of cerebral injury on intellectual performance. There he earned a verbal I.Q. of 74 and a performance I.Q. of 93 in the Wechsler scale, in contrast to his performance I.Q. of 72 two years previously. The psychologist further commented that the boy's best performances were on tests which ordinarily reveal the most impairment in a person following cerebral injury. He concluded that this child probably started life with nearly average cerebral equipment but suffered in development principally as the consequence of a severely impoverished early environment.

For those who know this boy in the context of his own family and who have had experience in observing his behavior both before he went to the state school and since he returned, the interpretation furnished by the psychologist fits the facts.

Both the family physician and the anthropologist found that the mother in this family had an unusually poor Spanish vocabulary. Perhaps this limited capacity in the verbal sphere accounts for the diagnosis of simple schizophrenia made by a psychiatrist in a hospital where the woman was receiving obstetrical care. She was also found to suffer from anemia and intestinal parasites. The psychiatrist further commented that this woman could not be expected to function outside of an institution. Actually, in the experience of those who have observed her in her own setting for four years, she has managed to care for the younger children within the very limited facilities available and has carried on negotiations with successive investigators from the Department of Welfare in an adequate manner.

The father's earning capacity is very limited due to lack of any special skill and poor knowledge of English. Even with the help of a supplementary allowance for the children given by the Department of Welfare, the family for several years were only subtenants in a basement apartment where cockroaches were rampant, and their house furnishings were limited to two beds, one crib, three chairs, and two kitchen pots. This meant that a child growing up in this family would have little opportunity to acquire a vocabulary and a limited experience in the sensory and motor spheres until he became old enough to play on the street.

The question may well be asked, What will happen to this child? The family situation has changed a little—the old woman from whom the family sublet the two rooms died, and there are now three rooms for seven people. The cockroaches have been cleared up and there is an additional bed. The father's earning capacity has not increased but he has kept the same job. The mother is concerned with the care of the smaller children. But when the boy comes home from school talking enthusiastically about the Presidents of the United States, neither she nor his father understand what he is talking about. There is little contact between parents and child.

But individuals who knew the boy three years ago and who are connected with local churches and recreational activities are still in the neighborhood, and they are the ones who must be relied upon to prevent this boy from running away again and from possibly joining an undesirable local gang. Nor are the problems of this family and the community finished. The third child was refused admission to school when she reached the age of six because she was considered too small, but eventually she and the three younger siblings will be tall enough to meet the standard for height set by the school authorities. The experience and education which these children receive at home is more limited than most in the area, and the question will pose itself again as to whether their deficiencies are organic and irreversible or are subject to remedial measures, provided such measures are available and can be vigorously and continuously applied.

Major disturbances of feeling state, thought, and behavior

in one member of a family, whether or not they are associated with mental retardation, can cast their shadows over other individuals in that family, as pointed out in Family 45. The illustrations can be multiplied indefinitely, and the family physician is in an advantageous position to observe the repercussions of disturbed behavior in one individual on the lives of other members of his family.

This middle-aged couple (Family 50) came to our attention after we tried repeatedly to raise a smile on the sad face of a large brown woman who was seen standing on the stoop all day long every day except in very cold weather. At the end of a few months we learned that she had seldom left the neighborhood since migration over twenty-five years ago. She lived with her husband, who seldom saw the light of day; he was examined at home. His muscles were flabby and weak. His slender frame supported a large head, with high brow, burning eyes, and a receding hair line—the sort of head one would expect to see in a Goya portrait of a Spanish nobleman. He explained in educated Spanish that he was the younger son of a well-to-do Spanish family in Puerto Rico. He migrated to New York thirty years ago at the age of twenty and soon thereafter married this dark-skinned woman whom he considered socially inferior to himself. But he has been unemployed for twenty years, and until recently she supported him by working in a small factory near by. For many years now he has gone out only briefly at night. He spends his time caring for a canary, writing poetry, lamenting his failure and his inability to do anything about it. The couple have a grown son who supports them.

This son goes to hospital emergency rooms frequently for relief from attacks of asthma. After he had made several visits to the family doctor's office, it became apparent that while he did not want to fail to support his parents, he also wanted to get married, and incidents related to this conflict often precipitated asthmatic attacks. He did marry and his asthma improved greatly.

His mother then tried to go to work, but the factory near by which formerly employed her had gone out of business, and she had no experience in traveling to distant parts of the city by subway and had no command of English. A neighbor who knew of an opening in the concern where she herself was employed offered to take her along. A few days later the woman came to the office complaining that she had been seized with nausea and vomiting on the morning that her neighbor called to take her to the new factory. Physical examination at this time revealed nothing remarkable, but the woman complained bitterly of her husband's inadequacies. She returned three times to the office in the course of the next six weeks with the same complaints. They developed each time following a call from the neighbor who was to take her to work. A few weeks later she was seen on the same stoop rocking a small child in a baby carriage and volunteered that she felt quite well. For this woman the uncertainties of employment away from the area, among strange people, were apparently very frightening and emphasized to her once more the chronic incapacity of her husband. Taking care of another woman's child (see Padilla) was something that other women did in the neighborhood and did not involve a new set of adjustments.

This case is remarkable in the sense that the problems which arose from a chronic disturbance of feeling state, thought, and behavior in the man in the family were reflected in some episodes of illness in other members, but eventually a working solution was reached by both mother and son with little outside help. Indeed, fortuitous circumstances and the personal resources of individuals living in the neighborhood may sometimes bring immediate relief to disturbed people. (See, for example, the case of Family 45 on p. 154.) An "appointment" with a social agency in a downtown office offers but an impersonal contact in the distant future.

Nevertheless, even in this group of eighty families, where every one may be said to have problems, a few families are outstanding for the disturbances of thought, mood, and behavior present in more than one individual in the family and in the consequent high utilization rate of medical and social services. The association between disturbances of thought, mood, and behavior and long-term dependency problems has already been discussed. (See Chapter VII, Welfare.) Other investigators, notably the Community Research Associates (1954), have also pointed out that 6 per cent of a population may absorb 50 per cent of the available health and social resources in the community.

It is suggested that more intensive study should be made of the household unit, not the individual only. Aside from any effect that constitutional factors which still defy measurement might have on explosive disturbed behavior, it seems that when such behavior is observed in one member of a particular family, episodes of similar behavior are more often noted in other members of that same family, in contrast to members of other family groups. Carefully matched family studies should be undertaken with the hope of elucidating factors to account for the marked differences between families living in the same social environment.

During the period of observation, one of the boys in Family 20 was arrested for shooting and wounding in the arm a Negro storekeeper on the block who had allegedly made an insulting remark about the Hispanos. In the same family two older boys were in prison for having stolen a car, one girl committed suicide the year following migration, a younger girl was dismissed from school for hitting the teacher, and a boy and girl of borderline intelligence were sent to state training schools because they were behavior problems in the special class to which they had been assigned. The mother spent most of her day in bed, claiming that she did her housework at night. During the two years of observation the father applied for many positions but did not find a job, except on the labor force of the Department of Welfare.

Similar problems were observed in Family 47, who have lived over twenty years in the neighborhood. The father is reported to have been hospitalized in a state hospital for a manic episode soon after migration, and has had periods of alternating depression and elation through the years. He has had a resection of the terminal ileum following many acute exacerbations of a regional ileitis. The twenty-four-year-old daughter became a drug addict. One boy and one girl were discharged from school, one for hitting a teacher, the other for assaulting a classmate. Both of these children received psychiatric care on an out-patient basis from two separate institutions which made no contact with the rest of the family.

The two families whose multiple behavior disorders have been enumerated can be matched with two other families (35 and 66) living on the same block. The time of migration, number of children, education of parents, and housing conditions are comparable, but disorders of behavior did not develop in Families 35 and 66.

The big broad smile on the mother's face (Family 35), making the family physician feel that climbing three flights of stairs was worth while, and the young boy's carrying the garbage out every evening under the watchful eye of his mother are small bits of evidence collected in the course of a family physician's visits suggesting that behavior problems in children are less likely to occur in families where consistent discipline and a warm affectionate relationship prevail. But the factors relevant to the development of disturbances of thought, mood, and behavior in individual families are still largely unknown. The devising of resources within the community for the control and management of disturbed individuals is of the greatest importance.

Summary. Ataques are a form of hysterical seizure common among Puerto Ricans, considered by them to be an appropriate and conventional reaction to catastrophe. The differential diagnosis between ataques and seizures arising as a result of a focal lesion in the brain or of a metabolic defect is made by the usual means.

Clusters of individuals with disorganized behavior were observed to occur in greater number in some families in this group as compared to other families. This observation is not unique, but means to investigate possible etiological factors for this phenomenon were not available. Emphasis is placed on the need for the development of better local facilities for the management of mental defectives and disturbed individuals in their homes and neighborhood.

XI. UTILIZATION OF
MEDICAL FACILITIES

Medical facilities available to the population living in the neighborhood in which this study was conducted include (1) private practitioners whose offices are located within a radius of a few blocks; (2) "Welfare doctors"; (3) Department of Health services; (4) the out-patient departments of municipal and voluntary hospitals located in the immediate neighborhood, and those in other parts of the city which do not limit their intake of patients to individuals living within specific districts; (5) the wards of these same hospitals.

A survey of the utilization of these services by Puerto Ricans in this area provides information concerning the circumstances under which individuals receive medical attention and incidentally throws some light on the problem of the general susceptibility to illness in this particular group. A few carry Blue Cross insurance through their unions, and at times these policies include the wage earner's family. In our experience, insured individuals in this particular group have little or no understanding of the services available to them through such policies, particularly where their families are concerned.

1. PRIVATE PRACTITIONERS

A few private medical practitioners are known to residents in the neighborhood, especially to the older migrants and to their adult children. These physicians have offices within a radius of a few blocks and hold office hours in the evening. The usual charge is $3 to $4 for an office visit and $7 to $8 for a house call. Some medication is usually included in this fee.

Individuals who can afford to spend the cash, especially those regularly employed, prefer to go to these physicians rather than "lose the day" (see Padilla) in an out-patient department. Visits to the physician's office and requests for house calls are usually made in the case of an acute illness. When cash fails and the acute illness has not subsided, other facilities are used. The names of two physicians were current in the neighborhood during the period of observation—one has died recently, the other graduated from medical school more than thirty-five years ago and does not have an appointment in a municipal or voluntary hospital. He is now assisted by a younger man, graduate of a foreign medical school, who also has no appointment in a municipal or voluntary hospital.

Residents of the neighborhood seeking a physician may also consult the Spanish-language newspapers, where advertisements appear daily listing the names of physicians, their office address, and the services they are prepared to render. *La Prensa,* surveyed during the month of June, 1956, carried the names of nineteen physicians, whose names were checked with the 1955 *Medical Directory of New York State.* Eleven of these did not belong to the county or state medical societies of the state of New York. Ten of the physicians who were registered in the *Directory* were graduates of foreign medical schools whose years of graduation ranged from 1907 to 1923. Nine of these nineteen physicians in *La Prensa* were not listed in the *Directory*. A review of *La Prensa* for January 24, 1957, carried the same nineteen names and three names which had not appeared in June, 1956. It need hardly be pointed out that advertising is unethical according to the principles of professional conduct set down by the county and state medical societies of the state of New York.

2. WELFARE DOCTORS

When an individual who is receiving public assistance is too ill to go to the out-patient department of a city hospital, he may call a physician through the Department of Welfare. Such a physician has been approved by the Department of Welfare and it pays his fee. This physician may only attend a client in his home on an emergency basis. The "Welfare doctor" is not well thought of by the individuals whom he attends (see Padilla), and no one within the hearing of the writer ever referred to one of these men by any other name than the "Welfare doctor."

3. DEPARTMENT OF HEALTH

In reviewing the histories given by the mothers and checking these with health station and well baby clinic records, it appears that out of the 122 children born in Manhattan who were under ten years of age, 113, or 93 per cent, had received complete immunization or were in the process of doing so. The nine children who had not been immunized came from three families (18, 20, 23), whose mothers claimed that pressure of too many small children made it impossible to bring a child to the health station. Many children who were of school age at the time of migration were vaccinated and received other types of immunizations on entering school in New York. Withdrawal of permission for the Salk vaccine following unfavorable newspaper publicity was noted in only two instances; however, these mothers (Families 7 and 54) showed marked anxiety on all subjects. The fact that health stations do not treat patients and that the child who is thought to require medication is sent to an out-patient department was perfectly understood, and the reproach "no me hacen na," they don't do anything for me, was never applied to the child health stations. Having observed clinic sessions in both hospital out-patient departments and health stations, we feel that the credit for greater acceptance by these patients of Department of Health clinics should go to the public health nurse, who may follow the same family over a period of months or even years and who comes to be regarded as a personal friend by the mother.

Individuals were willing to obtain an X-ray of the chest when this was recommended, and the majority of adults had had such an X-ray in the course of their lives. The attitude of this population towards hospitalization for tuberculosis is another matter and is discussed elsewhere (see p. 153). Migrants had had previous experience in bringing stool specimens for laboratory examinations and were quite willing to cooperate in this matter when the stool could be taken for them to the Central Laboratory for Tropical Diseases, which was a long distance from their homes.

Although the Health Department publicized the objectives of the cancer detection program in the neighborhood, in our observation the individuals who responded were those who had an overwhelming anxiety about their health.

Our contacts with the operation of the school health service were limited to the rendering of medical service to those children who came with a slip from a school doctor or nurse stating that the bearer required medical attention before returning to school. Since an intensive study of the school health service is being carried on under the auspices of the Health and Welfare Council of the City of New York, a discussion of this phase of the medical services available to the population will not be undertaken.

The utilization of many services available through the Department of Health appeared to depend upon the family's awareness of the individual's medical problem and their ability to communicate with the various agencies involved. (See Chapter VI, Language and Communication.) For instance, the second son in Family 35 is mentally retarded and suffers from severe myopia. Though glasses have been prescribed by the eye clinic of the school health service, the family cannot afford to buy them. They have requested but have not yet obtained an allowance for their purchase from the Department of Welfare, which gives supplementary aid to the family. From the mother's point of view, the boy is a good boy, and the fact that he cannot see to read is not the problem uppermost in her mind because she is occupied caring for her thirteenth child, who was born prematurely.

4. ADMISSION TO HOSPITALS

Hospital utilization was investigated in this group of eighty Puerto Rican families by taking medical histories and by searching the records of local municipal and voluntary hospitals. Only those hospital admissions which could be verified have been included in the count.

Those few individuals who carried some form of hospital insurance through their union were usually unaware of the benefits to which they were entitled. As far as we were able to determine, benefits for dependents were included in only five cases. Since these hospital insurance policies carried no provision for the payment of medical fees, none of the insured individuals with whom the matter was discussed had sought admission to a hospital except through the wards of municipal or voluntary hospitals. Therefore it is fair to assume that the number of hospitalizations recorded here account for practically the total number of hospitalizations for this population during the ten-year period 1945–1955.

The records of admissions to municipal hospitals for patients whose cases were closed more than ten years ago are unavailable as a practical matter. The attempt to trace hospital admissions which occurred before 1945 was therefore abandoned, and calculations on hospital utilization in this group of 420 people are based on the analysis of the records of 338 individuals—216 migrants who migrated between the years 1945 and 1955 and 122 children under ten years of age born in the United States. Records of the eighty-two individuals remaining do not form a part of this analysis; they include individuals who migrated before 1945 and young adults of Puerto Rican parentage whose reported hospitalizations took place before 1945.

In reviewing the family records, the high incidence of hospitalizations during the first year following migration is striking, whether the individual migrated one year ago or ten. Twenty per cent of 216 migrants were hospitalized within the first year following their migration. In the years following, the percentage of those hospitalized for the first time ranged from 10 to 15 per cent. These numbers are expressed as a percentage of all individuals in the sample who have been in New York the indicated number of years without a previous hospitalization. Therefore, the size of the group never hospitalized becomes progressively smaller each year. From the data in Table 10 and the analysis of the family records, one infers that for migrants in this group the proportion of the total population admitted to hospitals during the first year following migration is significantly higher than it is during subsequent years. Illustrations of what happens in individual cases suggest some of the factors which lie behind this high utilization rate.

The incidence of accidents in the first year following migration has already been pointed out (see Chapter III, Migration). The manner in which a cluster of hospital admissions may occur in the same family during the first year is shown by the case of Family 19. The mother started to hemorrhage in the fourth month of her seventh pregnancy a few months after arriving in New York. She was admitted to a city hospital where a curettage was performed. Four children under ten years of age were admitted to another hospital at the same time—all had the measles; the father was unable to stay home from work to care for them. Infectious diseases which developed in this family in later years did not require hospitalizations, even if they occurred at a time when the mother was expecting to be delivered, because her own mother had come to live in the same building and she had established a friendly relationship with neighbors, who took care of the children in case of emergency.

A high rate of hospital utilization in the first year may also be accounted for by the fact that those individuals suffering from chronic disease previous to migration are apt to seek treatment soon after arrival. Some of them have been sent by their doctors or their families for treatment of a specific illness. For instance, the young father in Family 48 was sharing his bed with his brother-in-law until the latter found a job and an apartment where he could bring his family in order that the mitral commisurotomy recommended for his youngest daughter in San Juan could be performed in New York.

A more extreme but similar situation was observed in Family 54. This woman had sold her bed and few household effects of Puerto Rico in order to pay the plane fare to New York for herself and her seven-year-old daughter. She brought with her a letter from a physician associated with the medical school in Puerto Rico recommending her to a colleague in a municipal hospital for the treatment of carcinoma of the cervix. She was admitted to the hospital within a month of her arrival and has had four admissions to this hospital over the past three years, as well as treatments in the out-patient department. The final diagnosis was carcinoma *in situ* and no metastases were found in the organs which were removed on hysterectomy.

From these data one might seek to answer two questions: (1) Are a group of people hospitalized in a given year likely to require an unusual amount of hospitalization, either high or low, the next year, and if so, for how many years does this unusual pattern exist? (2) Is this pattern for people hospitalized in year one of migration different from that of people first hospitalized in other years?

In answer to the second question, the curves suggest that there is no difference in pattern among the groups first hospitalized in various years. The curves cannot answer the first question without having some measure of the *usual* amount of hospitalization. We may, with a number of reservations, suppose that the usual number is seven admissions per year per 100 person years (using Dr. Anderson's figure for uninsured persons in urban centers of over 1,000,000 population; Anderson 1956). It does not appear that any of our curves approaches this low rate. If we assume that our four groups are uniform as to hospitalization patterns, we can then lump the results and observe the pattern for the entire hospitalized population. We get perhaps more reliable numbers by this manipulation and here see a suggested trend over the years.

TABLE 10

Rate of Hospitalization for 216 Migrants

Year since First Hospitalization	Number of Admissions	Number of Persons Exposed	Admissions per Year per 100 Persons Exposed
0	94	88	107
1	25	74	34
2	18	64	28
3	14	57	25
4	9	45	20
5	5	36	14

Evidently these hospitalized persons required an unusually large amount of hospitalization in the year after their first hospitalization, and this amount decreased for at least 4 additional years. Further, there is no reason to suppose that the decrease has ceased. More extended observation might reveal that it eventually approached Dr. Anderson's figure of seven. It might, on the other hand, prove to have overshot its ultimate value and eventually approach some value greater than fourteen.

Unfortunately, the New York City Department of Hospitals and the voluntary hospitals do not differentiate between Puerto Ricans and non-Puerto Ricans in recording hospital admissions, so that it is impossible to compare these hospital utilization rates with those of other groups of Puerto Ricans in New York City.

In the population of 216 migrants who form the basis of this discussion, 103 individuals were admitted to hospitals during the entire period of observation from 1945 to 1955. These individuals had a total of 199 admissions. (See Table 11.) Forty per cent of all admissions were to the obstetrical service. Normal maternity accounted for 81 per cent of this group. When individual family records are reviewed, it appears that admissions for normal maternity are distributed approximately equally over the first five years following migration and decline in later years as the proportion of admissions for obstetrical complications rises, a repetition of the well-known difficulties of the grand multipara. Eight postpartum tubal ligations were performed in this group (see Chapter VIII, Fertilization and Sterilization). A high admission rate to the maternity wards is to be expected, since Puerto Rican women are the most fertile group in New York at the present time. According to the standardized birth rates worked out by A. J. Jaffe of the Bureau of Applied Social Research at Columbia University for 1950, the birth rate per 1,000 population was 30 for the Puerto Rican population, 22.4 for the total nonwhite, and 19.4 for the total white population of New York City.

TABLE 11

*Diagnoses for 199 Hospital Admissions in 103
Individual Migrants, 1945–1955*

Obstetrics		79
Normal maternity	64	
Maternity and post-partum tubal litigations	8	
Maternity with complications	7	
Tuberculosis (5 individuals)		16
Major respiratory infections		15
Gynecology		14
Injury following trauma		13
Contagious diseases		12
Minor respiratory infections including ear, nose, and throat		6
Minor surgery including tonsillectomies		12
Major surgery		8
Mental disease and mental retardation (4 individuals)		6
Gastrointestinal disease		6
Miscellaneous		6
Rheumatic fever		3
Congenital defect		1
Poliomyelitis		1
Syphilis		1
Total		199

Note: When an individual is confined to a state institution for the mentally retarded or one for tuberculosis, each new calendar year that he is so confined has been counted as a new admission.

A high rate of admissions to hospitals prevails also among children born in the United States of Puerto Rican parents. Twenty per cent of these 122 children in our group were hospitalized during their first year of life, regardless of whether they were one year old or ten years old at the time of observation. Major respiratory diseases account for one third of the admissions during the first year, communicable diseases including pertussis for one fourth, and prematurity for one tenth. Prematurity does not figure on the list of admission diagnoses after the first year. Admissions for communicable diseases decline, but major respiratory infections account for the greatest number of hospital admissions for these children over the years. (See Table 12.) Calculations similar

TABLE 12

Diagnoses for 66 Hospital Admissions in 56
Children under 10, Born in the United States,
1945–1955

Major respiratory infections	17
Tonsillectomy	11
Contagious diseases	7
Prematurity	6
Miscellaneous	6
Injury following trauma	5
Gastrointestinal disease	4
Tuberculosis (2 individuals)	4
Congenital heart disease	2
Major surgery	2
Rheumatic fever	1
Minor respiratory infections	1
Total	66

to those in Table 10 were worked out for this group of children. But since the sample is about half the size of the migrant sample, the figures for the years following the first are too small to warrant presentation.

From these data one may conclude that this particular

population has a high rate of hospital utilization. But there are wide variations within the group itself. In order to compare utilization rates by families, the number of person years of exposure for each member of a family during the years 1945–1955 was calculated. These were then added together to obtain the sum of person years of exposure for each family. For instance, a family with four individuals who had migrated in 1951 would be said to have had five years of exposure per person or twenty years of family exposure, and if there were two recorded admissions for one or more members of the family since migration, the family would be said to have had a 10 per cent utilization rate.

The number of individuals living in the household was also counted, and an average was calculated for each group. A mean of 2.8 individuals was found for those households who had a 0 to 5 per cent utilization rate as compared to 6.3 individuals for those households who had a 30.1 to 40 per

TABLE 13

Percentage of Hospital Utilization by Families

Percentage	Number of Families	Average Number in Family
0–5	14	2.8
5.1–10	21	5.38
10.1–15	14	6.
15.1–20	13	5.92
20.1–30	9	5.9
30.1–40	3	6.3
40.1–50	3	4.
50.1 +	1	2.

cent utilization rate. (See Table 13.) In the Arsenal Health Study large households were found to have a greater number of medical problems than did smaller ones. (Ciocco, 1953.) In this group of Puerto Rican families who live under slum conditions, the crowding index rises with the size of the family, and it is reasonable to assume that crowding is a factor leading to a higher incidence of respiratory infections, whether this crowding occurs in army barracks or in tenements. (Bernstein 1957.) Besides, in our observation, an ambulance was called more frequently in large families, where the burden of caring for a sick child at home was greater than it was in a smaller family. An additional factor to be considered in the high hospital utilization rate for large families is that the greater the number of children, the greater the number of admissions for maternity.

In considering the seven families with the highest hospital utilization, one (Family 34) can be discarded as atypical for the particular group under study, since it is the only one involving an elderly couple; the woman died during the period of observation, following twelve admissions in eleven years for a multiplicity of diseases.

In two of the remaining six families (18 and 45), tuberculosis accounted for prolonged periods of hospitalization; in Family 45 two children were hospitalized with that disease. In five of these same six families with a 30 to 50 per cent hospital utilization rate, a diagnosis of a major disturbance of thought, mood, or behavior was made on one or both parents either by one of the family physicians or by a psychiatrist during the period of observation. A similar diagnosis involving one or both parents was made in 16 to 20 per cent of the remaining 73 families. A higher incidence of illness in families where a diagnosis of psychoneurosis had been made was observed in a study made in the eastern district of Baltimore. (Downes 1953.) The question whether the greater incidence of illness in families where one of the parents is diagnosed as suffering from a nervous disorder can be attributed primarily to constitutional factors or to greater stress created by the presence of a neurotic individual in the home remains unanswered.

Data supporting the constitutional theory are not available for this group, but observations were made pointing to the projection of a parent's anxiety on to the child and the subsequent illness of that child. For instance, the cervical carcinoma *in situ* of the woman in Family 54 was successfully treated, but her anxiety was not. Each time that she received a letter from the municipal hospital requesting her readmission for observation and evaluation of the carcinoma, she interpreted the communication as a sentence of doom and brought her child to the family physician because the child was "sick and would not eat." The child (age 7) was found to be grossly overweight and her mother admitted to spoon-feeding her. The child also suffered from nonspecific vaginitis which followed intensive masturbation that started when the child was left with a neighbor at the time of the mother's second admission to the hospital and was convinced that her mother would die.

By way of summarizing the subject of hospital and clinic utilization in this particular group of Puerto Rican families and pointing up the need for investigating many unanswered questions, a comparison of the number of hospital days and clinic visits for two families is presented in Table 14.

TABLE 14

*Comparison of Clinic Visits and Hospital Days for
Two Matched Families, 1953–1955*

Family 53	Age	Clinic Visits	Hospital Days
Father	38	24	2
Mother	35	3	14
Son	12	12	0
Son	9	12	0
Daughter	5	33	12
Son	4	62	13
Daughter	3	4	15
		150	56
Family 36			
Father	34	0	0
Mother	32	0	0
Son	12	5	0
Son	11	1	0
Daughter	9	1	0
Daughter	7	0	0
Daughter	6	11	0
Son	5	4	0
Daughter	2	3	0
		25	

Until Family 53 moved to a housing project (see Chapter V, Housing), the facilities of Mount Sinai Hospital were equally available to both these families, and during the period of observation, the conditions under which these two families lived were comparable. There were three rooms for nine people in Family 36 and two rooms for seven people in Family 53. In each case adults and children shared beds. Central heating was available in the case of Family 53, but Family 36 heated their home by means of the gas stove in the kitchen and two portable stoves.

The father in Family 36 was proud of the fact that although he had been laid off at times he had always been able to find work and received supplementary aid only because he had a large family. He had been hospitalized once for an appendectomy. All the children were found to have hypertrophied tonsils. Their mother said that she kept them home when they had colds—this happened rather frequently —and the children were absent on an average of thirty days during their first year at school and about fifteen days a year thereafter. She did not often take a sick child to the clinic, since she had no one with whom to leave the others, and no child had been sick enough to be admitted to the hospital. She herself had only been to the hospital for deliveries and was very thankful that a tubal ligation had been performed following the delivery of the seventh child. When calls were made at the home, the children were subdued and silent in the presence of the father and sucked their thumbs in the corner. When the father was not present, the mother was permissive and affectionate and the children were noisy and demanded the visitor's attention.

In Family 53, whenever a child appeared slightly ill, the mother wrapped him in a blanket and rushed to the hospital while the father stayed home with the rest of the family. She herself required frequent medical attention for a number of pelvic complaints. A hysterectomy was performed in the hope of correcting some of these conditions. This operation was not interpreted by her as a release from further child-bearing and as a means of putting an end to future hemorrhages, but meant that she no longer menstruated, and in her thinking a woman who ceased menstruating before the age of forty was sick *ipso facto*. A diagnosis of conversion hysteria was made, and she attended the psychiatric clinic for several months.

The man of the family had his first attack of asthma at the age of eighteen, eleven years before migration. He had been unemployed in Puerto Rico and, except for a few weeks on one occasion, had not been employed since migration nine years previously. His asthmatic attacks occurred now about once a month and were not very severe. He was described by psychiatrists as a passive, dependent individual and assisted his wife in the care of the children. While one cannot say why the children in Family 53 had bronchopneumonia repeatedly and those in Family 36 did not, there is no doubt that the very high utilization of hospital facilities by Family 53 can be explained in part by the extremely dependent attitude, chronic tension, and anxiety manifested by the parents in this family compared to those in Family 36.

5. OUT-PATIENT DEPARTMENTS AND CLINIC UTILIZATION

From the point of view of both the physician in the out-patient department and the Puerto Rican families in this study, it appears logical to discuss under separate headings visits to the emergency room and visits to a section of the out-patient department by appointment.

Since 1953 Mount Sinai Hospital has operated a reception ward where children are seen by a physician without previous appointment on payment of $1.00. When a course of parenteral medication is prescribed, the individual may return for not more than the number of visits required for the treatment of that episode of acute illness. Where more extensive study is indicated, patients are given an appointment in the regular out-patient department. While the number of visits to this reception ward increases annually, there are no figures to indicate what proportion of those using this service are Puerto Ricans. Also, it was not possible to determine from the records kept in Mount Sinai Hospital and other hospital emergency rooms how frequently the 420 individuals in this study made use of these services.

But judging from the reports of the patients themselves, going to "emergency" is a very popular means of seeking treatment in the case of acute illness and for obtaining relief when one does not have the time to wait for a clinic appointment. A young man (Family 51) with a high school education and with the ability to communicate with hospital personnel reported an average of twelve annual visits to the emergency rooms of several neighborhood hospitals over a period of years. He did not have a clinic card to any out-patient department and had not had any medical study or treatment beyond the therapy given for the control of an acute attack of bronchial asthma. He was aware of the fact that a "work-up" in the out-patient department of a hospital involved appointments for laboratory examinations on several different days and that each of these appointments would mean his losing half a day's work. Such a course, he felt certain, would result in the loss of his job, so he chose to seek treatment only for the acute emergency.

Probably an additional factor accounting for the popularity of the emergency room among Puerto Ricans is that something is done for the patient—either medication is prescribed, or the patient is admitted to the hospital, or he is told that he is not "muy grave" (seriously ill) as he feared. Illness among Puerto Ricans (see Padilla) is fraught with great anxiety, and in the minds of the patient and his family something must be done about it. Immediate action is felt to be necessary on the part of medical personnel, so that emergency treatment is preferred to the more lengthy process involved in "appointments."

Nevertheless, of the 420 individuals in the eighty families 348 or 80 per cent had a "clinic card" to the out-patient departments of one or more voluntary or municipal hospitals. When the records of these individuals were reviewed, three distinct patterns of clinic utilization became apparent: (1) the spasmodic, episodic visits to out-patient departments with incomplete "work-ups"; (2) continuing visits to several departments with varying complaints; (3) scheduled visits to a particular out-patient department for the treatment of a diagnosed condition.

A number of circumstances may surround clinic visits which fall into the first category. Indeed, the initiative for clinic utilization does not always come from the family but from school physicians, nurses, and social workers with whom the family comes in contact and who recommend medical attention for conditions of long standing which were not regarded as handicaps by the family in Puerto Rico. A number of clinic visits of this sort are apt to occur in the first year following migration.

Many times a course of clinic visits is undertaken by an individual in the setting of anxiety over a particular life situation for which this individual is seeking relief. The woman in

Family 1 suffered from secondary amenorrhea. After four visits to the gynecological department of a voluntary hospital over a period of three months, she came to the family doctor's office demanding that something be done for her. With her permission, the hospital chart was reviewed, and it was found that hypothyroidism was suspected in her case. All tests performed so far were normal, but the patient failed to cooperate in the study of vaginal cytology. Her husband was in the armed forces at the time, and she was concerned that on his return he might accuse her of being pregnant illegitimately if she were not menstruating. Visits to the hospital had not resulted in a return of her periods, so why should she continue to go there? The reasons for study were explained to her but since her period returned spontaneously she did not return to the clinic.

Clinic visits by several individuals in the same family may coincide in time with a crisis in the course of a major illness in one of the members of the particular family. The second child in Family 45 was released from a sanatorium for tuberculosis where he had spent thirty-three months. Shortly after his return home he was found to be suffering from ringworm of the scalp, for which over the next three months he received twenty out-patient treatments. He was disobedient and unruly at home, hitting his sisters and his mother; similar outbursts of temper occurred later in school. Coinciding with this crisis were the thirteen visits his mother paid to the outpatient department over a period of five months. This represented four separate episodes of illness on her part. She came first to the ear, nose, and throat clinic, where a diagnosis of chronic rhinitis was made. Two months later she visited the medical clinic, complaining of weakness and palpitations, and was discharged as euthyroid after five visits and satisfactory laboratory examination. The following month she came to the medical clinic, again complaining of insomnia and pruritus, and was sent to the skin clinic. The fourth episode involved acute pharyngitis, for which she was treated in the medical clinic by a physician who had not seen her before. During this same period she was taking her son for treatment of ringworm twice a week, and single clinic admissions are noted for the other two children, one for pain in the legs, the other for abdominal pain—in both of these cases the etiology was undetermined, and recommendations made for further investigation were not followed up.

Clinic utilization as described for Family 45 is representative of many situations involving spasmodic visits to an outpatient department. The boy's explosive behavior following his return from the sanatorium, at a time when her husband had deserted her, coupled with the necessity of frequent clinic visits for the treatment of ringworm, all created a very stressful situation for this woman and were associated with episodes of illness. She came to the clinic for treatment and reported that the tests for the thyroid helped her (no treatment was given in that particular clinic). Complaints in the other children, which might have been disregarded in less anxious times, were a source of alarm to her, and she brought them to the clinic only to be told that further investigations were necessary. The physical impossibility of taking all the tests required by the several departments, none of which was aware of the over-all problem in this family, is obvious. Subsequently the child's behavior problem was straightened out, and there were no more clusters of clinic visits for this family in the following year.

There are people, however, for whom going to the clinic becomes a way of life. At the age of forty-five, two years after migration, a woman (Family 2) made twelve visits to the out-patient department of one hospital over a period of four months. She had many complaints and was seen in four specialty clinics, but no definite diagnosis was made. The following year she was admitted to three different hospitals. The three admissions were for two and seven days respectively. Her complaints were nausea, vomiting, and leg pain following a fall in a store. All examinations were within normal limits. At the time that she was seen in the family physician's office at the request of the anthropologists, she was attending an out-patient department at regular intervals and outlined the recommended low fat diet in detail for the family physician. Later she was admitted to this same hospital for further study, but from the laboratory findings at this admission surgery was not considered necessary. The woman herself considered that another admission might be necessary within the next few months.

Her husband suffered from asthma and, according to her report, had been "unjustly hospitalized for tuberculosis" (see Chapter IX, Tuberculosis). His diet was different from hers. When he was seen at home, he showed the physician the medication prescribed by the out-patient department, which he kept on his night table with his clinic card and the slip for the next appointment. For this couple, whose son might have contributed to their support had he not been in prison for breaking and entering, illness represented a socially approved way of obtaining continuing help from the Department of Welfare, and additional medical examinations increased the importance and seriousness of their complaints in their own eyes.

A more rational use of clinic and hospital facilities was

observed where a patient had become an "interesting case" to one or more physicians in a hospital and a continuing relationship between physicians in the hospital and the patient was established. Following the successful delivery by Cesarean section of a woman (Family 11) in whom four deaths had occurred at term previously, she returned faithfully for antepartum care and a second section a year later (1956), although she had moved to the Bronx in the meantime. Similarly, individuals in the neighborhood who were receiving home care from a city hospital expressed appreciation of the service they were receiving and appeared "cooperative," following instructions given to them.

Summary. Compared to the urban population in the United States, this particular group of eighty Puerto Rican families has a higher than average hospitalization rate, especially in the first year following migration. Fear associated with illness and a desire for active treatment lead this population to use the emergency rooms of local hospitals frequently. Local physicians are also consulted in emergencies, but lack of funds usually do not permit completion of study or treatment.

There was widespread ignorance among this particular group both as to whether they carried hospital insurance through their union and as to the benefits to which they or their families might be entitled.

While families frequently found it impossible to follow through many appointments at different departments of a hospital because of the long waiting hours involved, individuals were responsive and cooperative where medical personnel expressed personal interest in them and provided continuity of treatment.

XII. SUGGESTIONS FOR A MEDICAL CARE PROGRAM

The data related to the eighty Puerto Rican families in this study and the clinical experience of physicians working in municipal hospitals indicate that both the incidence of illness and the use of hospital facilities is high among the Puerto Rican population of New York City who live in slum areas. Many of these families do not carry medical insurance, or when they do, it is inadequate to meet their needs. For this reason, at the present time Puerto Ricans in certain sections of New York City constitute a large part of the so-called medically indigent population who apply for medical care to the out-patient departments and wards of municipal and voluntary hospitals. Without discussing the merits of the question, it is a fact that the teaching of medical students, the training of house officers, and the continuing education of the attending staff are dependent upon the clinical material which becomes available through the medically indigent population.

This situation involves a reciprocal obligation: the physician hopes to learn and to heal where possible, the patient hopes to be relieved of his discomfort. In the case of medical and surgical emergencies, all the resources of a hospital are mobilized, and mutual satisfaction for both doctor and patient is likely to result. Similarly, when the patient presents an interesting and unusual case, many investigative and therapeutic procedures will be carried out and the patient will be the subject of continuing attention on the part of the physician. But for many patients who are neither emergencies nor interesting cases, and for many physicians, contact between the two groups at the out-patient department of a city hospital is a frustrating experience.

There are legitimate grounds for complaint on both sides. The patient would like to have something done for him. The physician would like the patient to have a complaint the investigation of which will lead to the diagnosis of a well-defined clinical entity so that rational therapy may be instituted. In order for the doctor to be able to fulfill this role, it is necessary for the patient to undergo a number of tests before treatment is prescribed. When the patient's complaints "do not add up" to a diagnosis, the laboratory findings are normal, and no pathology has been revealed following the examination of particular organs by specialists, the patient is told there is nothing wrong with him.

At this point both doctor and patient may feel that they have been imposed upon; the former because no disease has been diagnosed, the latter because his complaints have not been relieved. On the other hand, when one of the Puerto Ricans we have been discussing goes to a private physician in the neighborhood, symptomatic treatment may take the place of diagnostic study. For the most part, these particular physicians (see page 173) lack up-to-date training and the patients lack funds, so the combination is not conducive to the development of a continuing relationship between patient and family physician.

In large families, as we have seen, where more than one individual has complaints which require medical attention, attending clinics may become a full-time occupation for the mother of the family, and it is unusual for the physician who is taking care of one illness to be aware of what ails other members of the family, unless the disease is one that is known to be contagious or familial.

Fragmentation of the individual between clinics and lack of information concerning the total medical picture of the family are particularly detrimental where social and welfare problems are associated with health problems. The lapse of time between the first appointment to a medical clinic, the report to the Department of Welfare, the eventual referral to an employability clinic, may be so prolonged that the patient's complaints become fixed. Thus the individual who comes up for repeated examinations feels rejected by each new physician and becomes a malingerer in the eyes of that physician.

These observations are not new nor do they apply exclusively to Puerto Ricans. Indeed, during the past fifty years numerous measures to provide integrated medical care have been put into effect, including the development of the visiting nurse service and the home-care program now provided by city hospitals. But imagination and planning are needed to eliminate fragmentary impersonal medical care and inappropriate utilization of the facilities of large medical centers.

It is estimated by the Health Insurance Plan of New York that 70 per cent of the services rendered to their 500,000 enrollees are provided by three types of physicians: family physicians, pediatricians, and obstetrician-gynecologists. These are the physicians who have continuing and intimate relationships with their patients.

A plan is proposed here for the establishment of a family service center within the radius of a few blocks of a municipal or university hospital whose clientele is derived in large part from the medically indigent population living in the immediate neighborhood. In this family service center the family, not the disease, not the individual alone, would be studied and treated as a unit. Attending and resident physicians assigned to this center would serve for a period of several consecutive months. A team of obstetrician-gynecologist, pediatrician, and family physician, with scheduled clinic hours on the same day, could treat the same families, outside of emergencies, over the period of their assignment to the center, and these families could then be passed on to the next team. The proximity of patients to the center would make home calls feasible. Patients living within the determined radius who applied to the hospital for treatment would be referred to the family center.

The center should be equipped with a fluoroscope and portable electrocardiograph and have available the services of a nurse-technician for the performance of routine blood counts and urinalyses and the taking of additional laboratory specimens to be examined at the hospital. Where X-rays and complex laboratory procedures or the opinion of a specialist are indicated, the patient would be referred to the hospital with the assurance that after the completion of these examinations he would be seen again in the center by the physician who had sent him. When a patient is hospitalized or attended in the emergency room out of office hours, a record of this would be sent to the family service center. The continuity of contact between physicians and patients would be further encouraged by the opportunity for those physicians who had referred patients for treatment in the hospital to visit them on the wards and follow their course.

With the cooperation of the visiting nurses, the local health center, and other neighborhood social agencies, it should be possible for medical and social data on a given family to be concentrated within the family service center. This would enable a family with many problems to receive help in a coordinated fashion at the hands of a few people who had a continuing contact with all members of the family and eliminate the scattering of individuals and their problems among many agencies in remote parts of the city.

XIII. SUMMARY AND CONCLUSIONS

A large part of the world's population today consists of people who have much in common with the eighty Puerto Rican families we have been discussing. These people are now, or have been until recently, inhabitants of underdeveloped areas. This means that they have lived or continue to live in nonindustrialized regions of the earth where sanitary facilities, food supply, exploitation of natural resources, and industrial productivity are below the standard available in industrialized countries such as the United States and those of Western Europe.

But an increasing number of these people are learning within less than a generation to substitute tractors and combines for handmade plows. Men whose ancestors walked on mountain paths for centuries, bearing their burdens like pack animals, and women whose social life centered around the village washing trough are being introduced to the airplane and to the washing machine bought on credit, with little or no intermediate stage.

Where governments are able and willing to raise the necessary funds to make use of tried public health methods and to experiment with new approaches, the effects on the public health of the population in underdeveloped areas are now predictable. In time, the development of environmental sanitation, the mass application of specific immunizing and therapeutic procedures as an increasing number of these become available, the use of modern agricultural methods to raise the productivity of the soil, and the increased popular buying power which comes through industrialization result in a decline of infant and maternal mortality and a prolongation of life expectancy for that population. The population living on the island of Puerto Rico is in the midst of the process described, and the reports of the Department of Health of the Commonwealth as well as the industrial operation "bootstrap" proudly testify to the progress achieved along these lines in the last twenty years.

But leaping into mid-twentieth century industrial society is followed by the disruption of traditional ways of life with its manifold consequences. The Puerto Rican migrants to New York City, like the peoples of Asia and Africa, wish to "progress," to have a share in the more abundant food supply, the less arduous physical life, and the commercial entertainment which life in a metropolitan city provides. Environmental sanitation, including pure water and a safe milk and food supply, and the services of the Department of Health for immunization against specific diseases and the treatment of tuberculosis, parasitic, and venereal infections are free to all. As Dr. Leona Baumgartner, the Health Commissioner, said recently: "New York City is the healthiest largest city in the world." (*Life,* April 1, 1957.)

Nevertheless, the data on the eighty Puerto Rican families in this study, the clinical impression of physicians who treat Puerto Rican patients, the high incidence of new cases of tuberculosis (Lowell 1955 and 1956) and the high admission rate to mental hospitals (Malzberg 1956) reported for Puerto Ricans suggest that the general susceptibility to illness is high among Puerto Ricans in New York City as compared to other segments of the metropolitan population.

It may be argued that these Puerto Ricans are sick because they have not been exposed to the benefits of environmental sanitation long enough or in adequate measure to overcome their previous handicaps. Based on experience with other population groups, this position is in large measure valid, but not all health problems are soluble through environmental sanitation, better housing, and immunizations against specific diseases.

Among the eighty families studied there are marked differences between families as to the incidence of disease and hospital utilization. This observation is consistent with those of other investigators who found that in four widely separated and very different communities approximately 6 per cent of the total families living in them are absorbing a very large proportion of all their health assistance and adjustment services. These are the multi-problem families, and apparently every community has a hard core of them. The factors responsible for the development of a multi-problem family have not yet been determined.

When a congenital heart lesion, rheumatic fever, tuberculosis, mental deficiency, and a psychosis are found in one family, and another family originating from the same part of Puerto Rico, now living under the same conditions on the same block, is not so affected, students of man and nature may well ask what particular conditions—including repeated infections and debilitating diseases during pregnancy, inadequate nutrition, pathological personality traits, unfavorable economic and social conditions—may have so affected the parents and grandparents of these children that they have become more vulnerable to subsequent hardships. At the other end of the scale, the native Puerto Rican woman of twenty-six who has born six children in eight years, whose abdomen is firm, who has good teeth, no varicose veins, and does not drink milk presents a different kind of challenge.

We have also pointed out the existence·of a high incidence of hospital and clinic utilization in some families in·our group, and in other Puerto Ricans crowding the benches of out-patient departments, in whom objective evidence of significant disease was difficult to establish within the conventional framework of medical thinking. But these individuals are actually sick since they are unable to carry on the activities of their daily lives in the environment in which they live. In this connection, one may also consider the report of the New York State Department of Mental Hygiene concerning admissions to state hospitals: for the years 1949–1951, the rate of first admissions for dementia praecox for Puerto Ricans in New York City was almost twice that for non-Puerto Ricans. During this period, there was an average annual first admission rate of 400 Puerto Ricans to New York state hospitals as compared to 160–195 first admissions to the Insular Psychiatric Hospital in Puerto Rico.

The population of the island of Puerto Rico was estimated at 2,210,703 for 1950, which would mean an admission rate of .08 per 1,000 in that year, as compared to an admission rate of 1.4 per 1,000 for the Puerto Rican population of New York City, estimated at 275,200 for 1950.

But the number of hospital beds for mental patients available per 1,000 population in Puerto Rico is 0.99 compared to 6.04 beds per 1,000 population in the state of New York (Puerto Rico Department of Health and New York State Department of Mental Hygiene, personal communications, Oct.,

1957). That is, the difference in admission rates to mental hospitals between New York state and Puerto Rico does not necessarily reflect a difference in the incidence of schizophrenia among Puerto Ricans living in New York compared to those living in Puerto Rico. Indeed, the difference in hospital facilities between the two communities may be the most important factor in the difference between their admission rates.

While we have observed that some disturbed individuals come to New York or are sent there by their relatives, this probably is not significant in the difference in the admission rates to mental hospitals between New York state and Puerto Rico. Isolated clinical observations by the writer suggest that among Puerto Ricans in New York City who are admitted to state hospitals with the diagnosis of schizophrenia, there are many who suffer from what is coming to be known as the general maladaptation syndrome, which occurs in individuals subjected to chronic anxiety and frustration. Individuals so affected suffer from a decline in the higher integrative functions, the extent of which is indistinguishable from that observed in patients with organic brain disease. Some Puerto Ricans who are unable to adapt to the lower-class existence in metropolitan New York presumably fall in this category.

The activities of human beings are purposeful, motivated by aspirations, and directed towards goals. The "progress" goal, as Puerto Ricans see it, has been defined through these pages and in the Padilla volume. In order to progress, one must work, but in order to work one must have health. In New York, a man can no longer take pride in his biceps. He is expected to wield a pen or operate a complex machine if he is to be respected and progress. Family relationships take on a different character in the new environment, and parents have difficulty instilling "respeto" in their children.

Under these circumstances, illness may be an aspect of lack of success and may therefore become a justification for failure. Failure is inevitable where the discrepancy between an individual's aspirations and the limited employment opportunities open to him due to lack of schooling or special skill cannot be reconciled. To prove illness so that one may be cared for then becomes a vital necessity.

A good hospital will exhaust a large battery of tests to prove that there is nothing wrong with such an individual. Each new doctor, each additional test, confirms the man or woman in his conviction that he is sick and that he is not being helped. Finally, the social worker from the Department of Welfare resolves the duel with the family by a report of unemployability due to personality difficulties. If a cut in aid takes place, it is met with resentment on the part of the family, who consider that sickness entitles one to public assistance, and one must indeed be sick after seeing so many doctors who do nothing. "No me hacen na" (they don't do anything for me), is the Puerto Rican's final comment on this type of situation.

If healing is not to be found within the aseptic shrine of the medical center, where may the sufferer turn?

It has been demonstrated that the reaction of the organ systems of the body is the same in response to a variety of noxious stimuli. In a fistulous subject, the hyperemia which follows upon stroking the exposed surface of the gastric mucosa with a glass rod is indistinguishable from the hyperemia observed when the subject is angry and frustrated but the mucosa has not been traumatized. (Wolf 1948.) Obviously, these identical hyperemias require different treatment. Removing the glass rod is sufficient in the first case. An understanding of the causes for a man's anger and dealing with his behavior under the circumstances are required in the second case. And every clinician knows that the treatment of an angry man whose stomach is bothering him lies beyond the cause and effect relationship seen in the laboratory and postulated by Newtonian science.

Many factors are involved in the understanding and treatment of sick people, and the study of the relationship between disease and man's social environment is still in its infancy. Man is a purposive creature, imbued with aspirations, striving towards goals. In the case of the Puerto Ricans in this study, their goal is "progress," and when illness appears to be associated with failure to progress, to rise in the social scale, how is such illness to be treated?

At times, as a result of prolonged hospitalization or commitment to a training school, an individual acquires the tools which permit him to progress. The Puerto Rican child with rheumatic fever learns English and becomes familiar with American ways in a hospital for cardiac children. But often, as pointed out in these pages, the individual who returns home after prolonged hospitalization may be an emotional cripple, and gains which might have been achieved in an institution cannot be consolidated due to lack of community facilities. The drug addict's former companions are waiting on the same stoop a year later when he is discharged from prison or hospital.

Even so, occasionally a sick man is made whole. Apparently this is a matter of luck or the result of a careful manipulation of the environment by interested persons. In a family, school, church, settlement house, trade union, or neighborhood, when a dedicated individual with imagination who can mobilize some social or economic resources establishes and maintains a relationship with a man in trouble, things begin to happen. As a young American Negro who had become a member of the council of a local Baptist church in the neighborhood put it: "For the first time in my life I felt I was somebody." Or to quote a Puerto Rican boy who went to work on a New England farm: "The farmer's wife sees that I take my pill (prophylaxis for rheumatic fever) every morning. Everyone in town likes me and thinks I amount to something."

The current study has been focused on a segment of the Puerto Rican population, and it is hoped that as a result of the observations set forth, there will be groups in our society who will experiment with measures which may save some individuals from the suffering and disease that has always accompanied change in social structure. But the questions raised by the study of man in his social environment have implications beyond the range of this particular group of Puerto Ricans.

The Indians who leave their Andean communities and come to the city have a higher incidence of tuberculosis than those who remain in the altiplano. Formerly, crowding and unsanitary conditions in slum quarters were considered to be the only factors responsible for the severity of the disease in these people, but Dubos points out that the many social and psychological changes involved in a move from a rural to an industrial society may be equally responsible for the increase in the susceptibility of the host to the tubercle bacillus. In Brazil, individuals and social agencies working in the *favelas* (city slums) are impressed with the apparent increase of deaths from violence in populations moving to the city from rural areas. In the United States, the rise in the rate of admissions to mental hospitals in recent years has been pointed out many times. Indeed, even for those born and raised in the United States, life in the mid-twentieth century is filled with hazards and cannot be classified as entirely healthy when measured by the record of deaths from automobile accidents and coronary heart disease. Also, the popular appetite for tranquilizing drugs suggest that serenity is not one of the attributes of American life.

At the same time, great advances have been and are being made in the field of laboratory medicine. The physician, who is becoming increasingly expert in the manipulation of man's internal environment, may well consider that if an appropriate level of electrolytes and lipids is established and maintained in the blood, his patient is and will remain healthy, that is, able to live and to function. When all is not well, the patient returns to the laboratory and gets a checkup, which is expected to result in a restoration of homeostasis. At this point the patient expects the physician to provide him with instructions on how to live in the world.

It is the physician who signs a man's passport which permits him to go to school, to work, to marry. The conditions under which this man carries on his life's activities have an important bearing on his health, his ability to function, but the physician's knowledge of the effect on blood chemistry of the interaction between man and his total environment is still rudimentary. Intensive long-term studies of man in his habitat are needed. It is time that "we should try training ourselves to study human affairs by intense participation in human problems instead of by detachment from them. We should know by now that the most powerful moral influence flows from the terms in which morality is interpreted and that the interpretation of history is a decisive force of history." (Polanyi 1957.)

REFERENCES

Anderson, Nina A., Estelle W. Brown, and R. A. Lyon, "Causes of Prematurity," *American Journal of Diseases of Children,* 65 (1943), 523–34.

Anderson, Odin W., with Jacob Feldman. Family Medical Costs and Voluntary Health Insurance; a Nationwide Survey. New York, McGraw-Hill, 1956.

Army Regulation 40–115. *See* U.S. Army.

Bernstein, Stanley T. Observations on the Effects of Housing on the Incidence and Spread of Common Respiratory Diseases among Air Force Recruits. In press.

Blanco, Ana Teresa. Nutrition Studies in Puerto Rico. Rio Piedras, Social Science Research Center, University of Puerto Rico, 1946.

Ciocco, Antonio, Paul M. Densen, and Daniel G. Horvitz, "On the Association between Health and Social Problems in the Population," *Milbank Memorial Fund Quarterly,* July, 1953, pp. 265–90.

Community Research Associates, Inc. The Prevention and Control of Disordered Behavior in San Mateo County, California. July, 1954.

——— The Prevention and Control of Indigent Disability in Washington County, Maryland. July, 1954.

Downes, Jean, and Katherine Simon, "Characteristics of Psychoneurotic Patients and Their Families as Revealed in a General Morbidity Study," *Psychosomatic Medicine,* XV (Sept.–Oct., 1953), 463–74.

Dubos, Rene J., and Jean P. Dubos. The White Plague; Tuberculosis, Man and Society. Boston, Little, Brown, 1952.

Hanson, Earl P. Transformation, the Story of Modern Puerto Rico. New York, Simon & Schuster, 1955.

Hatt, Paul K. Backgrounds of Human Fertility in Puerto Rico. Princeton, Princeton University Press, 1952.

Hinkle, Lawrence E., Jr., and Norman Plummer, "Life Stress and Industrialism—the Concentration of Illness and Absenteeism in One Segment of a Working Population," *Industrial Medicine and Surgery,* 21 (Aug., 1952), 365–75.

Holmes, Thomas H., "Multidiscipline Studies of Tuberculosis," in Phineas J. Sparer, ed., Personality, Stress and Tuberculosis. New York, International Universities Press, 1956.

Holt, L. Emmet, Jr., and Rustin McIntosh. Pediatrics. 12th ed. New York, Appleton-Century-Crofts, 1953.

Jaffe, A. J. Demographic and Labor Characteristics of the Puerto Rican Population in New York City. New York, Bureau of Applied Social Research, Columbia University, Jan., 1954.

Lemkau, Paul V. The Epidemiological Aspects of Mental Deficiency. In press.

Lowell, Anthony M. Tuberculosis in New York City, 1954 and 1955. New York, Tuberculosis and Health Association, 1955 and 1956.

MacLeod, Robert B., "Teleology and Theory of Human Behavior," *Science,* 125 (March 15, 1957), 477–80.

Malzberg, Benjamin, "Mental Disease among Puerto Ricans in New York City," *Journal of Nervous and Mental Disease,* 123 (March, 1956), 263–69.

Mills, C. Wright, Clarence Senior, and Rose Cohn. The Puerto Rican Journey: New York's Newest Migrants. New York, Harper, 1950.

Nelson, Waldo E., ed. Textbook of Pediatrics. 6th ed. Philadelphia, Saunders, 1954

Padilla, Elena. Up from Puerto Rico. New York, Columbia University Press. In press.

Polanyi, Michael, "Scientific Outlook, Its Sickness and Cure," *Science,* 125 (March 15, 1957), 480–84.

Puerto Rico, Commonwealth of. Department of Health. Annual Reports, 1942–1953.

—— Department of Labor, Migration Division. A Summary of Facts and Figures. San Juan, March, 1956.

Robison, Sophia M. Social and Welfare Statistics of the New

York Puerto Rican Population. New York, Bureau of Applied Social Research, Columbia University, Jan., 1954.

Saunders, Lyle. Cultural Difference and Medical Care; the Case of the Spanish-Speaking People of the Southwest. New York, Russell Sage Foundation, 1954.

Stycos, J. Mayone. Family and Fertility in Puerto Rico. New York, Columbia University Press, 1955.

—— "Female Sterilization in Puerto Rico," *Eugenics Quarterly*, I, 3 (1954).

—— "The Pattern of Birth Control in Puerto Rico," *Eugenics Quarterly*, I, 3 (1954), 176.

Stycos, J. Mayone, K. Back, and R. Hill, "Contraception and Catholicism in Puerto Rico," *Milbank Memorial Fund Quarterly*, April, 1956, pp. 150–59.

Sutter, Jean, "Le mouvement dans le monde en faveur de la limitation des familles," *Population, Revue de l'Institut National d'Etudes Démographiques*, 10e année (avril–juin, 1955), 277–94.

Taback, Matthew, "Family Studies in the Eastern Health District: VI. Family Structure and Its Changing Pattern in Family Sociology: Summary and Conclusions," *Milbank Memorial Fund Quarterly*, Jan., 1955, pp. 5–49.

Tumin, Melvin M., and Arnold Feldman, "Status Perspective and Achievement: A Study of Education and the Class Structure in Puerto Rico," paper presented at the annual meeting of the American Sociological Society, Sept., 1955.

U.S. Army Regulation 40-115, 20 Aug. 1948, "Tables of Standard and Minimum Acceptable Measurements of Height, Weight, and Circumference of Chest."

U.S. Bureau of the Census. U.S. Census of Population: 1950. Vol. II, Characteristics of the Population. Vol. III, Census Tract Statistics. Washington, D.C., Government Printing Office, 1952.

Weiner, Louis. Vital Statistics in New York City's Puerto Rican Population. New York, Bureau of Applied Social Research, Columbia University, 1954.

Weiss, Samuel, and A. J. Jaffe, "The Labor Force and the Level of Living," *Monthly Labor Review*, 78 (Dec., 1955).

Wilner, Daniel M., and Rosabelle Prece Walkley. The Housing Environment and Mental Health. New York, American Association for the Advancement of Science, Dec., 1956.

Wolf, Stewart G., and Harold G. Wolff. Human Gastric Function; an Experimental Study of a Man and His Stomach. 2 ed., revised and enlarged. New York, Oxford University Press, 1947.

Wolff, Harold G. Stress and Disease. Monograph in Bannerstone Division of American Lectures in Physiology, edited by Robert F. Pitts. American Lecture Series, Publication No. 166. Springfield, Ill., Charles C. Thomas, Publisher, 1953.

—— "What Hope Does for Man," *Saturday Review,* Jan. 5, 1957, pp. 42–45.

Wolff, Harold G., Stewart G. Wolf, and Clarence C. Hare. Life Stress and Bodily Disease. Baltimore, Williams and Wilkins, 1950.

Woytinsky, Wladimir S., and Emma S. Woytinsky. World Population and Production; Trends and Outlook. New York, Twentieth Century Fund, 1953.

APPENDIX: CASE STUDIES
OF THE EIGHTY FAMILIES

The following case studies have been summarized from data collected from various sources. Identifying details have been changed to safeguard the privacy of the families concerned.

What is interesting is that in the sciences of man —and I include physiology—we can often make our best predictions on the basis of macroscopic observations and generalizations. The microscopists may eventually verify, or even correct, our statements, and they are beginning to do this in the fields of homeostasis and phenomenal constancy; but the fact remains that the initial hypothesis, the initial hunch, springs from an intuition as to whither man is going.

In a world that cries for a deeper understanding of man, however, a world in which physical science has granted enormous new powers to a human agent who has scarcely begun to understand himself, I think it is high time that the students of man stop pretending to be scientists in the traditional sense and settle down to the business of looking at man as he really behaves.

Robert B. MacLeod, "Teleology and Theory of Human Behavior," *Science,* 125 (March 15, 1957), 477–80

FAMILY 1

FATHER, 26 ══════ MOTHER, 24*

Son, 3

Medical: <u>Father</u>, 26, paresis left peroneal following trauma while in service. Frequent sick call in service. Periodic drinker. Passive aggressive man. <u>Mother</u>, 24, secondary amenorrhea, suspected hypothyroidism. <u>Son</u>, 3, NFTSD.† Feeding problem, frequent colds.

Hospitalization: Thyroid function study of mother not completed as patient saw no results.

Migration: All born in Manhattan. Father returned to Puerto Rico as a child.

Physical Characteristics: Mother obese, father wiry, child underweight. Color primarily light olive. Hair straight. Features Caucasoid.

Housing: Project in Staten Island.

English: Father and mother bilingual.

Education: Father primary education in Puerto Rico, high school incomplete Manhattan. Mother high school incomplete Manhattan.

Employment: Father inconstant plumber's helper. Mother occasionally employed in factory.

---

*Daughter of first marriage in Family 66.

†Children born in the United States whose condition at delivery was normal as checked in their hospital records bear after their identification the abbreviation NFTSD, which means "normal, full-term, spontaneous delivery."

217

Welfare: Father receives veteran's disability for injury to leg.

Family Type: Nuclear with own child, relying on extended Families 66, 15, and 40.

Religion: Roman Catholic.

Observations: Passive aggressive man with uncertain earning power, very dependent, married to woman very dependent on her own family.

FAMILY 2

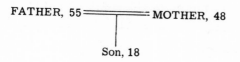

FATHER, 55 ══════════ MOTHER, 48

Son, 18

Medical: <u>Father</u>, 55, chronic bronchial asthma. Bilateral pulmonary tuberculosis moderately advanced recently treated and now arrested. Benign prostatic hypertrophy. <u>Mother</u>, 48, surgical menopause following uterine prolapse in Puerto Rico. Fall in store, no discernible injury. Multiple complaints—joint pains, epigastric pain, constipation. <u>Son</u>, 18, charged with breaking and entering, now in jail.

Hospitalization: Life of couple centers around visits to clinic. Three admissions to three separate hospitals following fall.

Migration: Five years ago.

Physical Characteristics: Color white. Hair straight. Caucasoid features. Tall, lean man. Obese woman.

Housing: Two people in three rooms. No separate bath. Central heating.

English: Fair.

Education: Parents grade school incomplete Puerto Rico. Son now in jail attended junior high school in Manhattan.

Employment: Couple do not work.

Welfare: Past two years.

Family Type: Couple now live alone.

Religion: Roman Catholic.

Observations: Middle-aged couple with chronic diseases migrated with adolescent son who became delinquent. Whole life now centered on their many ailments.

FAMILY 3

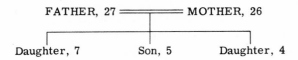

FATHER, 27 ══════ MOTHER, 26

Daughter, 7   Son, 5   Daughter, 4

Medical: Father, 27, always unstable. Accident at work resulting in skull fracture and partial blindness, followed by drug addiction and imprisonment for drug peddling. Mother, 26, no hospital or major illnesses. Minimal vitamin deficiency. Daughter, 7, NFTSD. Pertussis, bronchopneumonia first year of life. Numerous respiratory infections. Son, 5, NFTSD. Numerous respiratory infections and asthmatic attacks. Daughter, 4, NFTSD. Numerous respiratory infections and atopic dermatitis.

Hospitalization: Father did not follow through rehabilitation program for blindness. Few clinic visits by mother and children.

Migration: Mother and children born United States. Father migrated as young adult.

Physical Characteristics: Parents and children of short stature, asthenic. Mother light brown, wavy hair, Negroid features. Father and children dark olive, wavy hair, Negroid-Caucasoid features.

Housing: Three rooms for five people, no bath, no central heating.

English: Mother and children bilingual. Father adequate.

Education: Father unknown. Mother high school incomplete New York.

Employment: Mother does not work. Father irregularly employed before accident.

Welfare: Since father's accident three years ago.

Family Type: Nuclear family maintained by mother on welfare since father's imprisonment.

Religion: Roman Catholic.

Observations: Warm relationship between children and both parents observed on clinic visits. Possibly improved school attendance and fewer respiratory illnesses after father's incarceration. Mother very reserved but hinted at long-standing marital difficulties.

FAMILY 4

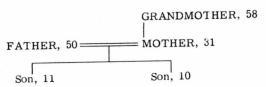

GRANDMOTHER, 58

FATHER, 50 ═══════ MOTHER, 31

Son, 11   Son, 10

Medical: Grandmother, 58, rheumatoid and osteoarthritis of knees and ankles. Father, 50, positive sputum for acid-fast bacilli found on routine examination. Left hospital against advice. Mother, 31, hypertension. Possible pituitary adenoma, work up not complete. Son, 11, ogivale palate speech defect. Asthma. Dental caries. Son, 10, asthma, dental caries.

Hospitalization: Entire family avoid hospitals as much as possible.

Migration: Father as young adult returned to Puerto Rico, married, and brought family after World War II. Grandmother came in past year.

Physical Characteristics: Entire family obese, light brown skin, kinky hair, Negroid features.

Housing: Four rooms for five people, bath and central heating.

English: Father and mother adequate, grandmother none, children bilingual.

Education: Grandmother never went to school. Parents grade school incomplete Puerto Rico.

Employment: Father hotel trade steady. Mother factory steady. steady.

Welfare: No record.

Family Type: Joint family, with grandmother caring for children while mother works and father spends his money outside home.

Religion: Roman Catholic.

Observations: Family disregards illness. Mother has assumed support of children in spite of father's being regularly employed.

FAMILY 5

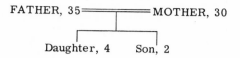

FATHER, 35 ══════════ MOTHER, 30

Daughter, 4   Son, 2

Medical: Father, 35, synechia left eye, partially blind.
Mother, 30, pneumonia during second pregnancy. Daughter,
4, NFTSD. No recorded illnesses. Son, 2, NFTSD. No recorded illnesses.

Hospitalization: Mother only for deliveries and pneumonia.

Migration: Father and mother as young adults.

Physical Characteristics: Father is wiry and appears vigorous. Mother petite, tending to obesity. All are predominantly light olive in color, with wavy hair and Caucasoid
features.

Housing: Four rooms for four people with private bath and
central heating.

English: All adequate.

Education: Father sixth grade Puerto Rico. Mother second
year high school Puerto Rico.

Employment: Father steady, auto mechanic.

Welfare: No record.

Family Type: Nuclear with own children.

Religion: Roman Catholic.

Observations: Father disregards defective vision, which is of
long standing, and family are working to improve their
home by doing own wallpapering.

FAMILY 6

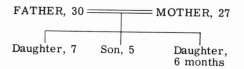

FATHER, 30 ========= MOTHER, 27

Daughter, 7   Son, 5   Daughter,
6 months

Medical: Father, 30, never examined. No hospital record.
Mother, 27, chronic pelvic inflammatory disease. Oopho-
rectomy age 24. Daughter, 7, NFTSD. Follicular tonsillitis
age 4. Son, 5, NFTSD. Bilateral strabismus corrected.
Fractured leg. Otitis media frequently. Daughter, 6 months,
NFTSD. Healthy.

Hospitalization: Mother three times for pelvic complaints.
Children clinic users for otitis media and respiratory infections.

Migration: Father and mother as young adults. All children
born in the United States.

Physical Characteristics: Color predominantly light olive.
Hair straight. Caucasoid features.

Housing: Three rooms for five people. No bath. Central
heating.

English: Parents adequate, children bilingual.

Education: Father unknown. Mother eighth grade Puerto Rico.

Employment: Father steady, hotel trade.

Welfare: No record.

Family Type: Nuclear with own children.

Religion: Roman Catholic.

Observations: Following numerous clinic visits and hospital
admissions for pelvic complaints, mother was referred to
psychiatry and responded to psychotherapy.

FAMILY 7

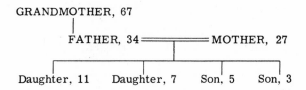

GRANDMOTHER, 67

FATHER, 34 ══════════ MOTHER, 27

Daughter, 11   Daughter, 7   Son, 5   Son, 3

Medical: Grandmother, 67, edentulous, emphysema. Sebaceous cyst excised since migration. Many complaints. Father, 34, vision of right eye impaired following accident at work in Puerto Rico. Very poor teeth, needs bridge. Mother, 27, frequent headaches, very anxious, complains of palpitations. Daughter, 11, asthma and tonsillectomy since migration. Speech defect. Nail biter. Daughter, 7, pertussis Puerto Rico. Tonsillectomy since migration. Nail biter. Son, 5, diphtheria since migration. Hypertrophied tonsils. Nail biter. Son, 3, NFTSD. Normal child.

Hospitalization: Children for tonsillectomies and diphtheria. Grandmother elective surgery. Permission for Salk vaccine canceled by mother.

Migration: Parents with children five years ago. Grandmother following year.

Physical Characteristics: Whole family are small and wiry. Color white to light olive. Hair wavy-straight. Caucasoid features.

Housing: Four rooms for seven people, bath and central heating.

English: Father and mother adequate. Grandmother fair. Children bilingual.

Education: Grandmother literate in Spanish. Children satisfactory. Father not recorded. Mother grade school incomplete.

Employment: Father machinist steady. Mother light factory intermittent.

Welfare: Grandmother since arrival. Others no record.

Family Type: Nuclear family with own children and paternal grandmother.

Religion: Roman Catholic.

Observations: Father disregards poor teeth, proud of being self-supporting. Mother refuses medical attention except on emergency basis. Children unruly outside home.

FAMILY 8

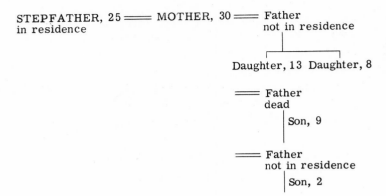

STEPFATHER, 25 ═══ MOTHER, 30 ═══ Father
in residence   not in residence

Daughter, 13   Daughter, 8

═══ Father
     dead
       Son, 9

═══ Father
     not in residence
       Son, 2

Medical: Stepfather, 25, no recorded major illnesses. Week-
end drinker. Mother, 30, obese. No recorded major illnesses. Daughter, 13, chronic conjunctivitis. Dental caries.
Son, 9, right inguinal hernia repaired. Tonsils 2 plus.
Daughter, 8, pertussis in first year of life. Systolic murmur at P-2 to be investigated. Dental caries. Son, 2,
measles age 1.

Hospitalization: No hospital admissions except for normal
deliveries. "Too busy to go to clinics."

Migration: Mother as young adult with infant daughter. Three
other children born New York. Stepfather as young adult.

Physical Characteristics: Mother and three older children
color brown, hair curly to kinky, Negroid features. Stepfather and son, 2, color pale olive, hair curly, Caucasoid
features.

Housing: Two rooms, no central heating, no separate bath.

English: Stepfather and mother adequate. Children adequate.

Education: Stepfather eighth grade Puerto Rico. Mother sixth grade Puerto Rico. All children excellent attendance record.

Employment: Stepfather steady hotel industry $60.00 a week. Mother steady factory.

Welfare: No record.

Family Type: Mother never married, successive sexual unions. All children with mother, some support from fathers. Similar pattern followed by mother's mother, who lives in same building.

Religion: Roman Catholic.

Observations: Strong maternal figure is carrying on the matriarchal pattern of caring for her children while marital partners succeed each other.

FAMILY 9

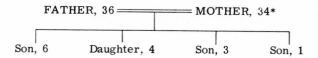

FATHER, 36 ══════ MOTHER, 34*

Son, 6   Daughter, 4   Son, 3   Son, 1

Medical: Father, 36, frequent tonsillitis since migration.
Mother, 34, no recorded illnesses. Son, 6, frequent tonsillitis since migration. Daughter, 4, frequent tonsillitis since migration. Son, 3, frequent tonsillitis since migration. Son, 1, NFTSD. Healthy.

Hospitalization: None except for delivery.

Migration: Father, mother, and three children less than three years ago.

Physical Characteristics: Parents under five feet, children small. Father and children light to dark olive in color, hair wavy, Caucasoid features. Mother light brown in color, hair straight, Caucasoid features.

Housing: Two rooms for six people. No bath. Central heating.

English: Father and mother fair. Children poor to none.

Education: Father and mother grade school incomplete Puerto Rico. Son, 6, refused admission to Manhattan public school because undersized.

Employment: Father worked in small restaurant, became unemployed two years after migration. Mother occasional light factory work.

Welfare: Accepted after father had been unemployed three months.

Family Type: Nuclear family with own children.

Religion: Roman Catholic.

Observations: Fourth child born within first year after migration. Family in crowded home with frequent tonsillitis. Father unskilled, was unable to find another job after small restaurant went out of business.

---

*Sister of woman in Family 80.

FAMILY 10

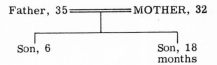

Father, 35 ══════ MOTHER, 32

Son, 6   Son, 18
                months

Medical: Father, 35, not examined and never seen by us. History of positive serology. Mother, 32, three spontaneous abortions pre-migration. Syphilis treated and cured ten years ago. Infectious hepatitis recently. Son, 6, negative serology. Scarlet fever recently. Son, 18 months, negative serology.

Hospitalization: Mother for treatment of syphilis and hepatitis.

Migration: Father and mother as young adults. Mother returned to Puerto Rico several times.

Physical Characteristics: Mother and children light olive in color, wavy hair, Caucasoid features.

Housing: Three rooms for three people. No central heating, no private bath.

English: Father unknown. Mother adequate. Son, 6, bilingual.

Education: Father unknown. Mother high school incomplete Puerto Rico.

Employment: Father laborer. Mother makes objects for sale at home, averaging $5.00-$8.00 a week.

Welfare: No record.

Family Type: Father lives with another woman but contributes $25.00 a week for support of his children and visits them and their mother from time to time.

Religion: Roman Catholic.

Observations: Syphilis successfully treated in this woman, followed by birth of two healthy children. This is an example of a Puerto Rican family with visiting father who contributes regularly to support of children.

FAMILY 11

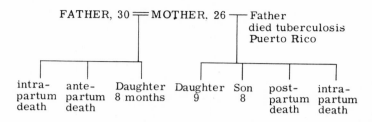

FATHER, 30 ⚬ MOTHER, 26 ─┬─ Father died tuberculosis Puerto Rico

| intra-partum death | ante-partum death | Daughter 8 months | Daughter 9 | Son 8 | post-partum death | intra-partum death |

Medical: Mother, 26, four fetal deaths at term, cholecyst-ectomy age 24, Cesarean age 25. Hookworm treated.
Father I, died tuberculosis Puerto Rico 1951. No active le-sion in other members. Father II, 30, acute rheumatoid arthritis age 28. Recovered. Pterygium removed age 28.
Dental extractions age 30. Daughter, 9, pertussis Puerto Rico. Son, 8, pertussis Puerto Rico. Hookworm treated.
Daughter, 8 months, Cesarean birth, artificial respiration. Now healthy.

Hospitalization: Antagonism to hospital arose following second fetal death in second marriage, but special prenatal care was secured resulting in live birth of daughter, now 8 months. Father anxious to have eye surgery.

Migration: Father as young man. Mother and children less than five years ago.

Physical Characteristics: Father dark olive in color, curly hair, Caucasoid features. Others light olive in color, straight hair, Caucasoid features.

Housing: Three rooms for four people. No bath. Central heating. Now moved to housing project.

English: Father adequate. Children bilingual. Mother fair.

Education: Father and mother grade school incomplete Puerto Rico.

Employment: Father sporadic. Mother does not work.

Welfare: Family have received assistance during two thirds of past four years.

Family Type: Nuclear family with own daughter and children of mother's previous marriage.

Religion: Protestant.

Observations: Mother with grave obstetrical problem treated successfully while father cared for family. He developed a persistent complaint and remained unemployed after wife's recovery, considering his minor complaints and eye lesions to be incapacitating.

FAMILY 12

HUSBAND, 45 ═══ WIFE, 39

Medical: Husband, 45, heavy drinker in youth. Accident at
work resulting in skull fracture. Paranoid schizophrenic.
Venereal disease in U.S. Army. Chronic bronchial asthma
under treatment. Rheumatoid arthritis, mild. Wife, 39,
idiopathic cerebral dysrhythmia.

Hospitalization: Both attend an out-patient department regularly.

Migration: Both as young adults.

Physical Characteristics: Color, both light olive. Hair wavy.
Features Caucasoid.

Housing: Three rooms for two people. No bath. Central heating.

English: Both adequate.

Education: Both grade school incomplete.

Employment: Man has been unemployed for several years.
Woman takes care of child of a working mother from time
to time.

Welfare: For past eight years.

Family Type: Childless couple.

Religion: Pentecostal.

Observations: Both are presumably unemployable due to
chronic illness, personality traits, age, lack of specific
skills and of education.

FAMILY 13

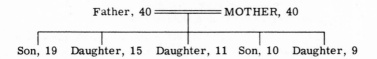

Father, 40 ══════ MOTHER, 40

Son, 19   Daughter, 15   Daughter, 11   Son, 10   Daughter, 9

Medical: Father, 40, not examined and never seen by us.
Mother, 40, syphilis and gonorrhea treated in Puerto Rico.
Negative serology United States. Tubes ligated post-partum
Puerto Rico. Frequent headaches, low back pain. Son, 19,
no recorded illness. Daughter, 15, rheumatic fever suspect
recently. Daughter, 11, skull fracture soon after migration.
Intestinal parasites treated recently. Fracture of big toe
past year. Son, 10, secondary anemia. Intestinal parasites
treated recently. Daughter, 9, asthma since migration.
Rheumatic fever suspect and truant from school.

Hospitalization: Children suspected of rheumatic fever.
Daughter, 11, hospitalized with skull fracture for three
months.

Migration: Parents and children within last three years.

Physical Characteristics: All white in color, with straight
hair and Caucasoid features.

Housing: Three rooms for six people. No separate bath. Central heating.

English: Mother and oldest daughter poor. Son, 10, bilingual.
Others, fair only.

Education: Father and mother unknown. Son, 19, one year
high school New York, has difficulty understanding English.
Daughter, 15, son, 10, satisfactory. Daughter, 11, unsatisfactory. Daughter, 9, truant.

Employment: Son, 19, factory worker. Mother intermittent
factory work. Visiting father contributes $15.00 a week.

Welfare: Not accepted.

Family Type: Mother with own children. Visiting father.

Religion: Roman Catholic and Pentecostal.

Observations: Family with visiting father and inadequate support, so mother tries to work and cannot care for youngest daughter, who is truant. Daughter, 11, hit by car first year of migration, always school problem.

FAMILY 14

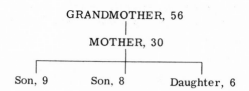

GRANDMOTHER, 56

MOTHER, 30

Son, 9   Son, 8   Daughter, 6

Medical: Grandmother, 56, many complaints. Blindness in left eye. Mother, 30, frequent minor injuries, two-year observation. Son, 9, healthy. Son, 8, carious teeth. Poorly nourished. Lymphadenopathy. Daughter, 6, bronchopneumonia three times, age 1 month, 1 year, 2 years. Frequent respiratory infections and sore throats. Fractured ankle. Anterior synechia following trauma of right eye.

Hospitalization: Daughter, 6, five times. Mother goes to emergency clinic and does not return for work-up.

Migration: Grandmother as young widow with mother age 6 months.

Physical Characteristics: Color predominantly dark olive. Hair kinky. Features Negroid.

Housing: Three rooms for five people. No separate bath. Central heating.

English: Grandmother none. Mother and children bilingual.

Education: Grandmother never attended school. Mother ninth grade United States.

Employment: Grandmother unemployed seven years. Mother intermittent factory worker.

Welfare: Over past six-year period family has received assistance approximately two thirds of the time.

Family Type: Mother separated, living with grandmother and children. Precarious intermittent support from separated husband.

Religion: Roman Catholic and Protestant.

Observations: Negro Puerto Rican woman raised in neighborhood by widowed mother. Separated. Finds children burdensome and does not have steady job.

FAMILY 15

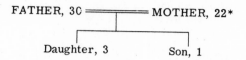

FATHER, 30 ══════ MOTHER, 22*

Daughter, 3   Son, 1

Medical: Father, 30, syphilis treated before marriage. Shoulder fracture five years ago. Mother, 22, obese, healthy. Daughter, 3, NFTSD. Primary tuberculosis, treated. Son, 1, NFTSD. Healthy.

Hospitalization: Tuberculosis treated in out-patient department after initial in-patient study. Entire family checked by Department of Health.

Migration: Father as young adult. Mother and children born in United States.

Physical Characteristics: Color light olive. Hair straight. Caucasoid features.

Housing: Three rooms for four people. No bath. Central heating.

English: Father adequate. Mother bilingual. Daughter, 3, learned to speak English during hospitalization.

Education: Father high school complete Puerto Rico. Mother high school incomplete Manhattan.

Employment: Father interstate trucking, regular. Mother does not work.

Welfare: No record.

Family Type: Nuclear family with own children living in same building with maternal grandmother.

Religion: Roman Catholic and Protestant.

Observations: Tuberculosis in child contracted in grandmother's home from visitor who was part of extended family.

---

*Daughter of first marriage in Family 66.

FAMILY 16

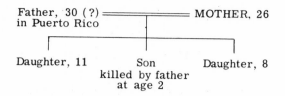

Father, 30 (?) ════════ MOTHER, 26
in Puerto Rico

Daughter, 11   Son   Daughter, 8
killed by father
at age 2

Medical: Father, 30 (?), in a state hospital in Puerto Rico after beating son, who subsequently died. Mother, 26, pneumonia first year after migration. Palpitations and "nervousness." Daughter, 11, mentally retarded behavior problem. Chronic blepharitis. Daughter, 8, frequent respiratory infections.

Hospitalization: Father in Puerto Rico. Mother pneumonia.

Migration: Mother with two infants.

Physical Characteristics: Color predominantly white-light olive. Hair straight. Caucasoid features.

Housing: Share three-room apartment with another family. Exact number of people in three rooms undetermined.

English: Mother and daughter, 11, poor. Daughter, 8, bilingual.

Education: Father unknown. Mother never went to school. Daughter, 11, mentally retarded. Daughter, 8, satisfactory.

Employment: Mother steady, cleaning establishment.

Welfare: No record.

Family Type: Mother with daughters whom she supports.

Religion: Roman Catholic.

Observations: Mother migrated after tragedy. Never having been to school and speaking little English, she is trying to support two children and is unable to cope with discipline of mentally retarded daughter. Help now being given by family agency.

FAMILY 17

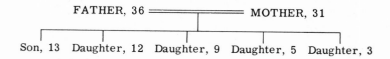

FATHER, 36 ══════════ MOTHER, 31

Son, 13   Daughter, 12   Daughter, 9   Daughter, 5   Daughter, 3

Medical: Father, 36, emphysema, chronic cough, no tuberculosis. Severe behavior disorder and periodic drinker.
Mother, 31, height 60 inches, weight 150 pounds. Rectocele
cystocele. Frequent upper quadrant pain, no gall bladder
disease diagnosed. Sebaceous cyst excised. Son, 13, corneal ulcer following trauma first year of migration. Daughter, 12, frequent otitis, tonsillitis, bronchitis every winter.
Daughter, 9, frequent otitis, tonsillitis, bronchitis every
winter. Daughter, 5, NFTSD. Frequent otitis, tonsillitis,
bronchitis every winter. Daughter, 3, high forceps term.
Frequent otitis, tonsillitis, bronchitis every winter.

Hospitalization: Frequent visits to emergency and out-patient
departments. Three children hospitalized first year after
migration.

Migration: Father first migrated as adolescent, traveling
back and forth until final migration with mother and three
children eight years ago.

Physical Characteristics: Predominantly light brown in color,
wavy hair, mixed Caucasoid-Negroid features.

Housing: Three rooms for seven people. No private bath.
Central heating.

English: Father and mother adequate. Children bilingual.

Education: Father and mother grade school incomplete. Children satisfactory.

Employment: Father building trades irregularly employed.
Mother does not work.

Welfare: Applied but not accepted three years ago.

Family Type: Nuclear family with own children. Parents are not legally married though living together fifteen years. Father has legal wife in Puerto Rico.

Religion: Protestant.

Observations: Father at times uses physical violence on wife, and episodes of illness in wife and children cluster around these outbursts.

FAMILY 18

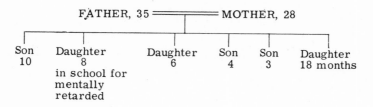

FATHER, 35 ═══════ MOTHER, 28

| Son 10 | Daughter 8 in school for mentally retarded | Daughter 6 | Son 4 | Son 3 | Daughter 18 months |

Medical: Father, 35, no recorded illnesses. Height 60 3/4 inches, weight 120 pounds. Periodic drinker. Mother, 28, malaria in second pregnancy. Hookworm with severe secondary anemia. Treated in pregnancy and relapsed thereafter. Para 6, grava 10, tubal ligation. Simple schizophrenia diagnosed by psychiatrist, not hospitalized. Son, 10, ran away from home many times. Committed to school for mentally retarded for one year. Daughter, 8, tuberculosis meningitis age 4. Committed to school for mentally retarded thereafter. Daughter, 6, febrile convulsions age 2. Pica age 2 to date. Son, 4, NFTSD, 7 pounds. Hit by car age 3, no concussion. Roach bites on buttocks. Son, 3, NFTSD, 7 pounds. Rachitic rosary. Daughter, 18 months, NFTSD, 5 pounds. Poorly developed, marasmic child.

Hospitalization: As noted above.

Migration: Father and mother with two oldest children as infants.

Physical Characteristics: Father light brown in color, kinky hair, Negroid features. Mother light olive in color, straight hair, Caucasoid features. Children dark olive in color, kinky hair, Negroid features. All children in this family are in lowest percentile for height and weight.

Housing: Seven people in two rooms. No separate bath. Central heating.

243

Fnglish: Father and mother fair. Son, 10, bilingual. Younger children none.

Education: Father and mother grade school incomplete Puerto Rico. Daughter, 6, not admitted to public school Manhattan because undersized. Entire family have very limited vocabulary in Spanish.

Employment: Father employed steadily, part time only, delivering groceries for Spanish shop.

Welfare: Partial support because of large family and father's low wage.

Family Type: Nuclear family with own children. Not legally married. Divorce has not been obtained since legal spouses in Puerto Rico could not be located in spite of efforts of social agencies.

Religion: Roman Catholic - Protestant

Observations: Chronic poor nutritional status of mother and children, limited verbal capacity, and personality problems of mother and children make this family one of the least susceptible to long-term medical and social treatment.

FAMILY 19

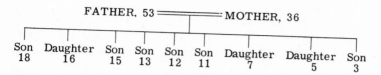

Medical: Father, 53, chronic cough and sinusitis. No X-ray obtained. Normal physical examination. Mother, 36, para 9, grava 10. Spontaneous abortion with hemorrhage first year after migration. "Ataques" (hysteria) under stress currently and in Puerto Rico. Episiotomy separated in puerperium eighth pregnancy. Son, 18, mumps and measles first year after migration. Obese. Daughter, 16, pneumonia first year after migration. Mumps and measles following year. Son, 15, mumps and measles first year after migration. Son, 13, mumps and measles first year after migration. Bronchopneumonia and otitis following year. Son, 12, mumps and measles first year after migration. Son, 11, mumps and measles first year after migration. Daughter, 7, NFTSD. Left ear drum scarred on physical examination. Daughter, 5, NFTSD. Croup three years ago. Internal strabismus. Son, 3, breech full term. Hypertension of undetermined etiology.

Hospitalization: Every member of the family but one, the father, has had one or more hospital admissions as recorded under dated illnesses above. Prolonged hospitalization for youngest child.

Migration: Father ten years ago. Mother and six children following year.

Physical Characteristics: Predominantly light olive in color, wavy hair, Caucasoid features.

245

Housing: Four rooms for eleven people. No bath. Central
heating.

English: Father and mother adequate. Children bilingual.

Education: Father and mother grade school incomplete. Son,
18, graduated from high school in 1956. All children in
school in appropriate grades, satisfactory. Three children
in high school.

Employment: Father in restaurant industry. Take home pay
$54.00 a week.

Welfare: $43.00 a week supplementary.

Family Type: Nuclear with own children. Maternal grandmother lives in same building.

Religion: Roman Catholic.

Observations: Family uses hospitals and clinics frequently.
Mother communicates easily and effectively with authorities, and all children are highly motivated to finish high
school. Welfare is accepted as a means to an end.

FAMILY 20

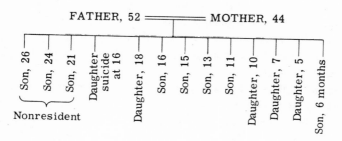

FATHER, 52 ══════════ MOTHER, 44

Son, 26
Son, 24
Son, 21
Nonresident

Daughter suicide at 16

Daughter, 18

Son, 16

Son, 15

Son, 13

Son, 11

Daughter, 10

Daughter, 7

Daughter, 5

Son, 6 months

Medical: Father, 52, diabetic since 1945. Controlled on insulin. Mother, 44, reversed sleep pattern. No pathology discovered. Son, 26, not examined. Son, 24, not examined. In jail for stealing car. Son, 21, not examined. In jail for stealing car. Daughter, suicide at age 16. Daughter, 18, severe behavior disorder. Son, 16, club foot. Mentally retarded. Son, 15, laceration scalp first year after migration. Son, 13, ventral hernia first year after migration. Severe behavior disorder. Mentally retarded. Son, 11, club foot. Mentally retarded. Daughter, 10, rheumatic fever suspected age 6. Daughter, 7, pneumonia age 4. Daughter, 5, pneumonia age 3. Son, 6 months, NFTSD, no Health Department care.

Hospitalization: Father attends clinic regularly for diabetes All children were sent to clinic for chronic conditions by family agency first year after migration, but have discontinued attendance.

Migration: Following onset of father's diabetes and loss of small landholdings, eldest sons migrated to join maternal grandmother. Remainder of family followed in two groups, two to three years later.

247

Physical Characteristics: All are light to dark olive, medium height and build, with straight hair and Caucasoid features.

Housing: Five now at home live in three rooms with no bath. Central heating. When children are released from institutions, they sleep in maternal grandmother's apartment in same building.

English: Father fair, mother none. Children adequate, becoming bilingual after institutional care.

Education: Father and eldest sons grade school complete Puerto Rico. Mother grade school incomplete Puerto Rico. All children behavior problems in school. Daughter, 18, and son, 16, discharged for this reason and now at home. Mentally retarded in state schools. All others of school age in Catholic boarding schools.

Employment: Father special labor force Welfare Department. Older sons do not contribute.

Welfare: Since migration to date. Recently closed as father was suspected of gambling.

Family Type: Nuclear family with own children. All but three are now scattered in jails, state schools, and boarding schools.

Religion: Roman Catholic.

Observations: Largest family in study. Disorganized and violent behavior manifested in several members. Many agencies involved.

FAMILY 21

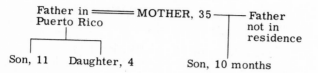

Father in ═══════ MOTHER, 35 ──────┬── Father
Puerto Rico   │   not in
                                    │   residence
┌──────────┬─────────┐   │
Son, 11   Daughter, 4   Son, 10 months

Medical: Mother, 35, chronic conjunctivitis. Tenderness over sigmoid, severe headaches. Son, 11, occasionally visits hospital emergency room for tonsillitis. Daughter, 4, club foot and imbecile. Son, 10 months, NFTSD. Congenital heart disease.

Hospitalization: Daughter, 4, in school for mentally retarded. Son, 10 months, under hospital management.

Migration: Mother and two children four years ago.

Physical Characteristics: Mother well built, color dark brown, hair kinky, Negroid features. Children dark in color, kinky hair, Negroid features. Son, 11, poor posture.

Housing: Three rooms for three people. No bath. Central heating.

English: Mother adequate, son bilingual, daughter not seen.

Education: Mother three years high school Puerto Rico. Son, 11, satisfactory. Daughter, 4, in institution.

Employment: Mother does not work.

Welfare: Since migration to date.

Family Type: Mother with no mate and three small children.

Religion: Roman Catholic.

Observations: Mother left alcoholic husband to come to the United States to improve her situation and that of her two children. Bore a child to another man, who deserted her. Two of the children have severe chronic congenital defects, and she has constant minor complaints associated with stress.

FAMILY 22

Father in Puerto Rico══MOTHER, 36

Twins died following Daughter, 14
Cesarean birth in
Puerto Rico

Note: Nephew, 10, whose mother died of tuberculosis in Puerto
 Rico, lives with family.

Medical: Mother, 36, contracted pelvis. Tubal ligation following birth of daughter. Minimal tuberculosis diagnosed after
 migration, now arrested. Daughter, 14, Cesarean birth.
 Pneumonia in Puerto Rico age 2. Chronic asthma and emotional problem. Very poorly developed. No tuberculosis.
 Nephew, 10, no tuberculosis. Dental caries. Nutritional deficiency.

Hospitalization: Mother several admissions for tuberculosis,
 leaving against advice. Daughter frequent visits to emergency room and clinics.

Migration: Mother alone with small daughter ten years ago.
 Nephew recent arrival.

Physical Characteristics: Predominantly dark olive in color,
 straight hair, Caucasoid features.

Housing: Formerly rooming house, now two rooms for three
 people. No bath. Central heating.

English: Mother and nephew fair. Daughter bilingual.

Education: Mother grade school incomplete Puerto Rico, reads
 Spanish. Daughter, in ninth grade, cannot read English.

Employment: Mother has worked intermittently.

Welfare: Family have received help for six out of ten years
 since migration.

Family type: Mother with no mate and two children.

Religion: Roman Catholic.

Observations: Chronic illness of mother and daughter have resulted in severe emotional problems in both and long-term dependency on welfare.

FAMILY 23

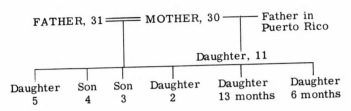

Medical: Father, 31, onset diabetes after migration, now controlled without insulin. Mother, 30, varicose veins. Placenta previa, death of premature baby, tubal ligation last year. Daughter, 11, scarlet fever first year after migration. Frequent otitis. Needs glasses for school. Daughter, 5, NFTSD. Bronchitis first year of life. First day en route to kindergarten hit by rock. Son, 4, NFTSD. Bronchopneumonia first year of life. Frequent colds and asthma. Son, 3, NFTSD. Bronchopneumonia first year of life. Daughter, 2, NFTSD. Chicken pox and bronchitis first year of life. Daughter, 13 months, lives with friend of family. Daughter, 6 months, NFTSD. Severe eczema, continuous rhinitis and pharyngitis. Milk only food.

Hospitalization: Emergency admissions for all dated illnesses.

Migration: Father single young adult. Mother young adult with infant daughter.

Physical Characteristics: Father well dressed, dark olive in color, wavy hair, Caucasoid features. Mother obese, white in color, wavy hair, Caucasoid features. Children predominantly light olive in color, wavy hair, Caucasoid-Negroid features.

Housing: Three rooms for eight people on fourth floor. No bath. Central heating.

English: Father adequate. Mother and younger children poor to none. Daughter, 11, bilingual.

Education: Father and mother grade school complete Puerto Rico. Daughter, 11, unsatisfactory.

Employment: Father steadily employed machinist ten years same concern.

Welfare: No record.

Family Type: Nuclear family with own children and daughter of mother's previous marriage. One of their own children has been taken over by a friend.

Religion: Roman Catholic.

Observations: Father is steadily employed at $80.00 a week and spends money on cards and women. Family is neglected, house very dirty, children poorly clothed. Medical care is sought only in emergency when desperately sick.

FAMILY 24

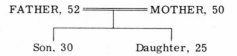

FATHER, 52 ════╤════ MOTHER, 50

Son, 30   Daughter, 25

Medical: Father, 52, poor visual acuity. Examination incomplete. Mother, 50, hysterectomy for fibroids twenty years
ago. Joint pains, mild rheumatoid arthritis. Son, 30, hit by
car as a child. Fissure in ano recently. Tonsillitis last
year. Normal male. Daughter, 25, not examined.
Hospitalization: Family claims to use private physicians. No
municipal hospital records found.
Migration: Father and mother as young adults thirty years
ago.
Physical Characteristics: Dark brown in color, kinky hair,
Negroid features.
Housing: Four rooms for four people.
English: Bilingual. Son has English accent in speaking Spanish.
Education: Mother and father grade school incomplete Puerto
Rico. Son high school complete Manhattan. Daughter high
school incomplete Manhattan.
Employment: Father steadily employed hotel business. Mother
cleaning in private home. Son licensed electrician. Daugh-
ter factory work.
Welfare: No record.
Family Type: Parents with two employed adult children at
home.
Religion: Protestant—Baptist.
Observations: Puerto Rican born parents, having migrated
thirty years ago, and their two Manhattan-born adult children identified with American Negro group.

254

FAMILY 25

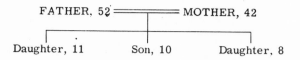

FATHER, 52 ══════════ MOTHER, 42

Daughter, 11   Son, 10   Daughter, 8

Medical: Father, 52, pneumonia shortly after migration. Eye
   injury eight years ago. Low back pain for many years.
   Mild osteoarthritis by X-ray. Mother, 42, essential hypertension discovered recently, asymptomatic. Severe varicose
   veins. Daughter, 11, NFTSD. Pertussis first year of life.
   Son, 10, NFTSD. Pertussis first year of life, nail biter at
   present. Daughter, 8, NFTSD. Otitis four years ago.

Hospitalization: Spotty use of out-patient department for minor complaints.

Migration: Father and mother as young adults. Children born
   in Manhattan.

Physical Characteristics: Father and children dark olive in
   color, curly hair, Caucasoid features. Mother light brown
   in color, kinky hair, Negroid features.

Housing: Three rooms for five people. No bath. Central
   heating.

English: All bilingual.

Education: Father not recorded. Mother grade school complete Puerto Rico.

Employment: Father metal worker currently; hotel business
   formerly.

Welfare: For several months eight years ago following eye
   injury at work.

Family Type: Nuclear family with own children.

Religion: Roman Catholic.

Observations: Complaint of chronic low back pain in father
   but manages to find work.

FAMILY 26

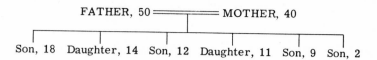

FATHER, 50 ══════ MOTHER, 40

Son, 18   Daughter, 14   Son, 12   Daughter, 11   Son, 9   Son, 2

Medical: Father, 50, fall with back injury at work year after
migration. Excision intervertebral disc and postoperative
psychosis following year. Arachnoiditis, conversion hysteria currently. Complains of back, head pain, insomnia.
Mother, 40, complains of weakness, fatigability, no pathology found. Son, 18, frequent headaches. Daughter, 14, rheumatic fever suspected recently. Son, 12, treated for Osgood
Schlatter's disease following trauma to knees. Daughter, 11,
frequent otitis. Son, 9, healthy. Son, 2, NFTSD. Healthy
child. Entire family was treated at home for severe respiratory infection during recent winter.

Hospitalization: Father has had four hospitalizations for treatment of injury and innumerable examinations by compensation, welfare, and hospital physicians. Infrequent use of
clinics by other members.

Migration: Father alone five years ago. Mother and children
following year.

Physical Characteristics: Predominantly white to light olive
in color, straight to wavy hair, Caucasoid features.

Housing: Eight people in four rooms, private bath, central
heating.

English: Father fair, mother poor, children bilingual.

Education: Father and mother grade school incomplete Puerto
Rico. Son graduated high school Manhattan, commercial
course. Other children satisfactory.

256

Employment: Father steady until accident. Mother does not work. Son now shipping clerk.

Welfare: Six months following accident to date.

Family Type: Nuclear family with own children.

Religion: Protestant.

Observations: Father of six children, now 50, previously self-supporting, sustained back injury a year after migration and continues unemployable, handicapped, and emotionally crippled three years later in spite of efforts of numerous agencies.

FAMILY 27

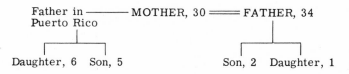

Father in ——— MOTHER, 30 ══ FATHER, 34
Puerto Rico

Daughter, 6   Son, 5   Son, 2   Daughter, 1

Medical: Father, 34, not examined. Mother, 30, thin, no major illnesses. Daughter, 6, NFTSD. Heart murmurs suggesting organic disease not investigated. Still sucks thumb.
Son, 5, NFTSD. Phimosis, rachitic rosary. Thumb sucking.
Pertussis first year of life. Son, 2, NFTSD. Blepharitis and
conjunctivitis last year. Daughter, 1, NFTSD. Otitis one
episode.

Hospitalization: None.

Migration: Father and mother as young adults. All children
born in New York.

Physical Characteristics: All primarily dark olive in color,
wavy hair, Negroid features.

Housing: Moved in 1956 and could not be located. Formerly
three rooms for six people, with neither bath nor central
heating.

English: Father bilingual, mother adequate.

Education: Father and mother not recorded.

Employment: Father seaman sometimes unemployed. Mother
helps out with factory work.

Welfare: No record.

Family Type: Nuclear family with own children and mother's
children from previous union.

Religion: Roman Catholic.

Observations: Older children born to mother out of wedlock.
Responsibility for all four children assumed by the father
of younger children.

FAMILY 28

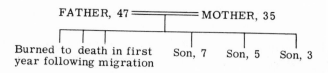

FATHER, 47 ══════╤══════ MOTHER, 35

Burned to death in first   Son, 7   Son, 5   Son, 3
year following migration

Medical: <u>Father</u>, 47, traumatic epilepsy with labyrinthine disease since migration. Bronchopneumonia three years ago. <u>Mother</u>, 35, obese, anxious. <u>Son</u>, 7, NFTSD. Feeding problem. Tonsils hypertrophied. <u>Son</u>, 5, NFTSD. Feeding problem. Tonsils hypertrophied. <u>Son</u>, 3, NFTSD. Feeding problem. Tonsils hypertrophied.

Hospitalization: Father on out-patient care.

Migration: Father and mother as adults with three children who died in fire first year of migration.

Physical Characteristics: Large man with stooping shoulders and uncertain gait. Obese, short woman. All children are small. Color predominantly dark olive, hair straight, Caucasoid features.

Housing: Three rooms for five people. No bath. Central heating.

English: Father and mother poor, children bilingual.

Education: Mother and father grade school incomplete Puerto Rico.

Employment: Father unemployed since fall through burning building.

Welfare: Continuous since accident.

Family Type: Nuclear with own children.

Religion: Pentecostal.

Observations: Fire in first year following migration resulted in death of three children and permanent disability of father.

FAMILY 29

MAN, 27 ══════ WOMAN, 33

Medical: Man, 27, lower abdominal pain and constipation, no
lesion of gastrointestinal tract. Mixed psychoneurosis. Improved. Woman, 33, spontaneous abortion four years ago.
Schistosomiasis discovered and treated past year. Dyspareunia recently. Improved.

Hospitalization: Psychiatric treatment of man by Spanish-
speaking physician in city hospital out-patient department
for six months. Woman finished course of treatment at
Health Department.

Migration: Both as young adults.

Physical Characteristics: Man asthenic, 120 pounds, light olive
color, curly hair, Caucasoid features. Woman plump, color
white, hair wavy, features Caucasoid.

Housing: Two people in three rooms. No separate bath. No
central heating.

English: Man adequate, woman poor.

Education: Both high school incomplete Puerto Rico.

Employment: Both are factory workers when not ill.

Welfare: No record.

Family Type: This man and woman have been living together
for the past two years. The man has two children in Puerto
Rico from a previous consensual union. The woman has a
child who lives with a relative in Puerto Rico in winter and
comes to stay with her during the summer.

Religion: Roman Catholic.

Observations: Man, apparently highly motivated in desire to
improve, used psychiatric out-patient department with
good results. Woman carried through schistosomiasis
treatment on recommendation of family clinic and accepted
interpretation given of man's emotional illness.

FAMILY 30

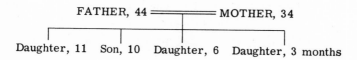

FATHER, 44 ═══════ MOTHER, 34

Daughter, 11   Son, 10   Daughter, 6   Daughter, 3 months

Medical: Father, 44, corneal scar following injury ten years
  ago. Long standing epigastric complaints, ulcer ruled out
  in recent medical study. Mother, 34, two spontaneous abortions after fourth pregnancy. Severe varicose veins. Tubal
  ligation. Daughter, 11, NFTSD. No major illness. Son, 10,
  NFTSD. No major illness. Daughter, 6, NFTSD. Mumps
  with encephalitis age 2. Daughter, 3 months, NFTSD. Well.
Hospitalization: Mother tubal ligation because of varicose
  veins. Earlier recommendation not carried through. One or
  two visits a year per child to out-patient department for mi-
  nor complaints.
Migration: Mother and father in late teens. Children born in
  New York. Father born in Argentina.
Physical Characteristics: Color predominantly light olive,
  hair wavy, features Caucasoid.
Housing: Six people in three rooms. No bath. Central heating.
English: Parents adequate. Children bilingual.
Education: Parents grade school complete before migration.
Employment: Father formerly in hotel business, now building
  superintendent.
Welfare: No record.
Family Type: Nuclear family with own children. Parents ap-
  pear congenial.
Religion: Roman Catholic.
Observations: Family apparently getting along without much
  friction or many illnesses.

261

FAMILY 31

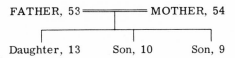

FATHER, 53 ======= MOTHER, 54

Daughter, 13   Son, 10   Son, 9

Medical: Father, 53, hand injury in Puerto Rico with amputa-
tion of index finger. Passive aggressive personality. History
of seizures. Osteoarthritis lumbosacral spine. Bilateral
epidydimitis. Mother, 54, hysterectomy for rectocele-
cystocele since migration. Daughter, 13, mentally retarded
by school tests. Effective at home. Son, 10, tuberculosis
diagnosed three years ago, now arrested. Son, 9, NFTSD.
Rheumatic fever age 4, now inactive.

Hospitalization: All members have been hospitalized for major illnesses listed. Father three times in psychopathic
ward of city hospital.

Migration: Parents with older two children ten years ago.

Physical Characteristics: Father tall, heavy man (190 pounds),
color light brown, kinky hair, Negroid features. Mother
obese, color white, straight hair, Caucasoid features. Children dark to light olive in color, hair wavy, Caucasoid features.

Housing: Moved to housing project.

English: Father fair to poor. Mother fair. Daughter, 13, adequate. Others bilingual.

Education: Father and mother grade school incomplete.
Daughter, 13, mentally retarded class.

Employment: Father construction foreman in Puerto Rico.
Employed one month in United States.

Welfare: Since a few months after migration.

Family Type: Nuclear family with own children.

Religion: Roman Catholic.

Observations: Father became unemployed soon after arrival and exhibited severe behavior disorder. A major chronic illness is present in each child.

FAMILY 32

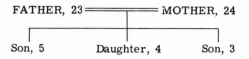

FATHER, 23 ══════════ MOTHER, 24

Son, 5   Daughter, 4   Son, 3

Medical: Father, 23, never examined. No hospital record. Mother, 24, history of convulsions before marriage. Breast abscess after first pregnancy. Returned to Puerto Rico for post-partum tubal ligation. Son, 5, NFTSD. Enuresis, hypertrophied tonsils. Daughter, 4, NFTSD. Enuresis, hypertrophied tonsils. Febrile convulsions age 2. Bronchopneumonia and iron deficiency anemia. Son, 3, born in Puerto Rico. Hypertrophied tonsils.

Hospitalization: Emergency use of both in- and out-patient departments municipal hospitals.

Migration: Father and mother as single, young adults, married in New York.

Physical Characteristics: Not recorded.

Housing: Moved 1956, could not be found. Formerly four rooms for five people with central heating but no private bath.

English: Not recorded.

Education: Not recorded

Employment: Father in hotel industry.

Welfare: No record.

Family Type: Nuclear with own children.

Religion: Roman Catholic.

Observations: Mother at age of 21 para two, grava three, returned to Puerto Rico for delivery and post-partum tubal ligation.

FAMILY 33

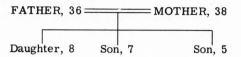

FATHER, 36 ══════════ MOTHER, 38

Daughter, 8   Son, 7   Son, 5

Medical: Father 36, peptic ulcer recently diagnosed, improved. Mother, 38, post-partum tubal ligation age 33. Several episodes bursitis. Frequent respiratory illnesses, back pain, constipation. Very anxious. Daughter, 8, NFTSD. Pertussis in first year. Frequent tonsillitis, tonsillectomy age 5. Sucks thumb. Son, 7, NFTSD. Frequent tonsillitis, tonsillectomy age 6. Sucks thumb, poor eater. Son, 5, frequent asthmatic attacks. Pneumonia age 1 and 4. Feeding problem.

Hospitalization: Mother takes children from one out-patient department to another, to family clinic, and to private doctor for frequent minor illnesses.

Migration: Father as a child, age 8. Mother young adult. Mother returned to Puerto Rico for birth of third child and tubal ligation.

Physical Characteristics: Father and children light olive in color, curly hair, Caucasoid features. Mother light brown in color, wavy hair, Negroid features.

Housing: Three rooms for five people, bath, central heating.

English: Father and children bilingual. Mother well spoken.

Education: Father high school incomplete United States. Mother high school incomplete Puerto Rico.

Employment: Father irregularly employed, now kitchen helper.

Welfare: No record.

Family Type: Nuclear with own children.

Religion: Protestant.

Observations: After Family 53, this family had the greatest number of recorded out-patient visits. Mother ambitious, disappointed woman married to ineffectual, poor provider.

FAMILY 34

HUSBAND, 70 ============ WIFE, 59

Medical: <u>Man</u>, 70, gonorrhea age 15, cholecystitis in
adult life. Back injury following fall. Chronic dislocated
hip. <u>Woman</u>, 59, died having had twelve hospital admissions
in past eleven years for multiplicity of diseases, including
cystitis, thrombophlebitis, congestive heart failure, and hypertension.

Hospitalization: As above.

Migration: Husband at turn of century as young adult. Wife
in 1930's.

Physical Characteristics: Husband white in color, gray,
straight hair, Caucasoid features. Wife not recorded.

Housing: Three rooms, bath, central heating.

English: Husband adequate. Wife not recorded.

Education: Husband grade school incomplete. Wife not recorded.

Employment: Husband started in factory, later failed in own
business, now living on ·compensation for injury and on
savings.

Welfare: No record.

Family Type: Retired childless widower, living alone.

Religion: Roman Catholic and Pentecostal.

Observations: The oldest individual in the group, living in re-
tirement in the neighborhood on his income.

FAMILY 35

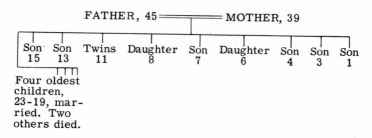

FATHER, 45 ══════════ MOTHER, 39

| Son 15 | Son 13 | Twins 11 | Daughter 8 | Son 7 | Daughter 6 | Son 4 | Son 3 | Son 1 |

Four oldest
children,
23-19, mar-
ried. Two
others died.

Medical: Father, 45, low back pain syndrome, normal laboratory and physical findings. Mother, 39, obese, edentulous,
cystocele retrocele. Grava 17, para 15. Low implantation
placenta age 39. Son, 15, tenia capitis, no severe illness.
Son, 13, severe myopia, needs glasses. Mental retardation.
Twin girl, 11, primary tuberculosis, inactive, not treated.
Mentally retarded. Twin boy, 11, tenia capitis. Frequent
respiratory infections. Daughter, 8, bulbar poliomyelitis
age 6, now recovered. Son, 7, NFTSD. No severe illness.
Daughter, 6, NFTSD. Mentally retarded. Scarlet fever
age 5. Son, 4, NFTSD. No severe illness. Son, 3, adopted
by friends, not examined. Son, 1, premature birth 4 pounds,
5 ounces. Bronchopneumonia first year of life.
Hospitalization: Family checked for tuberculosis on two occasions, no activity found. Minor illnesses disregarded.
Severe respiratory infection in all members simultaneously
observed during winter. Scarlet fever in daughter, 6, treated
at home by family clinic physician and also by visits to
emergency room.

Migration: Father eight years ago. Mother and children following year.

Physical Characteristics: Predominantly dark olive in color, straight hair, Caucasoid features.

Housing: Three rooms for eleven people. No bath. Central heating.

English: Father adequate, mother fair, older children bilingual.

Education: Father and mother grade school incomplete. Son, 15, in high school.

Employment: Father irregular factory work.

Welfare: Supplementary for large family since migration.

Family Type: Nuclear family with own children.

Religion: Pentecostal.

Observations: Strong family cohesion and adherence to religious tenets—no movies, no birth control, tubal ligation refused. Son, 3, is being reared by friends under informal adoption agreement.

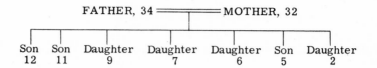

FATHER, 34 ══════╤══════ MOTHER, 32

| Son | Son | Daughter | Daughter | Daughter | Son | Daughter |
| 12 | 11 | 9 | 7 | 6 | 5 | 2 |

Medical: Father, 34, appendectomy since migration. Episodic
epigastric pain, ulcer not demonstrated. Mother, 32, ascaris in childhood, no parasites demonstrated currently.
Hypertrophied tonsils. Appendectomy during fifth pregnancy.
Post-partum tubal ligation for multiparity. Son, 12, thumb
sucking. Hypertrophied tonsils. Son, 11, thumb sucking.
Hypertrophied tonsils. Internal strabismus. Daughter, 9,
thumb sucking. Hypertrophied tonsils. Daughter, 7, thumb
sucking. Hypertrophied tonsils. Daughter, 6, NFTSD.
Thumb sucking. Hypertrophied tonsils. Son, 5, NFTSD.
Thumb sucking. Hypertrophied tonsils. Daughter, 2, NFTSD.
Well baby. Hypertrophied tonsils.

Hospitalization: "Too busy to go to clinic." Children have frequent respiratory infections treated at home or in emergency room.

Migration: Father and mother as adults with three children.

Physical Characteristics: Color predominantly white to light
olive, hair straight to wavy, Caucasoid features.

Housing: Three rooms for nine people. No bath, no central
heating. On file for project three years.

English: Father adequate. Mother and younger children poor.
Older children bilingual.

Education: Father high school complete Puerto Rico. Mother
and son, 12, in health class. Son, 11, also underweight, not
in health class.

Employment: Father hotel trade, periodic layoffs.

Welfare: Partial.

Family Type: Nuclear family with own children. Dominating father, permissive mother.

Religion: Roman Catholic.

Observations: Presence of hypertrophied tonsils and frequent tonsillitis in mother and all children in large family living in crowded quarters is not surprising. Thumb sucking persists in twelve-year-old child and is prominent in all but youngest.

FAMILY 37

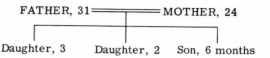

FATHER, 31 ══════════ MOTHER, 24

Daughter, 3   Daughter, 2   Son, 6 months

Medical: Father, 31, abdominal surgery Puerto Rico following stabbing. Right hydrocele. Mother, 24, abortion, probably induced, recently. Daughter, 3, NFTSD. Tonsillitis at
1. Daughter, 2, NFTSD. Well baby. Son, 6 months, NFTSD.
Well baby.

Hospitalization: All children taken regularly to well baby
clinic.

Migration: Father and mother as single young adults.

Physical Characteristics: Light olive to white color. Hair
wavy. Caucasoid features.

Housing: Two rooms for five people. No separate bath. No
central heating.

English: Father adequate. Mother making great progress.

Education: Father and mother grade school incomplete Puerto
Rico.

Employment: Father skilled mechanic steadily employed.
Mother occasionally employed in factory.

Welfare: No record.

Family Type: Nuclear with own children. Father supports
child of previous union and has extramarital affairs.

Religion: Roman Catholic.

Observations: Young family struggling with problem of man's
extramarital affairs.

FAMILY 38

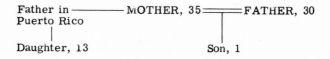

Father in ——————— MOTHER, 35 ══════ FATHER, 30
Puerto Rico
Daughter, 13   Son, 1

Medical: Father, 30, healthy male. Mother, 35, syphilis
treated and cured. Obese. Edentulous. Arthritis right el-
bow. Daughter, 13, congenital syphilis treated. Severe myopia. Mentally retarded. Son, 1, NFTSD. Healthy child.
Hospitalization: Syphilis adequately treated.
Migration: Father as single adult. Mother with man of pre-
vious union.
Physical Characteristics: Mother and children dark brown in
color, kinky hair, Negroid features. Father light brown in
color, curly hair, Caucasoid features.
Housing: Four people in three rooms. No separate bath. Cen-
tral heating.
English: Father adequate. Mother and daughter fair.
Education: Parents grade school incomplete Puerto Rico.
Daughter cannot read or write.
Employment: Father steadily employed light factory work.
Welfare: No record.
Family Type: Father previously married to woman older than
himself, now trying to get divorce in order to marry mother
of this only son, age 1. Mother has had two previous consen-
sual unions and other children.
Religion: Roman Catholic.
Observations: Apparently no dissension in current family set-
up. Mother not concerned over retardation of daughter, who
takes good care of baby.

273

FAMILY 39

FATHER, 53 ══════╤══════ MOTHER, 50

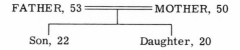

Son, 22   Daughter, 20

Medical: Father, 53, not examined. Mother, 50, not examined.
Son, 22, two attacks of rheumatic fever and rheumatic heart
disease in childhood. Tonsillectomy performed later. Obesity developed in adolescence to date. Rheumatic heart disease inactive. Mitral stenosis and insufficiency currently.
Daughter, 20, mastoiditis with mastoidectomy in childhood.
Infected wound right foot recently.

Hospitalization: Son with rheumatic fever attended hospital
and clinic regularly since age 4 and spent three years in
cardiac convalescent home.

Migration: Father and mother 1928 as young adults. All children born Manhattan.

Physical Characteristics: Color predominantly light olive,
hair wavy, features Caucasoid.

Housing: Four rooms for four people with bath and central
heating.

English: Mother and father adequate. Daughter and son bilingual.

Education: Mother and father not recorded. Son, 22, high
school graduate United States. Daughter high school incomplete.

Employment: Father and son regularly employed.

Welfare: No record.

Family Type: Father and mother live in neighborhood. Daughter married recently and lives in neighborhood. Son married non-Puerto Rican and lives in South.

Religion: Daughter and son Protestant. Parents not recorded.

Observations: Son on return from convalescent home became identified with Protestant group, breaking away from Puerto Ricans, later leaving neighborhood for another city, where he married a non-Puerto Rican. In contrast, sister married Puerto Rican in neighborhood.

FAMILY 40

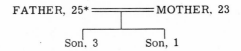

FATHER, 25* ══════ MOTHER, 23

Son, 3   Son, 1

Medical: Father, 25, episodic epigastric pain, no ulcer demonstrated. Mother, 23, healthy. Son, 3, scarlet fever, bron-
chitis, otitis media age 2. Son, 1, otitis media age 1.
Hospitalization: For children's illnesses. Would appreciate
pediatric care by own physician.
Migration: Entire family born in the neighborhood.
Physical Characteristics: Father light olive in color, hair
straight, Caucasoid features. Mother and children light
brown in color, hair kinky, Negroid features.
Housing: Two rooms for four people, bath and central heating.
English: Bilingual.
Education: Father completed high school Manhattan under G.I.
bill. Mother high school complete Manhattan.
Employment: Father mechanic. Mother works when he is laid
off.
Welfare: No record.
Family Type: Nuclear family with own children closely asso-
ciated with grandmothers on both sides.
Religion: Protestant.
Observations: Couple under 30 of Puerto Rican parentage
born in neighborhood continuing to live there in order to
remain close to own parents.

───────

*Son of first marriage in Family 66.

FAMILY 41

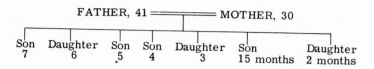

FATHER, 41 ══════╤══════ MOTHER, 30

| Son 7 | Daughter 6 | Son 5 | Son 4 | Daughter 3 | Son 15 months | Daughter 2 months |

Medical: Father, 41, fall at work five years ago, no pathology lumbar spine found. Moderate narrowing mid-portion both sacroiliac joints by X-ray. Mother, 30, polydactylism. Son, 7, beefy tongue. Daughter, 6, carious teeth. No other apparent defects. Pertussis age 4. Son, 5, beefy tongue. Son, 4, NFTSD. Beefy tongue. Daughter, 3, NFTSD. Beefy tongue. Son, 15 months, NFTSD. Stomatitis. Daughter, 2 months, NFTSD. Normal baby.

Hospitalization: No hospitalizations except for delivery. Outpatient departments have declared father employable.

Migration: Father as young adult went back and forth several times. Mother with three eldest children arrived five years ago.

Physical Characteristics: Predominantly light olive in color, hair wavy, Caucasoid features.

Housing: Three rooms for nine people. No bath. Central heating.

English: Mother and father poor to none. Father going to English school in Manhattan. Two oldest children adequate. Younger children not recorded.

Education: Father and mother grade school incomplete Puerto Rico.

Employment: Father, employed in small business enterprise in Puerto Rico, unemployed since fall which occurred at work.

Welfare: Past five years.

Family Type: Nuclear with own children.

Religion: Roman Catholic and Pentecostal.

Observations: Father has not been employed since accident and demonstrates to physician his inability to walk. Lack of specific trade, age, poor English, and hopes of large compensation settlement combine to make this man probably unemployable.

FAMILY 42

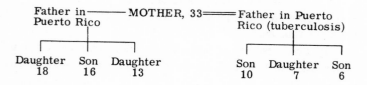

Father in———— MOTHER, 33====Father in Puerto
Puerto Rico   Rico (tuberculosis)

Daughter   Son   Daughter   Son   Daughter   Son
   18   16   13   10   7   6

Medical: Father of younger children was hospitalized for tuberculosis on arrival. Now cured and living in Puerto Rico. No evidence of active tuberculosis in mother and children. Mother, 33, frequent migraine headaches. Dizzy and nauseated. Daughter, 18, dysmenorrhea. Hookworm treated. Infected ear lobe. Became pregnant and married past year. Son, 16, not examined. Daughter, 13, hookworm treated. Son, 10, atopic dermatitis "delicado." Hookworm treated. Daughter, 7, NFTSD. Tonsillectomy four years ago. Son, 6, NFTSD. Hyperactive, poor eater, "bravo."

Hospitalization: No hospitalizations outside of normal deliveries.

Migration: Mother, father of younger children, and three older children ten years ago.

Physical Characteristics: Mother light olive in color, wavy hair, Caucasoid features. Father of older children said to be Negro—these are noticeably dark brown in color, with kinky hair and Negroid features, in contrast to three younger, who resemble mother.

Housing: Originally three rooms, including kitchen, for seven people, with no bath and no central heating. Later family moved to six-room apartment in cleaner building near by, a fourth-floor walk-up with central heating and no bath.

English: Mother fair. Children bilingual.

Education: Mother grade school incomplete Puerto Rico.

279

Daughter, 18, left high school in New York to get married and lives near by. Others satisfactory.

Employment: Mother does not work.

Welfare: One year after migration to date.

Family Type: Mother and father of younger children came to New York with three children of mother's previous consensual union and since his institutionalization she has lived alone with the children, of whom there are now five at home since eldest daughter's marriage.

Religion: Roman Catholic.

Observations: Mother compulsive neat woman for whom poor housing conditions were very stressful. Successful adaptation of family without male figure to support by Welfare.

FAMILY 43

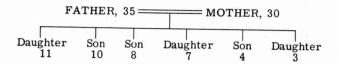

FATHER, 35 ══════ MOTHER, 30

| Daughter | Son | Son | Daughter | Son | Daughter |
| 11 | 10 | 8 | 7 | 4 | 3 |

Medical: Father, 35, not examined. Mother, 30, no major illnesses. Post-partum tubal ligation. Daughter, 11, pertussis in Puerto Rico. Athlete's foot. Son, 10, pertussis in Puerto Rico. Athlete's foot. Son, 8, tonsils hypertrophied. Daughter, 7, tonsils hypertrophied. Otitis media at age 5. Son, 4, tonsils hypertrophied. Otitis media at age 4. Daughter, 3, NFTSD. Acute enteritis paratyphoid B at age 1, cured.

Hospitalization: Post-partum tubal ligation in private hospital by private physician, cost $225.00. No major illnesses except for youngest daughter.

Migration: Mother came first with children five years ago. Father followed a few months later.

Physical Characteristics: Father light olive in color, curly hair, Caucasoid features. Mother light brown in color, curly hair, Caucasoid features. Children light olive to dark in color, wavy hair, Caucasoid features.

Housing: In 1955 moved on own initiative to six-room apartment in Brooklyn, paying $1,200.00 for "furniture" and $50.00 monthly rent.

English: Father fluent, mother fair, older children bilingual.

Education: Father grade school complete. Mother grade school incomplete Puerto Rico.

Employment: Father skilled machine-tool operator steadily employed at $80.00 a week.

Welfare: No record.

Family Type: Nuclear family with own children.
Religion: Roman Catholic and Protestant.
Observations: Regularly employed father, skilled workman, under 40, almost white, favor upward mobility of family.

FAMILY 44

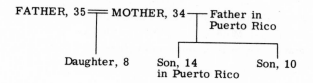

FATHER, 35 ⚌ MOTHER, 34 — Father in
Puerto Rico

Daughter, 8   Son, 14   Son, 10
            in Puerto Rico

Medical: Father, 35, appendectomy recently. Weekend drinker.
Mother, 34, weight 94 pounds. Vitamin B deficiency. Many
gastrointestinal complaints, no definite diagnosis. Anxious.
Son, 10, bronchitis 1953. Enuresis, thumbsucking. Inatten-
tive, hyperactive in school. Vitamin B deficiency. Daughter,
8, NFTSD. No enuresis. Feeding problem. Follow up fall
1956: Son, 10, spent summer in Puerto Rico with father.
Returned with older brother to spend winter with mother
and stepfather. Father, mother, daughter hospitalized for
acute food poisoning during summer. Son, 14, fine teeth.
No intestinal parasites. Gained 5 pounds in two months
after arrival in the United States.

Hospitalization: Sporadic and in emergencies.

Migration: Ten years ago.

Physical Characteristics: Father, mother, daughter light to
dark olive in color, hair wavy, Caucasoid features. Sons
light brown in color, hair kinky, Caucasoid features.

Housing: Three rooms for four people. No bath. Central
heating.

English: Father adequate, mother fair, children adequate.

Education: Mother and father grade school incomplete.

Employment: Father light factory subject to layoff. Mother
intermittent.

Welfare: Applied for and accepted at time of father's illness.
Closed several months later. Family reemployed.

Family Type: Nuclear family with own child and one or two children of mother's previous marriage.

Religion: Roman Catholic and Protestant.

Observations: Mother immature and anxious, with many complaints, has frequent quarrels with husband.

FAMILY 45

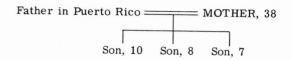

Father in Puerto Rico ══╤══ MOTHER, 38

Son, 10   Son, 8   Son, 7

Medical: Mother, 38, chronic rhinitis. Palpitations, weakness, pain on swallowing, insomnia, diagnosed euthyroid. Son, 10, pruritis. Pharyngitis. Mantoux positive-satisfactory periodic chest X-rays 1949 to date. Son, 8, hospitalized for tuberculosis thirty-three months, now arrested. Severe behavior problem on return from hospital. Ringworm of scalp. Nose fracture. Son, 7, hospitalized for tuberculosis twelve months, now arrested. Leg pain, etiology undetermined. Walked at 2, enuresis until 5. Frequent abdominal pain, undiagnosed etiology.

Hospitalization: Cluster of clinic visits by mother at time of husband's desertion. Hospitalizations as above.

Migration: Mother and father with first-born infant.

Physical Characteristics: Color predominantly light olive. Hair wavy. Caucasoid features.

Housing: Moved to housing project. From rooming house to three-room apartment to housing project over course of ten years.

English: Mother fair. Sons bilingual.

Education: Mother not recorded.

Employment: Mother does not work.

Welfare: Since father's desertion.

Family Type: Father returned to Puerto Rico in October, 1952, applying for divorce. Mother living alone with three sons.

Religion: Protestant.

Observations: Tuberculosis contact in rooming house year following migration. Hospitalization of son, 8, from age 2 1/2 to 5, second son, 7, from age 6 months to 18 months. Chronic marital difficulties culminating in father's desertion, mother's illness, and severe behavior problem of son, 8.

FAMILY 46

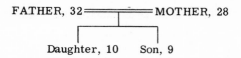

FATHER, 32 ══════ MOTHER, 28

Daughter, 10   Son, 9

Medical: Father, 32, syphilis in youth, cured. Respiratory infections, headache, chest pain, rhinitis since marriage. Mother, 28, pneumonia age 4. Otitis in childhood. Vague gastrointestinal complaints since marriage. Three induced abortions. Daughter, 10, NFTSD. Frequent colds. Son, 9, NFTSD. Otitis age 2-5.

Hospitalization: Family use private physician for minor ailments of children, voluntary hospital for delivery.

Migration: Mother and father born in New York of parents migrating before 1930. Children also born in New York.

Physical Characteristics: Color white.

Housing: Four rooms in one of better buildings, now moved.

English: All bilingual.

Education: Parents high school graduates.

Employment: Father skilled machinist with $70.00 a week take-home pay, now steadily employed. Mother intermittently employed in clerical job.

Welfare: No record.

Family Type: Stable couple with own children.

Religion: Protestant.

Observations: Young couple of Puerto Rican parentage who have delayed move to better neighborhood in order to remain near parents, his mother and her widowed grandmother, age 72. Marital relations have been strained when the father was unsteadily employed.

FAMILY 47

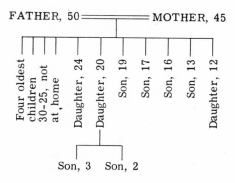

FATHER, 50 ══════ MOTHER, 45

Four oldest children 30-25, not at home | Daughter, 24 | Daughter, 20 | Son, 19 | Son, 17 | Son, 16 | Son, 13 | Daughter, 12

Son, 3   Son, 2

Medical: Father, 50, pneumonia age 18. Committed to state
institution for alcoholism with psychotic reactions twenty
years ago. Acute pyelonephritis and benign prostatic hypertrophy ten years ago. Regional ileitis and resection of
terminal ileum one year ago. Mother, 45, post-partum hemorrhage after last delivery. Four oldest children, 30-25, not
examined. Daughter, 24, drug addict since age 18. Under psychiatric care. Daughter, 20, rheumatic fever in childhood.
Son, 19, in Army, not examined. Son, 17, rheumatic heart
disease ten years ago. Treated in psychiatric out-patient department for two years, now discharged. Son, 16, eczema
age 1. Burns on legs age 4. Epilepsy age 10. Son, 13, no major illness or hospital record. Daughter, 12, severe eczema
after birth. Under care psychiatric clinic past three years.
Grandson, 3, apparently healthy. Grandson, 2, apparently
healthy.

Hospitalization: All dated illnesses above involve admission
to hospital.

Migration: Father as young adult. Mother as school girl. All
children born in the United States.

288

Physical Characteristics: Color white to light olive. Hair fine, curly. Caucasoid features.

Housing: Three rooms. No bath. Central heating.

English: Parents bilingual. Younger children speak no Spanish. Others poorly.

Education: Father and mother not recorded. Daughter, 24, in state training school for delinquents age 16. Son, 16, no school five years because of epilepsy. Illiterate. Daughter, 12, suspended because of slapping teacher and pupils. No child went beyond grammar school.

Employment: Father hotel industry steady past ten years except for illness, irregular formerly.

Welfare: Family have been known to Department for twenty-three years and have received help during half of this period. Daughter, 20, now deserted, also receiving public assistance for her children.

Family Type: Older children have left home, but daughter deserted by her husband has returned with two children.

Religion: Roman Catholic.

Observations: Family with the greatest number of problems and the longest dependency record in series. Compare with Family 20 for similar situation in recent migrant.

FAMILY 48

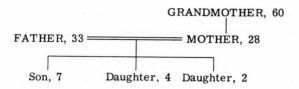

GRANDMOTHER, 60

FATHER, 33 ══════════ MOTHER, 28

Son, 7   Daughter, 4   Daughter, 2

Medical: Grandmother, 60, arteriosclerotic heart disease,
mild. Tension headaches, improved. Father, 33, episodic
epigastric pain. Spasticity duodenal bulb by X-ray, no ulcer
crater seen on two examinations. Mother, 28, frequent tonsillitis, cryptic tonsils. Tonsillectomy age 26, improved.
Spontaneous abortion age 27. Son, 7, hypertrophied tonsils.
Vomits easily. Hookworm treated. Daughter, 4, pharyngitis
age 2, "delicada." Daughter, 2, respiratory infection and
diarrhea age 1.

Hospitalization: Spasmodic.

Migration: Father first ten years ago. Returned to Puerto
Rico. Later migration with family four years ago.

Physical Characteristics: Color predominantly light olive to
white. Hair curly. Caucasoid features.

Housing: Moved on own initiative in 1956 to five-room apartment in neighborhood with bath and central heating. Formerly three rooms for six people with no bath and no central
heating.

English: Father adequate. Grandmother none. Mother and
younger children fair to poor. Son, 7, bilingual.

Education: Father high school incomplete. Mother and grandmother grade school incomplete Puerto Rico.

Employment: Father steadily in hotel trade.

Welfare: No record.

Family Type: Nuclear with own children plus maternal grandmother.

Religion: Roman Catholic.

Observations: Father, ambitious, has gastrointestinal symptoms associated with stress, accepts reassurance. Upward
mobility has started with move to better quarters.

FAMILY 49

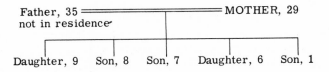

Father, 35 ══════════════════ MOTHER, 29
not in residence

Daughter, 9   Son, 8   Son, 7   Daughter, 6   Son, 1

Medical: Mother, 29, photophobia, conjunctivitis. Obese, 5
feet, 150 pounds. Edentulous. Spontaneous abortion age 26.
Daughter, 9, hit by car year of migration, no fracture. Son,
8, tonsillitis age 7. Son, 7, hospitalized for measles and
bronchopneumonia year of migration. Daughter, 6, otitis
age 5. Son, 1, NFTSD. Otitis age 1.

Hospitalization: Apparently few illnesses or clinic visits.

Migration: Mother and father six years ago. Children following year.

Physical Characteristics: Mother light olive in color, hair
wavy, Caucasoid features. Children dark olive in color,
hair kinky, Negroid features.

Housing: Three rooms for six people. No bath. Central
heating.

English: Mother fair, children bilingual.

Education: Mother grade school incomplete Puerto Rico. Children satisfactory.

Employment: Mother does not work. Separated husband contributes irregularly.

Welfare: Since father deserted.

Family Type: Woman, separated from common-law husband,
with five small children. Her sister and parents live in
same building.

Religion: Roman Catholic.

Observations: Father has visiting privileges. Children live in
large part with mother's relations in same building. Apparently few illnesses.

FAMILY 50

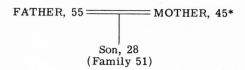

FATHER, 55 ════╤════ MOTHER, 45*

Son, 28
(Family 51)

Medical: Father, 55, chronic simple schizophrenia. Malnu-
trition. Mother, 45, no major illnesses. Vascular headaches, occasional gastrointestinal disturbance.

Hospitalization: Father never hospitalized. No medical service beyond that provided by family clinic.

Migration: Mother and father as single young adults.

Physical Characteristics: Father cachectic, color white; curly
black hair, Caucasoid features. Mother sturdy, brown skin,
straight hair, Negroid features.

Housing: Three rooms for two people. No bath. Central
heating.

English: Father adequate. Mother none.

Education: Father high school complete Puerto Rico. Mother
grade school incomplete Puerto Rico.

Employment: Father formerly in hotel industry. Mother formerly employed in neighborhood cleaning establishment, now
tends children. Son contributes.

Welfare: No record.

Family Type: Middle-aged couple with one son who is now married and lives in Brooklyn.

Religion: Roman Catholic.

Observations: Father spends entire time indoors caring for
canary and writing poetry. Mother visits with neighbors,
and the two rarely speak to each other.

———
*Sister of woman in Family 69.

FAMILY 51

FATHER, 28* ══════════ MOTHER, 26

Son, 1

Medical: Father, 28, chronic and acute bronchial asthma improved. Mother, 26, two induced abortions in previous marriage. Son, 1, NFTSD. Healthy.

Hospitalization: Before marriage father went to emergency room several times weekly for treatment of asthma; now no longer.

Migration: All born in Manhattan.

Physical Characteristics: Father light brown in color. Hair curly. Caucasoid features. Mother white, hair bleached blonde, Caucasoid features. Son light olive in color.

Housing: Brooklyn since marriage.

English: Both bilingual.

Education: Both high school graduates Manhattan. Father one year university in Puerto Rico.

Employment: Father office worker, steady. Mother saleswoman in Park Avenue dress shop before pregnancy.

Welfare: No record.

Family Type: Nuclear family with own child. Child of mother's previous marriage cared for by relatives.

Religion: Protestant.

Observations: Young couple born in neighborhood of Puerto Rican parents struggling to get into American middle class.

_____

*Son of couple in Family 50.

FAMILY 52

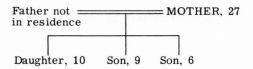

Father not ══════════ MOTHER, 27
in residence

Daughter, 10   Son, 9   Son, 6

Medical: Mother, 27, syphilis and parasites treated in Puerto
Rico, cured. Palpitations, easy fatigability, anxious.
Daughter, 10, ascaris treated since migration, "delicada."
Pertussis in Puerto Rico. Son, 9, alopecia aerata. Head-
aches, 20/20 vision. Son, 6, scarlet fever first year after
migration. Ascaris treated since migration.
Hospitalization: Limited to emergencies.
Migration: Mother left common-law husband who did not sup-
port her to join her own mother in New York five years ago.
Physical Characteristics: Mother pale olive in color, hair
kinky, Negroid features. Children dark olive in color, hair
kinky, Negroid features.
Housing: Three rooms. No bath. Central heating.
English: Mother fair. Children bilingual.
Education: Mother grade school incomplete Puerto Rico.
Employment: Mother worked a few months after arrival.
Welfare: Since mother stopped working.
Family Type: Woman living with children and no mate.
Religion: Roman Catholic.
Observations: Mother migrated with children hoping to better
her lot, appears frustrated by inability to work and become
independent of Welfare.

FAMILY 53

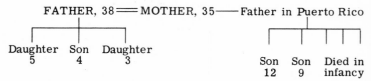

FATHER, 38 ═══ MOTHER, 35 ──── Father in Puerto Rico

Daughter   Son   Daughter
5   4   3

Son   Son   Died in
12   9   infancy

Medical: Father, 38, asthma for twenty years. Passive, dependent. Gastrointestinal complaints, no pathology discovered. Mother, 35, anorexia, loss of weight, dyspareunia,
frequent colds, anxious. Varicose veins age 28. Vaginal
hysterectomy and anterior posterior colporrhaphy age 32.
Conversion hysteria age 34. Diagnostic curettage age 35
for menorrhagia. Son, 12, tonsillectomy first year after
migration Frequent respiratory infections every winter.
Son, 9, frequent asthma and tonsillitis. Daughter, 5, NFTSD.
Bronchopneumonia twice in first year of life. Frequent tonsillitis every winter. Hepatitis age 5. Son, 4, bronchopneumonia first and second years of life. Frequent asthma.
Daughter, 3, bronchopneumonia first year of life. Frequent
asthma.

Hospitalization: Greater number of recorded episodes of illness and visits to clinic than any other family in study.

Migration: Father nine years ago. Mother with sons of previous union following year.

Physical Characteristics: Color predominantly light olive.
Hair straight. Caucasoid features.

Housing: Housing project 1955. Formerly rooming house,
then two rooms for seven people, with central heating and
no bath.

English: Father fair. Mother adequate. Older children bilingual.

296

Education: Father grade school incomplete Puerto Rico.
Mother high school incomplete Puerto Rico.

Employment: Father has worked only a few months for past twenty years. Mother occasionally employed light factory work.

Welfare: Since mother arrived with children.

Family Type: Nuclear family with own children and those of mother's previous union.

Religion: Roman Catholic.

Observations: Both parents suffer from neuroses of long standing, panic in face of children's frequent episodes of illness, and have become increasingly dependent on hospital personnel.

FAMILY 54

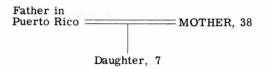

Father in
Puerto Rico ═══════════ MOTHER, 38

Daughter, 7

Medical: Mother, 38, carcinoma cervix grade 2 diagnosed in
Puerto Rico, treated with radiation and hysterectomy in New
York. Final diagnosis carcinoma cervix in situ. No metastases. Daughter, 7, pertussis before migration. Mastur-
bates, nonspecific vaginitis. Anxious, enuresis.

Hospitalization: Carcinoma treated in municipal hospital.

Migration: Two years ago to seek treatment for carcinoma.

Physical Characteristics: Obese mother and child. Color
white. Hair straight. Caucasoid features.

Housing: Two rooms. No bath. Central heating.

English: Mother poor. Daughter fair.

Education: Mother not recorded.

Employment: Mother has not worked in New York.

Welfare: Since arrival.

Family Type: Woman with one child and no mate.

Religion: Protestant.

Observations: While carcinoma has been adequately treated,
woman's anxiety and bewilderment persist and foster similar feelings in child. Panic à deux.

FAMILY 55

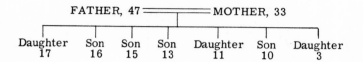

FATHER, 47 ══════════ MOTHER, 33

Daughter	Son	Son	Son	Daughter	Son	Daughter
17	16	15	13	11	10	3

Medical: Father, 47, urinary infection normal kidneys by X-ray. Mother, 33, stillbirth. Tubal ligation with Cesarean section three years ago. Daughter, 17, otitis. Son, 16, not examined, no hospital record. Son, 15, otitis one year after migration. Son, 13, apparently healthy. Daughter, 11, pertussis one year after migration. Son, 10, measles one year after migration. Daughter, 3, Cesarean, birth weight 5 pounds, 10 1/2 ounces. Bronchitis in first year of life.

Hospitalization: Hospitalization for all recorded illnesses one year after migration and for delivery.

Migration: Entire family, except youngest, five years ago.

Physical Characteristics: Not recorded.

Housing: Formerly three rooms for nine people. No bath. Central heating. Moved in past year and could not be located.

English: Not recorded.

Education: Not recorded.

Employment: Father in hotel industry.

Welfare: Hospital records indicate supplementary allowance for large family since one year after migration.

Family Type: Nuclear with own children.

Religion: Roman Catholic.

Observations: Apparently good health record following many illnesses in first year of migration. Study incomplete as family moved and could not be found.

FAMILY 56

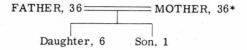

FATHER, 36 ══════ MOTHER, 36*

Daughter, 6   Son, 1

Medical: Father, 36, bilateral pterygia. Essential hyper-
tension (mild). Mother, 36, ascaris treated in Puerto Rico.
Daughter, 6, occasional tonsillitis. Son, 1, NFTSD. Well.
Hospitalization: For delivery only and well baby clinic.
Migration: Father, mother, and daughter four years ago.
Physical Characteristics: Color primarily light olive, hair
straight, Caucasoid features.
Housing: Three rooms for family and one or two transient
relatives.
English: Father and mother adequate.
Education: Father and mother grade school incomplete Puerto
Rico.
Employment: Father steady office building superintendent.
Mother intermittent factory work.
Welfare: No record.
Family Type: Nuclear with own children.
Religion: Protestant.
Observations: Family ambitious to "get ahead," do not wish
more children.

---

*Younger sister of woman in Family 70.

FAMILY 57

FATHER, 27════════MOTHER, 24
|
Daughter, 1

Medical: Father, 27, tonsillitis 1951. Frequent respiratory
infections. Mother, 24, periodic epigastric pain, no pathology demonstrated by X-ray. Daughter, 1, NFTSD. Tantrums. No major illness.

Hospitalization: Father in Army hospital overseas. Mother
sporadic visits to clinics. Daughter health station.

Migration: Father and mother as single adolescents.

Physical Characteristics: Father dark olive in color, hair
wavy, Caucasoid features. Mother dark brown in color, hair
kinky, Negroid features. Daughter dark olive in color, hair
kinky, Negroid features.

Housing: Three rooms for three people. No bath. Central
heating.

English: Father and mother bilingual.

Education: Father high school incomplete Puerto Rico. Mother
high school complete Manhattan.

Employment: Father shipping clerk. Mother would-be night
club singer.

Welfare: No record.

Family Type: Nuclear with own child.

Religion: Roman Catholic.

Observations: Parents migrated as adolescents and man had
two years overseas in Army. No major illnesses, but
mother's frustrated ambitions as a singer and father's buying car on time and wrecking it are subjects of dissension.

FAMILY 58

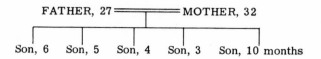

FATHER, 27 ══════ MOTHER, 32

Son, 6   Son, 5   Son, 4   Son, 3   Son, 10 months

Medical: Father, 27, tonsillectomy age 24, week-end drinker.
Mother, 32, dental caries, anxious, cries easily. Son, 6,
NFTSD. Tonsils hypertrophied. Son, 5, NFTSD. Tonsils
hypertrophied. Son, 4, NFTSD. Tonsillectomy 1954. Son, 3,
NFTSD. Tonsils hypertrophied. Impetigo last year. Son,
10 months, NFTSD. Healthy.

Hospitalization: No hospital admission except for tonsillectomies and deliveries. Few clinic visits.

Migration: Father single adolescent. Mother young adult.

Physical Characteristics: Father and mother white in color,
hair blond, Caucasoid features. Children light olive in
color, brown straight hair, Caucasoid features.

Housing: Four rooms. No bath. No central heating.

English: Father and mother adequate.

Education: Father grade school complete Puerto Rico. Mother
grade school incomplete Puerto Rico.

Employment: Father steadily employed as painter.

Welfare: No record.

Family Type: Nuclear with own children. Mother's sister
and brother-in-law live in same building.

Religion: Roman Catholic.

Observations: Principal problem appears to be father's philandering, to which mother reacts with tears and scenes.

302

FAMILY 59

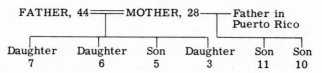

FATHER, 44 ===== MOTHER, 28 ———— Father in
Puerto Rico

| Daughter | Daughter | Son | Daughter | Son | Son |
| 7 | 6 | 5 | 3 | 11 | 10 |

Medical: Father, 44, bronchopneumonia age 40. Normal
male. Mother, 28, varicose veins. Post-partum tubal ligation, anorexia, weight loss, abdominal pain, no pathology
found recent hospital admission. Son, 11, old burn scar
abdomen. Son, 10, perforation right drum. Daughter, 7,
premature, mentally retarded, history of seizures. Esopho-
ria left eye with lateral nystagmus both eyes 1955. Normal electroencephalogram. Healed primary tuberculosis
1955. Herpetic stomatitis. Daughter, 6, frequent tonsillitis
and otitis. Son, 5, otitis 1951. Gastroenteritis 1953. Frequent tonsillitis. Daughter, 3, frequent tonsillitis and
otitis.

Hospitalization: Mentally retarded daughter institutionalized
for a brief period in 1953. Clinic and hospital shopping
since then. Others emergency ambulance calls.

Migration: Father and mother as young adults. Sons by first
marriage arrived from Puerto Rico one fall and returned
following spring.

Physical Characteristics: Color predominantly light olive.
Hair wavy to kinky. Caucasoid features.

Housing: Four rooms for eight people. No bath. Central
heating.

English: Mother and father bilingual. Sons fair to adequate.
Daughter, 7, poor. Younger children bilingual.

Education: Father and mother grade school incomplete.

Employment: Father steady restaurant business. Mother child tending intermittently.

Welfare: Six months while sons from first marriage were in New York. Now closed.

Family Type: Nuclear family with own children and children from mother's previous marriage. Couple not legally married due to lack of divõrce documents.

Religion: Protestant.

Observations: Mother guilty and unhappy over retarded child for whom she refuses institutional care. Impulsive, inconsistent discipline, and disorderly home.

FAMILY 60

HUSBAND, 52 ══════ WIFE, 61

Medical: Husband, 52, gonorrhea as young man. Rheumatoid-osteoarthritis knees and ankles severe. Pneumonia age 50. Wife, 61, tonsils hypertrophied. Ruptured appendix and hysterectomy age 40.

Hospitalization: Couple disregards doctor's instructions and makes very limited use of medical facilities.

Migration: Husband and wife as young adults before 1930.

Physical Characteristics: Husband dark brown in color, hair kinky, Negroid features. Wife white in color, hair straight, Caucasoid features.

Housing: Three rooms. Bath. Central heating.

English: Husband bilingual. Wife none.

Education: Husband not recorded. Wife no schooling.

Employment: Husband steadily employed in factory except when acutely ill. Wife takes care of children occasionally.

Welfare: No record.

Family Type: Childless couple.

Religion: Roman Catholic.

Observations: White woman married to Negro man. Early history not obtainable. Both proud not to be on Welfare.

305

FAMILY 61

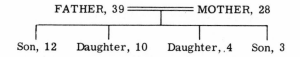

FATHER, 39 ══════ MOTHER, 28

Son, 12   Daughter, 10   Daughter, 4   Son, 3

Medical: Father, 39, gonorrhea ten years ago. Cured. Healthy.
Mother, 28, post-partum tubal ligation in Puerto Rico.
Wrist fracture recently. Obese, anxious. Son, 12, possible
coarctation of aorta not investigated. Daughter, 10, bronchitis age 5. Daughter, 4, NFTSD, frequent tonsillitis. Son, 3,
frequent tonsillitis and otitis.

Hospitalization: Sporadic by mother, who also uses many patent medicines and herbs.

Migration: Father after World War II. Mother and children
following year. Daughter, 10, has been back several times
to Puerto Rico. Youngest son born in Puerto Rico where
mother returned to obtain post-partum ligation.

Physical Characteristics: All are light to dark brown in color
with Negroid features and kinky hair.

Housing: Three rooms for five people. No bath, no central
heating.

English: Father bilingual. Mother and daughter, 10, fair.
Son, 12, bilingual.

Education: Father not recorded. Mother grade school incomplete Puerto Rico.

Employment: Father steady merchant seaman.

Welfare: No record.

Family Type: Nuclear with own children.

Religion: Mother practices spiritualism. Father opposed to
this. Son, 12, Protestant.

306

Observations: Mother very anxious, impulsively asks help in various directions, including spiritualists. Considers herself a medium.

FAMILY 62

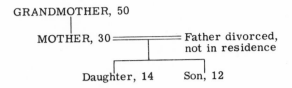

GRANDMOTHER, 50

MOTHER, 30 ══════ Father divorced, not in residence

Daughter, 14   Son, 12

Medical: Grandmother, 50, oophorectomy as young woman in Puerto Rico. Healthy. Mother, 30, headaches, palpitations, compulsive, gastrointestinal complaints. Daughter, 14, NFTSD. Behavior problem. Son, 12, NFTSD. Behavior problem.

Hospitalization: No record of hospitalization in past ten years.

Migration: Grandmother with mother as infant.

Physical Characteristics: Light to dark brown in color, hair kinky, Negroid features.

Housing: Three rooms. No central heating. No bath.

English: All bilingual.

Education: Grandmother one year high school Puerto Rico. Mother high school incomplete New York.

Employment: Grandmother steady light factory. Mother saleswoman.

Welfare: No record.

Family Type: Three generations living together under domination maternal grandmother.

Religion: Protestant.

Observations: Domination of maternal grandmother is resented by grandchildren who are behavior problems at school and mother reacts with many gastrointestinal complaints.

FAMILY 63

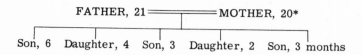

FATHER, 21 ══════════ MOTHER, 20*

Son, 6   Daughter, 4   Son, 3   Daughter, 2   Son, 3 months

Medical: Father, 21, loss of weight, easy fatigability, normal
chest X-ray. Mother, 20, tuberculous lymphadenitis age 15
and 16. Appendectomy age 16. Adhesions age 17. Oophori-
tis age 19. Headaches, weight gain, fatigue. Son, 6, furuncu-
losis age 1. Enuresis, feeding problem. Daughter, 4, pyloric
stenosis age 1. Repeated otitis. Son, 3, diarrhea (nonspecific) age 1. Frequent respiratory infections. Daughter,
2, frequent respiratory infections and diarrhea age 1.
Son, 3 months, NFTSD.

Hospitalization: Entire family checked for tuberculosis. Three
older children hospitalized within first year of life. Mother
seeking help from many sources.

Migration: Father as adolescent. Mother born in neighborhood.

Physical Characteristics: Color light olive, hair wavy to
straight, Caucasoid features.

Housing: Formerly two rooms for six people. No bath. Central heating. Moved out to New Jersey with maternal grandmother (Family 64).

English: Father adequate. Mother bilingual.

Education: Father high school incomplete Manhattan. Mother
one year high school Manhattan.

Employment: Father nonunion painter. Mother does not work.

Welfare: No record.

Family Type: Nuclear family with own children closely associated with maternal grandmother.

─────────

*Daughter of couple in Family 64.

Religion: Protestant.

Observations: Mother almost daily visitor to family clinic with children with many ailments. Marital and houskeeping problems.

FAMILY 64

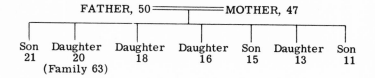

FATHER, 50 ══════════ MOTHER, 47

Son	Daughter	Daughter	Daughter	Son	Daughter	Son
21	20	18	16	15	13	11
	(Family 63)					

Medical: Father, 50, not examined. Mother, 47, 159 pounds, 52 inches. No major illness. Son, 21, committed to institution for delinquent boys age 14. Went West to work on farm. Daughter, 18, erythema nodosum age 13. Pregnant at 14. Daughter, 16, left-handed. Appendectomy age 14. Son, 15, no major illness. Daughter, 13, no major illness. Son, 11, struck by car, fracture humerus age 7.

Hospitalization: Hospitalizations for emergencies. Mother had home deliveries.

Migration: Parents as young adults. All children born Manhattan.

Physical Characteristics: Color light olive, hair straight, Caucasoid features.

Housing: Parents, eldest daughter (Family 63), and younger children recently moved to undeveloped community (no sewage or electricity) in New Jersey. Second daughter and her children living with in-laws in Ohio.

English: Father and mother adequate. Children bilingual.

Education: Parents not recorded. No children have gone beyond ninth grade. Daughter, 18, could not read on graduation from ninth grade.

Employment: Father steady hotel industry.

Welfare: No record.

Family Type: Nuclear family with own children.

311

Religion: Protestant.

Observations: Two daughters became pregnant under 16 years of age and son became delinquent. Home always disorganized and parents show little affection for their children.

FAMILY 65

MOTHER, 35══Husband in Puerto Rico

Son, 18

Medical: Mother, 35, train accident in Puerto Rico age 28.
No major illnesses. Reported weight gain 25 pounds since
migration. Son, 18, mild acne of face, no major illnesses.
Hospitalization: No clinic records found. Report occasional
service by private physician for respiratory infection.
Migration: Mother and son after World War II.
Physical Characteristics: Color light olive, hair straight,
Caucasoid features.
Housing: Three rooms for two people. No bath. Central
heating.
English: Mother poor. Son bilingual.
Education: Mother grade school incomplete Puerto Rico. Son
high school incomplete New York.
Employment: Mother and son factory workers.
Welfare: No record.
Family Type: Mother migrated with ten-year-old son and
second husband. Second husband left for Puerto Rico re-
cently. Neighbors report he drank and was abusive.
Religion: Roman Catholic.
Observations: Few illnesses reported. Family apparently able
to solve own problems.

FAMILY 66

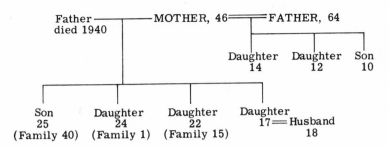

Medical: Father, 64, obese, hypertensive cardiovascular disease. Mother, 46, obese. Induced abortion ten years ago. Major respiratory infection recently. Daughter, 17, healthy. Husband of daughter, 18, not examined. Daughter, 14, NFTSD. Obese. No major illness. Daughter, 12, NFTSD. Obese. No major illness. Son, 10, NFTSD. Obese. Secondary anemia, slight. No major illness.

Hospitalization: Family uses clinics very little. Call local doctor in case of acute illness.

Migration: Mother and first husband as young adults. Father about fifteen years ago.

Physical Characteristics: Color light olive, hair straight, features Caucasoid.

Housing: Four rooms, bath, central heating, number of occupants variable.

English: Father none. Mother adequate. Children bilingual.

Education: Father never attended school. Mother grade school complete Puerto Rico. Daughter, 17, high school incomplete Manhattan.

Employment: Father steady, porter. Married daughter, 17, and her husband factory workers.

Welfare: No record.

Family Type: This family is center of an extended family involving mother's many relatives and married children who come in and out constantly and may take up residence for several months.

Religion: Protestant.

Observations: Mother and all children have rounded contour of endomorphs. Cluster of minor illnesses in an otherwise healthy family have been observed in times of stress, for example, following death of a favorite uncle.

FAMILY 67

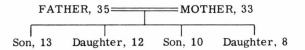

FATHER, 35══════════MOTHER, 33

Son, 13   Daughter, 12   Son, 10   Daughter, 8

Medical: Father, 35, fracture. Gross tremor of hands. Heavy
drinker past ten years. Mother, 33, post-partum tubal li-
gation Puerto Rico. Left shoulder pain. Secondary anemia.
Son, 13, no major illnesses. Daughter, 12, pertussis in
Puerto Rico. Son, 10, feeding problem, secondary anemia.
Trichuris in stool. Bilateral genu valgum. Daughter, 8,
bilateral genu valgum. Bilateral otitis media.
Hospitalization: No hospital admissions. Few clinic visits.
Migration: Entire family four years ago.
Physical Characteristics: Color light olive, hair straight,
Caucasoid features.
Housing: Three rooms for six people. No bath. Central
heating.
English: Father and children adequate. Mother poor.
Education: Father grade school incomplete Puerto Rico.
Mother no schooling.
Employment: Father steady restaurant industry. Mother does
not work.
Welfare: No record.
Family Type: Nuclear family with own children.
Religion: Roman Catholic. Children go to parochial school.
Observations: Drinking does not appear to interfere with
father's steady employment and his being a good provider.
Home appears stable and discipline consistent.

316

FAMILY 68

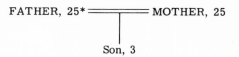

FATHER, 25* ═══════ MOTHER, 25

Son, 3

Medical: Father, 25, no major illness. Mother, 25, incomplete
abortion with D & C before birth of son. Prolonged labor.
Son, 3, frequent respiratory infections. Very apprehensive
of physicians.

Hospitalization: Child taken to pediatric clinic when necessary.

Migration: All born in the United States.

Physical Characteristics: Father and son light brown in color,
hair wavy, Caucasoid features. Mother white in color, hair
straight, Caucasoid features.

Housing: Three rooms for three people. Bath. Central
heating.

English: Parents bilingual. Son none.

Education: Father high school complete Manhattan. Mother
high school incomplete Manhattan. Child placed in nursery
school to learn English.

Employment: Father steady skilled toolmaker. Mother does
not work.

Welfare: No record.

Family Type: Nuclear family with own child with close association with extended family living in neighborhood.

Religion: Protestant.

Observations: Family have skills and economic potential to
move out of neighborhood but remain near relatives. Mother
wants no more children and regrets husband's not permitting
her to work.

_____

*Son of couple in Family 69.

FAMILY 69

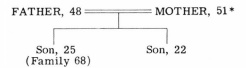

FATHER, 48 ========= MOTHER, 51*

Son, 25   Son, 22
(Family 68)

Medical: Father, 48, not examined. No hospital record. Mother, 51, ulcerative colitis, chronic. Obese. Menopausal depression age 45. Son, 22, drug addict, onset age 16. Several hospitalizations. Not improved.

Hospitalization: State hospital admission for depression. Continuing use of existing hospital facilities for treatment of drug addiction.

Migration: Parents as young adults. Sons born in Manhattan.

Physical Characteristics: Color light brown, hair wavy to straight, Caucasoid features.

Housing: Four rooms for three adults. Bath. Central heating.

English: Mother fair, improved to adequate in past two years. Others bilingual.

Education: Father high school incomplete Puerto Rico. Mother grade school incomplete Puerto Rico. Son high school incomplete Manhattan.

Employment: Father steady. Subway conductor same concern twenty years. Mother seasonal factory worker.

Welfare: No record.

Family Type: Nuclear family with adult son.

Religion: Protestant.

Observations: Mother's colitis has fluctuated with course of son's drug addiction.

---

*Sister of woman in Family 50.

FAMILY 70

Father in Puerto Rico ══╤══ MOTHER, 39*
┌─────────────┴─────────────┐
Daughter, 19   Daughter, 17

Medical: Mother, 39, fistula in ano and hemorrhoidectomy in
Puerto Rico. Chronic constipation and low back pain. Al-
lergic rhinitis. Daughter, 19, no major illnesses. Daughter,
17, no major illnesses.

Hospitalization: Mother underwent satisfactory check up at
cancer detection center. No clinic records on daughters.

Migration: Parents with teen-age daughters.

Physical Characteristics: Mother somewhat obese. Color
light olive, straight hair, Caucasoid features. Both girls
good posture, dark olive in color, kinky hair, Caucasoid
features.

Housing: Three rooms for three adults. No bath, no central
heating.

English: Mother fair. Daughters bilingual.

Education: Mother grade school incomplete. Daughter, 19,
high school complete Manhattan. Daughter, 17, hopes to
finish high school.

Employment: Mother and elder daughter factory workers.

Welfare: No record.

Family Type: Father has apparently returned to Puerto Rico.
Mother and adolescent daughters living together.

Religion: Protestant.

Observations: Family without a man functioning and self-
supporting. Mother does not consider symptoms incapacitating, and since anxiety was allayed by cancer study
declines medical care.

─────────

*Oldest sister of woman in Family 56.

FAMILY 71

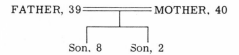

FATHER, 39 ══════ MOTHER, 40

Son, 8   Son, 2

Medical: Father, 39, no major illnesses. Healthy. Mother, 40,
120 pounds on migration, 186 pounds now. Two Cesarean
sections (borderline pelvis). Ventral hernia repaired with
recurrence two years later and postoperative infection of
wound. Son, 8, Cesarean birth. Obese. Tonsillectomy age
5. Son, 2, Cesarean birth. Well child.
Hospitalization: Mother prognosticated over necessary repair
of hernia. Few clinic visits.
Migration: Mother and father as young adults.
Physical Characteristics: Light olive in color, wavy hair,
Caucasoid features.
Housing: Four people in three rooms. No separate bath. Cen-
tral heating.
English: Father and mother adequate, children bilingual.
Education: Father and mother grade school incomplete Puerto
Rico.
Employment: Father steady, steward on ship.
Welfare: No record.
Family Type: Nuclear family with own children. Maternal
grandmother and maternal aunt live in neighborhood.
Religion: Not recorded.
Observations: Apart from mother's major medical problem
family appear well.

FAMILY 72

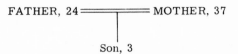

FATHER, 24 ════╤════ MOTHER, 37

Son, 3

Medical: Father, 24, Osgood Schlatter disease ten years ago.
Thin, 125 pounds, 5 feet 8 inches. Stammers, nail biter.
History of vertigo, anisoiconia, no definite diagnosis.
Mother, 37, short, 160 pounds. Cesarean section, fetal dis-
tress. Pregnant, EDC November 1956. Son, 3, Cesarean
birth. Healthy.

Hospitalization: No interest in further diagnostic study.

Migration: Father as adolescent. Mother as young divorced
adult.

Physical Characteristics: Father light brown in color, kinky
hair, Negroid features. Mother and son dark olive, hair
wavy, Caucasoid features.

Housing: Three rooms for three people. Bath. Central
heating.

English: Father and mother adequate.

Education: Father high school incomplete Manhattan. Mother
grade school incomplete Puerto Rico.

Employment: Both adults employed steadily in hotel trade.

Welfare: No record.

Family Type: Mother had children by previous union not now
under her care. Child five-day boarder in another home.
Nuclear family with own child, another expected. Woman
thirteen years older than man.

Religion: Roman Catholic.

Observations: Motherly wife appears to fill man's needs.
Health questions appear unimportant compared to joint
earning power.

FAMILY 73

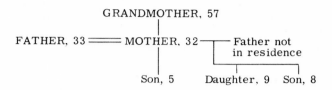

GRANDMOTHER, 57

FATHER, 33 ══════ MOTHER, 32 ─┬─ Father not
in residence

Son, 5   Daughter, 9   Son, 8

Medical: Grandmother, 57, pulmonary tuberculosis (now inactive) diagnosed three years ago. Diabetes mellitus diagnosed ten years ago. Ulceration big toe right foot on two
occasions. Bronchitis every winter. Mother, 32, "ataques"
since adolescence, following generalized convulsions considered to be on hysterical basis New York voluntary hospital. Pruritus severe recently. Father, 33, pneumonia ten
years ago. Brachial plexus syndrome? Daughter, 9, NFTSD.
Obese. Appendectomy age 7. Behavior problem. Enuresis.
Son, 8, thin. High forceps delivery. Pain in legs and abdomen, no pathology found. Son, 5, NFTSD. Tuberculosis
cutis diagnosed age 4. Diarrhea and high fever age 4.
Hospitalization: Grandmother has left hospital against advice
on two occasions. Periodic checking of family by Health
Department carried through.
Migration: Father young adult. Mother age 20. Grandmother
young adult.
Physical Characteristics: Grandmother and son, 5, light olive
in color, straight hair, Caucasoid features. Father dark
olive in color, kinky hair, Negroid features. Mother and
daughter, 9, light brown in color, wavy hair, Negroid features. Son, 8, white in color, wavy hair, Caucasoid features.
Housing: Formerly six or seven people in four rooms. No
separate bath. Central heating. Moved to Bronx.

322

English: Grandmother none. Remainder of family bilingual.

Education: Grandmother never attended school. Father grade school incomplete Puerto Rico. Mother high school incomplete Manhattan.

Employment: Father steady hotel trade. Mother factory work intermittently.

Welfare: No record.

Family Type: Extended family with mother's nieces residing at times with family. Also occasionally children from husband's previous marriage.

Religion: Protestant.

Observations: Mother dependent on own mother and fearful of offending her. Has "ataques" in times of crisis. Discipline inconsistent, with grandmother playing one child against another. Father stabilizing influence.

FAMILY 74

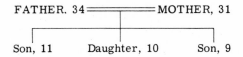

FATHER, 34 ━━━━━━━━ MOTHER, 31

Son, 11   Daughter, 10   Son, 9

Medical: Father, 34, left indirect inguinal hernia, not treated.
Mother, 31, tension headaches many years, anxious. Post-
partum tubal ligation in Puerto Rico. Son, 11, high forceps
delivery. Feeding problem. Vitamin deficiency. Daughter,
10, low forceps delivery, feeding problem. Respiratory infections. Son, 9, frequent otitis and tonsillitis.
Hospitalization: Mother takes children and relatives to many
physicians and clinics. Father declines repair of hernia
though insured.
Migration: Father as young adult. Mother as small child with
frequent revisits to Puerto Rico.
Physical Characteristics: Color white to light olive. Hair
straight. Features Caucasoid.
Housing: Five people in three rooms. Separate bath. Central
heating.
English: Whole family bilingual.
Education: Father grammar school incomplete Puerto Rico.
Mother high school incomplete Manhattan.
Employment: Father hotel industry; same position since mi-
gration.
Welfare: No record.
Family Type: Nuclear family with own children, with numer-
ous nieces, nephews and grandmothers.
Religion: Roman Catholic.
Observations: Frequent visits to physicians for this woman
is apparently a way of relieving anxiety.

FAMILY 75

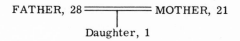

FATHER, 28 ══════╤══════ MOTHER, 21

Daughter, 1

Medical: Father, 28, bronchial asthma chronic and acute, no
symptoms in the Army. Mother, 21, obese, 30 pound weight
gain in six months. Excessive intake of food. Attacks right
upper quadrant pain not investigated. Daughter, 1, healthy.

Hospitalization: Father uses veteran's hospital for treatment
of asthma.

Migration: Father 1949. Mother 1953.

Physical Characteristics: Color white to light olive. Hair
curly. Caucasoid features.

Housing: Three rooms for three people. No bath. Central
heating.

English: Father bilingual. Mother fair.

Education: Father high school complete Puerto Rico. Mother
grade school incomplete Puerto Rico.

Employment: Father steady, printer. Mother does not work.

Welfare: No record.

Family Type: Nuclear family with own child. No other relatives in evidence.

Religion: Protestant.

Observations: Mother's admitted overeating with recent weight
gain and depressed aspect suggest onset of stresses. Nature of these is not clear, but family is not seeking help at
present.

FAMILY 76

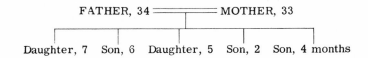

FATHER, 34 ══════════ MOTHER, 33

Daughter, 7   Son, 6   Daughter, 5   Son, 2   Son, 4 months

Medical: Father, 34, syphilis treated. Mother, 33, syphilis
treated. Cholecystectomy. Post-partum tubal ligation, varicose veins. Daughter, 7, congenital syphilis and osteo-
chondritis treated. Occasional enuresis, nail biter. Son, 6,
NFTSD. Negative serology. Normal child. Daughter, 5,
NFTSD. Normal child. Son, 2, NFTSD. Normal child. Son,
4 months, NFTSD. Normal child.

Hospitalization: Syphilis successfully treated. Otitis and
pharyngitis from time to time treated at clinic.

Migration: Father as infant. Mother as adolescent "to get a
change."

Physical Characteristics: Father and mother light brown in
color, hair wavy, Negroid features. Children dark olive in
color, hair curly, Caucasoid features.

Housing: Three rooms for seven people. No bath. No central
heating. Rent and heat $78.00 one winter month.

English: All bilingual.

Education: Father high school incomplete Manhattan. Mother
grade school incomplete Puerto Rico.

Employment: Father, steady. Merchant seaman. Mother does
not work.

Welfare: No record.

Family Type: Nuclear family with own children. Mother had
child by previous consensual union, child in Puerto Rico.
Father also had previous common-law marriage.

Religion: Roman Catholic.

Observations: Father is steady provider. Mother shrugs shoulders and comments on situation, "no es bueno, no es malo."

FAMILY 77

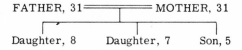

FATHER, 31 ══════╤══════ MOTHER, 31

| Daughter, 8 | Daughter, 7 | Son, 5 |

Medical: Father, 31, dilated inguinal ring. Tonsillar hypertrophy. Mother, 31, tonsillectomy age 27. Menorrhagia
age 31. Daughter, 8, primary tuberculosis, inactive, not
treated. Daughter, 7, perforated left ear drum. Carious
teeth. Son, 5, carious teeth.

Hospitalization: Family checked for tuberculosis.

Migration: Entire family after World War II.

Physical Characteristics: Color white. Hair straight. Caucasoid features.

Housing: Three rooms for five people. No bath. Central
heating.

English: Father and mother adequate.

Education: Father and mother grade school complete Puerto
Rico.

Employment: Father factory worker night shift. Mother on
day shift in factory.

Welfare: Applied during period of unemployment. Withdrawn.

Family Type: Nuclear family with own children, both parents
working, no other relatives in evidence.

Religion: Roman Catholic.

Observations: Family anxious to get ahead. Both parents
working on different shifts, very irritable and punitive with
children.

328

FAMILY 78

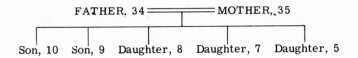

FATHER, 34 ========= MOTHER, 35

Son, 10   Son, 9   Daughter, 8   Daughter, 7   Daughter, 5

Medical: Father, 34, "blind as a child." Myopia corneal opac-
ity. Mother, 35, post-partum tubal ligation Puerto Rico.
Cloasma. Tonsils hypertrophied. Carious teeth. Son, 10,
and Son, 9, carious teeth. Pediculosis. Daughter, 8, carious
teeth. Prognathism. Enuresis. No major illness. Daughter,
7, occasional otitis. Tonsils hypertrophied. Daughter, 5,
pharyngitis and scabies age 2.

Hospitalization: No admissions. No regular clinic visits except for checking man's vision. Few emergency visits.

Migration: Father after World War II. Mother and children
following year.

Physical Characteristics: Color dark olive. Hair kinky. Negroid features.

Housing: Two rooms for seven people. No bath. Central
heating.

English: Father and mother none. Children poor.

Education: Parents have never attended school. School reports language handicap with children. Daughter, 7, absent
102 times in first grade.

Employment: Father factory worker unemployed most of the
time. Mother does not work.

Welfare: Past two years.

Family Type: Nuclear, with own children. No relatives in
evidence.

Religion: Roman Catholic.

Observations: Parents have never been to school, speak no
English, are unable to discipline children. Have no awareness of health problems beyond father's poor vision.

FAMILY 79

MOTHER, 44══════Father not in residence

Twin daughters, 10

Medical: <u>Mother</u>, 44, Cesarean section age 34. Rheumatoid
arthritis knee joint. Mild hypertension. Menopause
"ataques." Senile vaginitís. <u>Twin I</u>, premature 4 pounds.
More aggressive. Pale, thin. <u>Twin II</u>, premature 3 pounds,
4 ounces. Shorter "mas umilde," pale.

Hospitalization: Frequent clinic visits.

Migration: Mother age 32, single. Became pregnant following
year.

Physical Characteristics: Color white. Hair straight. Caucasoid features.

Housing: Building torn down. Moved 1955, not found.

English: Mother poor. Children bilingual.

Education: Mother grade school incomplete.

Employment: Mother does not work.

Welfare: Since mother became pregnant.

Family Type: Mother with two children and no mate.

Religion: Protestant.

Observations: Older woman impregnated and abandoned
shortly after arrival in Manhattan now living in anxiety with
many complaints and little sympathy for twin daughters.

FAMILY 80

HUSBAND, 47══════WIFE, 45*

Medical: Husband, 47, eye infection in childhood. Trauma
·to right eye at work in Puerto Rico. Pterygium excised
age 46. Recurrence of same. Vision O.D. 15/200, O.S.
20/40. Wife, 45, all children died in infancy. Bronchitis
first year after migration. Menopause.
Hospitalization: Husband had eye surgery but declines re-
habilitation program.
Migration: Since World War II.
Physical Characteristics: Color light olive. Hair straight.
Caucasoid features.
Housing: Three rooms for two people. No bath. Central
heating.
English: Poor.
Education: Husband grade school incomplete Puerto Rico.
Wife never attended school.
Employment: Husband in restaurant industry when injured;
now light factory.
Welfare: No record.
Family Type: Childless couple help out Family 9 from
time to time.
Religion: Roman Catholic.
Observations: Husband somewhat confused by medical
recommendations but declines to accept visual handicap
as reason for applying for Welfare.

———
*Sister of woman in Family 9.

THE PUERTO RICAN EXPERIENCE

An Arno Press Collection

Berle, Beatrice Bishop. **Eighty Puerto Rican Families in New York City:** Health and Disease Studied in Context. New Foreword by the author. 1958

Blanco, Tomas. **El Prejuicio Racial en Puerto Rico.** (Racial Prejudice in Puerto Rico). 1948

Carroll, Henry K. **Report on the Island of Porto Rico;** Its Population, Civil Government, Commerce, Industries, Productions, Roads, Tariff, and Currency, With Recommendations. 1899

Cebollero, Pedro A. **A School Language Policy for Puerto Rico.** 1945

Chiles, Paul Nelson. **The Puerto Rican Press Reaction to the United States, 1888-1898.** 1944

Clark, Victor S., et al. **Porto Rico and Its Problems.** 1930

Coll Cuchí, José. **Un Problema en América.** (The American Problem). 1944

Colon, Jesus. **A Puerto Rican in New York and Other Sketches.** 1961

Enamorado Cuesta, J[ose]. **Porto Rico, Past and Present:** The Island After Thirty Years of American Rule. A Book of Information, Written for the American Reading Public, in the Interest and for the Benefit of the People of Porto Rico. [1929]

Fernández Vanga, Epifanio. **El Idioma de Puerto Rico y El Idioma Escolar de Puerto Rico.** (Language and Language Policy in Puerto Rico). 1931

Fleagle, Fred K. **Social Problems in Porto Rico.** 1917

Friedrich, Carl J. **Puerto Rico: Middle Road to Freedom.** 1959

Gallardo, José M., editor. **Proceedings of [the] Conference on Education of Puerto Rican Children on the Mainland (October 18 to 21, 1970).** 1972

Geigel Polanco, Vicente. **Valores de Puerto Rico.** (Puerto Rican Leaders). 1943

Institute of Field Studies, Teachers College, Columbia University. **Public Education and the Future of Puerto Rico: A Curriculum Survey, 1948-1949.** 1950

Jaffe, A[bram] J., editor. **Puerto Rican Population of New York City.** 1954

New York [City]. Welfare Council. **Puerto Ricans in New York City:** The Report of the Committee on Puerto Ricans in New York City of the Welfare Council of New York City. 1948

Osuna, Juan José. **A History of Education in Puerto Rico.** 1949

Perloff, Harvey S. **Puerto Rico's Economic Future:** A Study in Planned Development. 1950

Puerto Rican Forum. **The Puerto Rican Community Development Project:** Un Proyecto Puertorriqueño de Ayuda Mutua Para El Desarrollo de la Comunidad. A Proposal For a Self-Help Project to Develop the Community by Strengthening the Family, Opening Opportunities for Youth and Making Full Use of Education. 1964

Puerto Ricans and Educational Opportunity. 1975

The Puerto Ricans: Migration and General Bibliography. 1975

Roberts, Lydia J. and Rosa Luisa Stefani. **Patterns of Living in Puerto Rican Families.** 1949

Rosario, José C[olombán]. **The Development of the Puerto Rican Jíbaro and His Present Attitude Towards Society.** 1935

Rowe, L[eo] S. **The United States and Porto Rico:** With Special Reference to the Problems Arising Out of Our Contact with the Spanish-American Civilization. 1904

Siegel, Arthur, Harold Orlans and Loyal Greer. **Puerto Ricans in Philadelphia:** A Study of Their Demographic Characteristics, Problems and Attitudes. 1954

[Tugwell, Rexford G.] **Puerto Rican Public Papers of R. G. Tugwell, Governor.** 1945

United States-Puerto Rico Commission on the Status of Puerto Rico. **Status of Puerto Rico:** Report of the United States-Puerto Rico Commission on the Status of Puerto Rico, August 1966. 1966

United States-Puerto Rico Commission on the Status of Puerto Rico. **Status of Puerto Rico:** Selected Background Studies Prepared for the United States-Puerto Rico Commission on the Status of Puerto Rico, 1966. 1966

United States Senate. Select Committee on Equal Educational Opportunity. **Equal Educational Opportunity for Puerto Rican Children (Part 8):** Hearings Before the Select Committee on Equal Educational Opportunity of the United States Senate. 91st Congress, 2nd Session, Washington, D. C., November 23, 24 and 25, 1970. 1970

Van Middeldyk, R. A. **The History of Puerto Rico:** From the Spanish Discovery to the American Occupation. 1903

Wakefield, Dan. **Island in the City:** The World of Spanish Harlem. 1959

White, Trumbull. **Puerto Rico and Its People.** 1938